Environmental Management in Canada

Environmental Management in Canada

Editors
Brett Ibbotson
John-David Phyper

McGraw-Hill Ryerson Limited
Toronto New York Auckland Bogotá Caracas
Lisbon London Madrid Mexico Milan New Delhi
San Juan Singapore Sydney Tokyo

Environmental Management in Canada

First published in 1996 by
McGraw-Hill Ryerson Limited
300 Water Street
Whitby, Ontario, Canada
L1N 9B6

1 2 3 4 5 6 7 8 9 0 TRI 4 3 2 1 0 9 8 7 6 5

Canadian Cataloguing in Publication Data

Phyper, John-David
    Environmental management in Canada

Includes index.
ISBN 0-07-551723-X

1. Industrial management - Environmental aspects -
Canada. 2. Environmental policy - Canada. 3. Corporate
planning - Canada. I. Ibbotson, Brett. II. Title.

HD69.P6P58 1994   658.4'08   C94-932511-2

Publisher: Joan Homewood
Production Coordinator: Sharon Hudson
Cover Design: Jan Scharlach
Page Makeup: Pages Design
Editor: Don Loney/Word Guild

Printed and bound in Canada

To my parents for their unfailing support,
and to Debra for her patience and encouragement
B.G.I.

To my loving wife, Christine, and my family
and friends for their support
J.-D.P.

Table of Contents

LIST OF FIGURES

LIST OF TABLES

Preface

THIS BOOK IS PRIMARILY DIRECTED
toward helping those people who are responsible for designing, implementing and maintaining environmental management systems for businesses and organizations in Canada. It reflects the cumulative experience of people from several disciplines. By having contributing authors who include engineers, lawyers, accountants and scientists, it is hoped that readers will be better prepared to face the multi-disciplinary challenges that environmental management issues can pose.

Although the authors are well aware of the rapidly changing nature of environmental management, it still was a struggle to incorporate late-breaking information from many sources. Despite the efforts made to ensure that the information is current and accurate, it is inevitable that some facts or notions will become stale in short order. We are more confident that the underlying themes and main components will withstand the test of time.

The authors welcome suggestions for ways to improve the book and information on any errors or misinterpretations that may have been included.

List of Contributors

ONE OF THE GOALS OF WRITING this book is to examine environmental management from the perspectives of various disciplines. To that end, the list of contributors includes individuals whose areas of expertise include engineering, the law, trade, accounting and public communication, as well as Canadian companies that are trying to grapple with the many challenges presented by environmental management.

ROSS BURNS

Ross Burns is Responsible Care® Coordinator with the Department of Public Affairs and Environment, Novacor Chemicals. Having 12 years of marketing, logistics and environment, health and safety experience at Novacor's head office in Calgary, Ross has represented Novacor at a senior level with the Canadian Chemical Producers' Association and the U.S. Chemical Manufacturers' Association.

Ross is a 1990 recipient of the CCPA's Award of Merit for his outstanding contributions to Responsible Care® implementation in Canada. He is currently Vice Chairman of Novacor's Responsible Care® Council.

TEK CHIN

Tek Chin is a professional engineer with extensive experience in high-technology process operation, technical management and business development both in Canada and Asia. Tek was the Senior Policy Advisor with the Department of Public Affairs and the Environment, Novacor Chemicals until June 1994. He represented Novacor, Polysar and Petrosar at a senior level with the Canadian Petroleum Products Institute.

Tek was also the Chairman of the Board of Lambton College (1992–95), Sarnia, Ontario, Canada. He is a 1993 recipient of the Government of Canada 125th Anniversary Commemorative Medal, as well as other awards for outstanding contributions to environmental conservation within the petroleum industry.

ROGER COTTON

Roger Cotton is a Partner and Head of the Environmental Law Group at Tory Tory DesLauriers & Binnington. Mr. Cotton has written numerous articles on environmental compliance, regulatory processes, environmental liabilities, and corporate due diligence. He was appointed Chair of the Law Society of Upper Canada's Certification Committee on Environmental Law. He is also Chair of Ontario Hydro's Environmental Advisory Committee, and a past National Chair of the Environmental Law Section of the Canadian Bar Association. He is the General Editor of Butterworth's *Canadian Environmental Law*. Mr. Cotton regularly advises major industry sectors, particularly pulp and paper, mining, chemical and manufacturing, on environmental issues.

Mr. Cotton obtained his LL.B. from the University of New Brunswick, his LL.M. from Osgoode Hall Law School and was called to the Bar in Ontario in 1982.

SAM FENIMORE

Sam Fenimore is an Information Systems Analyst with Novacor Chemicals working throughout the company at both the plant and corporate levels. Sam's background includes teaching and private business. Currently he is also an M.B.A. candidate at California Coast University and is working on a thesis entitled, "Characteristics of information systems in key areas of environment and safety."

HUGH HOWSON

Hugh Howson has a B.Sc. from the University of Waterloo in Mechanical Engineering. He became intensely involved in environmental issues while working for Quaker Oats and ultimately became their first National Manager of Environmental Affairs. He is past chairman of the Canadian Manufacturers' Association environmental committee, sits on several committees under the auspices of CSA for the development of Canadian environmental guidelines, chaired the CSA small business environmental program and represented Canada at the ISO environmental technical committee meetings. He has a deep personal commitment to environmental issues, was involved with Canada's input to the United Nations Agenda 13, and has been involved in several reviews of environment and trade, especially as it pertains to GATT and NAFTA.

BRETT IBBOTSON

Brett Ibbotson received his Bachelor of Applied Science and Master of Engineering degrees in civil engineering from the University of Toronto. He has been an environmental engineering consultant for the past 19 years. During that time, he has participated in a wide range of projects across Canada, in the United States and in the Caribbean. A founding principal of Angus Environmental Limited, he has written more than 40 articles and technical papers on risk assessment, site remediation, and environmental compliance.

GREG JUDD

Greg Judd is a Manager in the Restructuring and Advisory Services group (RAS) of Deloitte & Touche Chartered Accountants. He has experience in the management and sale of toxic waste-contaminated properties as they affect lenders, business operators and involvement with government regulatory agencies. Recent environmental engagements have included the operation and sale of a large retail gasoline chain and liquidation of a portfolio of mortgage properties for a financial institution.

JOHN–DAVID PHYPER

John-David Phyper received his B.A.Sc. and M.A.Sc. (chemical engineering) and M.B.A. degrees from the University of Toronto. He has been working in the environmental field for the past 12 years including several years as Coordinator of the Air and Water Quality for Stelco Inc. He has participated in hundreds of environmental audits and site assessments and is currently assisting several companies in implementing ISO. John is founding principal of Phyper & Associates Ltd., an environmental engineering consulting firm, and Environmental Software Associates Ltd., a software firm specializing in environmental issues.

THOMAS RAHN

Thomas Rahn is a Senior Associate with LURA Group (Toronto and Halifax), based in Toronto. He has spent 10 years participating in, designing and carrying out public consultation and community planning programs. As part of the multi-disciplinary team at the LURA Group he has provided services in strategic and community planning, public consultation, and communications on environmental issues for a wide variety of clients. The LURA Group has been a pioneer in developing processes that involve a diversity of people in productive and creative decision-making, often around contentious issues.

DANIEL SCHMID

Dan Schmid is the Auditing Supervisor with 3M's Corporate Environmental Technology & Services (ET&S) organization. He is responsible for 3M's corporate environmental auditing programs. He is a participant in the Corporate Responsible Care process and in the development of 3M global auditing services.

Dan has been with 3M's environmental auditing group since 1986 and with 3M corporate environmental group since 1976. Dan holds a B.S. degree in Environmental Studies from Bemidji State University and is a Qualified Environmental Professional (QEP) and a Certified Hazardous Material Manager (CHMM).

Dan is currently on the Board of Directors of the Industrial Council on Environmental Management, a Minnesota-based professional organization. He has also served on the Board of Directors for the Institute for Environmental Auditing and is a member of the Environmental Auditing Roundtable and CHMM organizations.

THOMAS ZOSEL

Tom Zosel is Manager, Pollution Prevention Programs, in 3M's Corporate Environmental Technology & Services (ET&S) organization. He graduated from the University of Wisconsin with a degree in Chemical Engineering. He has been with 3M for 27 years, 21 of which have been in the environmental area.

In his present position, Tom is responsible for following major legislative actions, for directing waste minimization initiatives and for managing 3M's internationally recognized Pollution Prevention Pays (3P) Program.

He currently serves on U.S. EPA's Clean Air Act Advisory Committee, is past–chair of the American Institute of Chemical Engineers Centre for Waste Reduction Technologies and is a frequent author and speaker on pollution prevention and industry's response to environmental issues.

Acknowledgements

THIS BOOK REPRESENTS THE efforts of many people. The authors acknowledge the many useful comments and suggestions received from co-workers, friends, and colleagues. Special thanks are extended to Andrew Pitt, environmental engineer at Phyper & Associates Limited, and Paul MacLean, Principal at ÉEM Inc., for their assistance and suggestions during the preparation of selected chapters.

1

Introduction

by
Brett Ibbotson
Angus Environmental Limited

1.1 OVERVIEW

Over the last couple of decades, the environment has emerged as an important agent of change. Laws and regulations have been established to protect and manage the environment. The interconnections between the environment and economics, trade, and culture have become increasingly apparent. The environment has become a factor that influences marketing, politics, and investment.

Not so long ago, most environmental issues were addressed in a relatively simplistic manner. For example, laws were enacted that set maximum emission rates, pollution control equipment was installed, and monitoring programs were implemented. In North America, many of the more obviously damaging practices were stopped or greatly curtailed.

While improvements are evident, there is a growing sense that over the long term something better, more permanent and pervasive, needs to be done. For most companies and organizations, some difficult issues will need to be addressed for that next level of improvement to be reached. Examples of these issues include:

- Should a company or organization be content to comply with legal requirements or should it strive to meet a higher level of performance?
- Should environmental responsibilities be assigned as full-time activities or be part of other job functions?
- Should incentives for employees be tied to environmental performance?
- Do companies need to trade off the prospects of short-term profitability for long-term sustainability?

Reactions to the environmental challenge cover a broad spectrum. Some companies and organizations are trying to meet the challenge head on, with various degrees of success. Others ignore or dismiss it. Some recognize the need to change but are frozen by indecision as to how to proceed or are waiting to see how others fare in their efforts. Yet others continue to address environmental issues on the same piecemeal or *ad hoc* basis as they have in the past.

To offer advice on how to proceed, business theorists have stepped forward with amalgams of activities and philosophies that have names like TQEM, "sustainable development," and "going green." Some companies and organizations have adopted their own names and acronyms. Brief comments on a couple of these philosophies are offered in Section 1.4.

The generic term **environmental management system** (EMS) is employed in this book to represent the totality of all things a company or organization does to manage its environmental affairs and monitor its effects on the environment. The term EMS is not new or catchy, but it is direct and unambiguous.

This book is intended to help people develop and implement an effective EMS. The terms "manager" and "company" are used frequently, but the discussions are equally applicable to people with other titles and to other types of organizations.

1.2 FUNDAMENTAL PRINCIPLES

The approach to EMS described in this book is based in large part upon three fundamental principles.

Principle No. 1: An EMS must take into account the internal components and external factors that are relevant to a company or organization.

Internal components are the functional resources that a company can use to deal with challenges. These resources are broken down into three components. "Operational" components include the procedures that a company utilizes and the standards by which it judges its efforts. "Organizational" components include the ways that responsibilities are assigned and the internal reporting system that is used. "Cultural" components include characteristics of the work environment that influence intangibles such as morale, ethics, and respect.

External factors include those things outside a company that shape the environment in which it operates. Examples include laws, accounting practices, and public expectations. Figure 1.1 provides further examples for both the internal components and external factors.

The managers of a company must understand the relative importance of each internal component and external factor and determine how they will influence their EMS. Some companies may choose to strive for very high environmental standards, perhaps as a way to appeal directly to the marketplace. Other companies may be more bottom-line oriented and want an EMS that minimizes the liabilities associated with regulatory non-compliance.

FIGURE 1.1
INTERNAL COMPONENTS AND EXTERNAL FACTORS

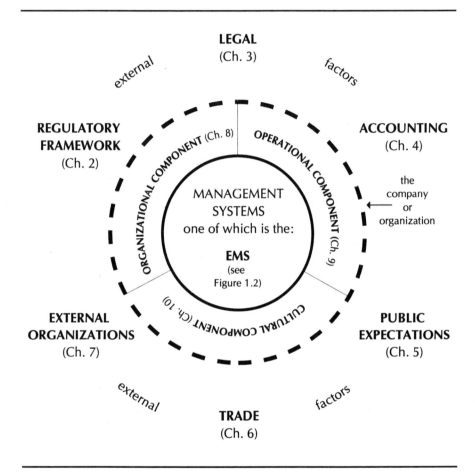

Principle No. 2: To have the best chance of doing the most good, an EMS needs to address the technical, political, and cultural (TPC) dynamics of a company.

First put forward as a framework for solving problems in organizations (Tichy, 1983), the TPC theory is used in this book as a means of ensuring that all three dynamics are addressed when implementing an EMS. For example, assigning a senior manager to environmental affairs (a political dynamic) may do little good if staff have not received environmental training (a cultural dynamic). Similarly, the ability of the new manager to bring about improvements may be hampered if he or she is not given the budget to upgrade pollution control equipment (a technical dynamic).

The TPC theory mirrors the internal components described in Principle No. 1. The operational component corresponds to the technical dynamic, the organizational component corresponds to the political dynamic, and the cultural component corresponds to the cultural dynamic.

Principle No. 3: The EMS should be incorporated into, and not kept separate from, the company's general management system.

The EMS should be integrated into the general principles of the company's management system, whatever that may be (e.g. total quality management, management by objectives, etc.). Integration, both vertical and horizontal, is a key to successful implementation of an EMS. Elements of an EMS which can be integrated into a company's management system include:

- a philosophical commitment by senior management to environmentally sound and sustainable practices
- the allocation of sufficient resources to support recommended actions
- the integration of environment stewardship into all areas of business
- employee involvement and empowerment
- vertical and horizontal distribution of environmental information
- striving for continuous improvement
- setting performance goals and monitoring performance
- taking corrective action at the root cause of inadequate performance

A recent study conducted by the Business Roundtable in the United States examined several companies to determine common elements of successful pollution prevention programs (The Business Roundtable, 1993). Several common elements were identified in those programs that echo aspects expressed in the three fundamental principles described above:14

- All facilities had strong management support.
- The facilities understood their corporate and plant cultures, and implemented programs in a way that worked in those cultures.
- Facilities were successful when they were given the freedom to choose the best method to reach goals.
- Facilities had the ability to report progress against selected goals or initiatives on a monthly or quarterly basis.
- Driven by government regulations, facilities spent more resources on compliance activities than on pollution prevention activities. Facilities expressed the desire to move the balance of resources toward pollution prevention.

1.3   STEPS IN DEVELOPING AN EMS

Eight steps which can be taken to develop an EMS are shown in Figure 1.2. Since two of the steps direct attention back to earlier steps, the process is iterative and can also be used to maintain and improve an EMS.

FIGURE 1.2
STEPS OF AN EMS

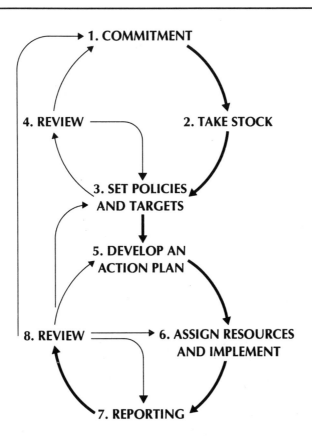

Note: The Step 4 Review occurs less frequently than the Step 8 Review.

Steps 1 through 4 occur at senior or upper levels of an organization. The effectiveness of Steps 1 through 3 is scrutinized in Step 4 and the findings can prompt a review and/or revision of any or all of the first three steps. It is anticipated that this iterative review-and-revise process will occur infrequently, perhaps on the order of once every few years, with the flexibility to initiate a review and revision whenever needed.

While the process described by Steps 1 through 4 might be thought of as "corporate" in nature, Steps 5 through 8 focus on day-to-day operations. In larger companies, there might be specific sets of Steps 5 through 8 for each operational unit, division, factory, product line, etc.

The effectiveness of Steps 5 through 7 is scrutinized in Step 8 and the results can prompt a review and/or revision of the previous three steps. It is anticipated that this iterative review-and-revise process will occur frequently, perhaps on the order of once every six to 24 months, with the flexibility to initiate a review and revision whenever needed.

The prime objective of this book is to help people understand and use these steps so that they can develop and implement an effective EMS. Many of the subsequent chapters examine the ways that the internal components and external factors noted in Section 1.2 can influence an EMS. Table 1.1 highlights chapters and sections that are particularly relevant to each of the eight steps.

Step 1 - Commitment

Ideally, everyone in an organization shares a common understanding of a corporate goal and works cooperatively towards achieving that goal. There is no better place for such a commitment to originate than from the highest level in a company.

In some companies, senior staff create a corporate environmental policy or statement and distribute it widely within the company as a way of communicating this commitment. This may include posting copies in common areas such as cafeterias, conference rooms, and even lobbies. There also is a growing practice of including an environmental policy in annual statements.

Distributing copies of a corporate policy is seldom sufficient in itself. True commitment must also be evident in the actions and attitudes of a company's officers and directors. Staff will see through the insincerity of a policy that exists only on paper.

Commitment at a senior level is discussed further in Section 8.1. Initial sections of Chapters 12 and 13 describe the role of commitment in two case studies.

Step 2 - Taking Stock

It is difficult to plan a journey if you don't know where you are. The second step in developing an EMS is to take a dispassionate, critical look at how well an organization is doing at managing its environmental affairs.

Table 1.2 presents a simple set of questions that a company or manager can use to take stock. These questions are best suited for the first time a company undertakes Step 2. Subsequent returns to Step 2 likely will see a manager modify the questions to become more specific to the company's needs and/or reflect lessons learned.

Step 3 - Setting Policies and Targets (Points of Reference)

The corporate policy described in Step 1 is often broadly worded and requires that other supporting documents that are more focused in scope be prepared. Equally important to the setting of policies is establishing targets or points of reference that can subsequently be used to determine if the policy is being met.

Many candidates for targets and points of reference exist, such as regulatory requirements, industrial codes of practice, voluntary programs and EMS guidelines. Some of the chapters in this book describe possible sources of targets. Chapter 2 represents a review of the regulatory framework (federal, provincial, and municipal) that an EMS may need to address. Chapter 7 provides brief summaries of publications by external organizations and standard-setting associations. Moreover, Chapters 2 through 10 examine the ways in which internal components and external factors can affect the setting of policies and targets and other elements of an EMS in Canada.

Selecting an appropriate point of reference may hinge upon satisfying one or more of the following questions:

- Is it consistent with other company policies and targets?
- Is it being employed by similar companies?
- Is it being employed by your customers or suppliers?
- Will it reduce waste (and/or save money)?
- Will it mitigate potential incidents of non-compliance and civil litigation?
- Could it contribute to a defense of "reasonable care" or "due diligence"?
- Are the resources available to implement and maintain it? EMS guidelines developed outside an organization or generic codes of practice should not be accepted without first considering these types of questions.

Step 4 - Review (of Steps 1 through 3)

Step 4 reflects the inevitability that sound environmental management must respond to the ever-changing influences. Even a good EMS needs to be updated or improved from time to time, and Step 4 is intended to prompt senior staff into asking questions such as:

- Does the company's overall approach to environmental management need to be reassessed?
- Are the corporate environmental policies, guiding principles, and targets appropriate?
- Is the organization truly committed to the policies and guiding principles, and achieving the targets?

While a timetable for this type or review should be set (perhaps once every few years), there must be flexibility to initiate a review and revisions whenever there is due cause. A Step 4 review could indicate that only Step 3 needs to be revisited or it could suggest that the entire process starting at Step 1 needs to be considered.

There are at least two options for conducting a detailed review of an EMS:

- An environmental benchmark review would identify the deficiencies in the structure and/or components of an EMS. This type of review is analogous to the "Initial review" described in British Standard 7750-94 (see Chapter 7).
- An environmental audit would examine both regulatory compliance and conformity with corporate policies and guiding principles, as well as other EMS standards if required. The practice of conducting environmental audits is discussed in detail in Chapter 11.

Step 5 - Develop an Action Plan

In most situations, the policies and targets set in Step 3 will lead to the realization that improvements or alterations will need to be made to one or more of the operational, organizational, or cultural components of the EMS. The extent of these improvements can range from minor (such as installing a new monitoring device) to substantial (such as a large training initiative or the expanding of environmental staff).

An action plan should be developed that identifies the tasks and resources needed to provide the desired improvements. It may be necessary to assign priorities to the improvements if it is apparent that the improvements require substantial amounts of time, effort, or other resources.

Step 6 - Assign Resources and Implement the Action Plan

No plan can succeed if the available resources are insufficient or are used ineffectively. The lack of resources to implement needed improvements can be the cause for initiating a review of Steps 1 through 3.

How a company implements a plan of action is best left to the people directly involved — the officers, managers, and staff of a company or organization. This step can be costly and time consuming. Chapters 12 and 13 provide case studies that relate the experiences of two international companies.

Step 7 - Reporting

The improvements made in Step 6 should contribute to the generation or distribution of information that will be used to assess whether or not policies or targets are being met, and if not, why.

Like most other aspects of an organization, it is essential that accurate and representative information be distributed in a timely manner. The flow of environmental information can be in response to both internal and external requirements. People at all levels of an organization may need environmental information to determine how they are performing, to see the effect of improvements, and be alerted to adverse changes.

The types of information and the level of detail required will change from person to person. The operator of a pollution control device may need to see detailed performance results, while a senior executive may need to see general trends or be apprised of non-complying events.

External information needs continue to increase steadily. Regulatory agencies require written notification for many types of activities and events. As noted in some of the legal cases described in Chapter 3, failure to report environmental information in a timely manner has become one of the most frequent sources of charges and penalties.

Also increasing is the frequency with which environmental information is being shared with members of the public and other stakeholders. Understanding the expectations of these readers is the focus of Chapter 5.

Step 8 - Review (of Steps 5 through 7)

While Step 4 involves the review of environmental management practices on a corporate level, Step 8 can be as specific as a review of one type of activity or practice, or it can be broadened to be a review of an operational unit of a company or a factory.

Increasingly, this type of review is being referred to as an environmental audit (see Chapter 11).

Growing numbers of companies are setting timetables for conducting environmental audits. Depending upon factors such as potential to cause environmental damage and the complexity of environmental legislation, a company might plan to audit activities or facilities every one to three years. Regardless of the timetable, there must be the flexibility to initiate a review and revisions whenever the need arises.

If an audit conducted in Step 8 indicates that relatively minor improvements are necessary, it could be satisfactory to re-enter the process at Step 6 or at Step 7 (if the improvement involved only the flow of information). If an audit conducted in Step 8 found more serious deficiencies, it could suggest re-entering the process at Step 3 or even Step 1.

Table 1.1
CROSS-REFERENCE OF CHAPTERS AND SECTIONS TO EMS STEPS

EMS Step	Relevant Chapters and Sections	
1) Commitment	7.3	as expressed by industrial associations
	8.1	as expressed by several Canadian companies
	12.1	case study - Novacor
	13.1, 13.2	case study - 3M

2) Taking Stock	Ch 7	guidance from non-government organizations
	8.1	as a first step in setting policy
	13.2	case study - 3M
3) Setting Policies and Targets	Ch 2	regulatory considerations
	Ch 3	legal considerations
	Ch 4	financial considerations
	Ch 6	trade considerations
	Ch 7	guidance from non-government organizations
	8.1	principles and objectives
	12.2, 12.3	case study - Novacor
	13.2, 13.3	case study - 3M
4) Review of Steps 1 through 3	8.4	management reviews
	Ch 11	environmental audits
5) Develop an Action Plan	9.2, 9.3	pollution and spill prevention
	12.3	case study - Novacor
	13.2	case study - 3M
6) Assign Resources and Implement Action Plan	8.2	organization structure, resource allocation
	10.2	training programs
	12.4	case study - Novacor
	13.3	case study - 3M
7) Information Flow	3.3	legal reporting requirements
	4.3, 4.4	reporting environmental costs
	Ch 5	public involvement and communication
	8.3	types of reports
	9.4, 9.5	environmental manuals, monitoring
	9.7	interaction with external stakeholders
	10.3	communicating achievements
	11.6	environmental audit reports
	12.4	case study - Novacor
8) Review of Steps 5 through 7	3.4, 11.3	legal considerations
	Ch 11	environmental audits
	12.5	case study - Novacor

Table 1.2
SUGGESTED QUESTIONS FOR TAKING STOCK

1) Do you have a corporate environmental policy?
2) Has a senior person (i.e. director, vice-president, etc.) been given overall responsibility for environmental issues?
3) Is a reporting system in place for environmental issues?
4) Do all employees know about the policy and reporting system?
5) Are there environmental policies, procedures, and/or standards in place for individual units, divisions, factories, plants, etc.?
6) Is at least one employee per division or facility devoted to environmental compliance issues?
7) Does that employee know the requirements of environmental legislation?
8) Have these requirements been integrated into policies, procedures, standards, and training?
9) Are monitoring data assessed and summarized on regular intervals and distributed internally?
10) Are programs in place to prevent pollution (e.g. purchasing policies)?
11) Are spill response programs in place?
12) Do you have a program in place that includes environmental audits?
13) Do you know which aspects of your operations pose the greatest environmental risks for the organization?
14) Do you know what other stakeholders (customers, shareholders, suppliers) expect of the way you manage environmental issues?

1.4 OTHER APPROACHES TO ENVIRONMENTAL MANAGEMENT

As noted in Section 1.1, several approaches to environmental management have been put forward. No one approach has proven itself to be so superior that the others have lost all support. Indeed, the innumerable ways in which companies and organizations differ among one another virtually assures that there must be several viable approaches to environmental management. It is this search for the "right" approach that every company and organization must make for itself.

In the past few years, the term Total Quality Environmental Management (TQEM) has gained some degree of popularity. TQEM is a variation of Total Quality Management (TQM), a concept that advocates continuous improvement as the cornerstone of sound management principles. The full-scale adoption of the TQM model to environmental issues may not be appropriate. Increasing numbers of regulatory agencies and standard-setting organizations are treating environmental issues in substantially different ways than quality issues. This difference is evident in the recent decision by the International Organization for Standardization (ISO) to establish two distinct technical committees for Environment (ISO 14 000) and Quality (ISO 9 000).

There also are some environmental management approaches that focus on going "beyond compliance." Given the possible fines, spectre of imprisonment, and increasing public disapproval of environmental offenders, compliance must be the basic goal of an EMS. Based on the authors' experience, very few companies comply with all of the requirements of environmental legislation all of the time. We believe that a company must learn to walk before it runs. Once a company has compliance under control, it can then set its sights on a higher level of performance.

REFERENCES

The Business Roundtable. November 1993. *Facility Level Pollution Prevention Benchmarking Study.* Prepared with the AT&T QUEST (Quality, Engineering, Software, and Technologies) Benchmarking Group.

Tichy, N.M. 1983. *Managing Strategic Change: Technical, Political and Cultural Dynamics.* John Wiley & Sons Ltd.

2

Regulatory Framework

---

by
J.D. Phyper, Phyper & Associates Limited
Brett Ibbotson, Angus Environmental Limited

2.1 THE EMPHASIS PLACED ON COMPLIANCE

An assumption that underlies many EMS standards/guidelines (e.g. the Canadian Standards Association CSA Z750 or British Standards Institute BS7750) and corporate environmental policies is that striving to comply with all pertinent environmental legislation is a key objective of an EMS. Other environmental issues such as sustainable development, environmentally friendly design, or life cycle analysis may come to be key components of an EMS over time, but compliance must be the first priority of an EMS.

As legislation becomes more complex and pervasive, achieving compliance becomes increasingly difficult. This is further complicated by the broadening reporting requirements being imposed by government agencies and jurisdictions. These trends, along with the strengthened resolve in many jurisdictions to prosecute companies and individuals that do not achieve compliance, have resulted in many companies increasing their efforts to meet legislative requirements.

This chapter provides an overview of environment legislation in Canada. It describes the roles of the different levels of government, the types of regulatory instruments agencies use, and commonly encountered types of legislative requirements. A detailed discussion of the regulatory requirements in each province is beyond the scope of this book. It is thus critical that environmental managers be familiar with the legislation that is relevant to the facilities they manage.

2.2 ROLES OF VARIOUS LEVELS OF GOVERNMENT

Environmental management activities undertaken at the federal level can be divided into three main categories. One is the environmental management of federal facilities, such as many airports, harbours, and government installations. The second is regulating environmental issues where more than one province is involved. Examples include interprovincial transportation by road, transportation by rail and airplane, and discharges that may be deleterious to fish or to navigable waters. The third category is regulating issues deemed to be in the national interest, such as the import or export of goods and wastes, transboundary movement of air pollutants, the proper management of special materials (such as polychlorinated biphenyls), and the registration of new chemicals prior to being imported or produced on a commercial scale.

Provincial jurisdiction includes regulating emissions to air, discharges to water, waste management, road transportation within the province, natural resource management, and environmental impact assessments. Federal regulations can be used by provincial agencies if province-specific regulations have not been passed.

The divisions between federal and provincial responsibilities are not always clearly set out. There are duplications and gaps, and instances where both may apply. In a recent ruling, the Ontario Court of Appeal ruled that federally regulated industries are subject to provincial environmental laws of "general application" (Templegate, 1994).

Tables 2.1 and 2.2 present environmental acts at both the federal and provincial levels, respectively. Note that there may be several regulations under a particular act which govern the release, storage, handling, or disposal of chemicals.

Municipal governments largely undertake roles assigned to them by provincial governments. Typically, municipal governments are authorized to impose environmental requirements on activities within their jurisdiction or that use their facilities. Many municipalities have established by-laws for discharges to municipal wastewater treatment systems and noise control. An increasing number of municipalities are becoming involved in the siting and operation of solid waste management facilities, and some have established environmental protection offices or departments.

Two municipalities, Montreal Urban Community (MUC) and Greater Vancouver Regional District (GVRD), have entered into agreements with their respective provincial governments whereby they have jurisdiction for air emissions and components of solid waste management in addition to discharges to municipal sewer systems. The City of Toronto has expanded its role by establishing an Environmental Protection Office and passing by-laws regulating ozone-depleting substances.

Table 2.1
FEDERAL ENVIRONMENTAL ACTS

Canadian Environmental Protection Act (CEPA)
- Authorizes the Minister of the Environment to set environmental quality objectives, codes of practice, and guidelines. These are not legally binding, but are useful in determining standards of due diligence or acceptable levels of contaminants.
- Controls toxic substances throughout Canada, from cradle (manufacture and importation) to grave (disposal).
- Contains reporting and clean-up requirements in the case of toxic substances.
- Regulates nutrients such as phosphorus and other cleaning agents.
- Protects the environment from activities within the jurisdiction of federal government such as those relating to federal lands, international air pollution, and ocean dumping.

Fisheries Act
- Prohibits the carrying out of a work or undertaking that results in the harmful alteration, disruption, or destruction of fish habitat or the deposit or causing or permitting the deposit of material which is deleterious to fish in water frequented by fish.
- "Deleterious substance" is defined as one which would degrade or alter the quality of water so as to render the water deleterious to fish or fish habitat.
- Administered by Environment Canada but may be enforced by provincial agencies where delegation has taken place.

Transportation of Dangerous Goods Act
- Regulates the manner in which dangerous goods are transported interprovincially and internationally.
- Applies to all movements of dangerous goods within, into or out of Canada by any mode of transport.
- "Dangerous Goods" is defined in the act as "a product, substance or organism included by its nature or by the regulations in any of the classes listed in the schedule".

Table 2.2
PROVINCIAL ENVIRONMENTAL ACTS

ALBERTA
- Clean Air Act
- Clean Water Act
- Environmental Protection and Enhancement Act
- Hazardous Chemicals Act
- Transportation of Dangerous Goods Control Act
- Oil and Gas Conservation Act
- Pipeline Act
- Municipal Government Act
- Public Health Act
- Agricultural Chemicals Act
- Land Surface Conservation and Reclamation Act

BRITISH COLUMBIA
- Environment Management Act
- Waste Management Act
- Transport of Dangerous Goods Act
- Municipal Act
- Health Act
- Pesticide Control Act
- Mines Act
- Environment and Land Use Act
- Environment Management Act and Utilities Commission Act

MANITOBA
- Environment Act
- Dangerous Goods Handling and Transportation Act
- Municipal Act
- Public Health Act
- Pesticides and Fertilizers Control Act
- Waste Reduction and Prevention Act
- Ozone-depleting Substances Act

NEW BRUNSWICK
- Clean Environment Act
- Clean Water Act
- Transportation of Dangerous Goods Act
- Municipalities Act
- Health Act
- Pesticides Control Act
- Mining Act

TABLE 2.2, continued

NEWFOUNDLAND
- Department of Environment and Lands Act
- Waters Protection Act
- Municipalities Act
- Department of Health Act
- Pesticides Control Act
- Waste Material (Disposal) Act
- Dangerous Goods Transportation Act

NORTHWEST TERRITORIES
- Environmental Protection Act
- Environmental Rights Act
- Transportation of Dangerous Goods Act
- Public Health Act
- Pesticide Act
- Forest Protection Act

NOVA SCOTIA
- Environmental Protection Act
- Water Act
- Dangerous Goods and Hazardous Wastes Management Act
- Dangerous Goods Transportation Act
- Municipal Act
- Health Act
- Ozone Layer Protection Act
- Pest Control Products Act
- Recycling Act

ONTARIO
- Environmental Bill of Rights
- Environmental Protection Act
- Health Protection and Promotion Act
- Ontario Water Resources Act
- Municipal Act
- Conservation Authorities Act
- Dangerous Goods Transportation Act
- Pesticides Act
- Mining Act
- Gasoline Handling Act
- Waste Management Act

TABLE 2.2, continued

QUEBEC
- Environment Quality Act
- Transport Act
- Cities and Towns Act
- Municipal Code of Quebec
- Public Health Protection Act
- Pesticides Act

SASKATCHEWAN
- Environmental Management and Protection Act
- Air Pollution Control Act
- Dangerous Goods Transportation Act
- Water Corporation Act
- Ozone Depleting Substances Control Act
- Public Health Act
- Pest Control Products Act
- Pollution (By Livestock) Control Act

YUKON
- Dangerous Goods Transportation Act
- Environment Act
- Public Health Act
- Noise Prevention Act

2.3 TYPES OF REGULATORY INSTRUMENTS

Several types of instruments are used by government agencies in Canada to manage or regulate environmental issues:

i) Provincial and Federal Acts, Regulations, Standards

ii) Permits, Certificates of Approval, Certificates of Authorization, licenses required by Acts

iii) Orders (e.g. stop, clean-up, prevention, or control orders)

iv) Municipal by-laws

v) Codes of Practice, Policies, Criteria, Objectives, and Guidelines

Acts or statutes are passed by parliament or the provincial legislature. Acts are typically general in nature in terms of requirements (e.g. an act may prohibit creating "adverse effects") and have a broader policy perspective. **Regulations** are made pursuant to authority set out in an act and provide specific operational details on the general powers listed in the act. **A bill** is a proposed law that following passage by legislature becomes an act or regulation.

Permits, certificates, and licenses are issued to specific parties by federal or provincial agencies. Such instruments are required by some acts and regulations.

Orders are issued to specific parties by federal or provincial agencies usually in response to failure by the party to comply with an act or regulation, or on the strong suspicion that non-compliance could occur.

Municipal by-laws are similar to regulations because they depend upon and are authorized by provincial statute. They typically cover water discharges, development, and land-use planning.

Codes of practice, policies, criteria, objectives, and guidelines are used by federal and provincial agencies to address many environmental issues. These types of instruments are also created by joint federal-provincial organizations, such as the Canadian Council of Ministers of the Environment. The CCME develops codes of practice and environmental criteria, and manages the National Contaminated Sites Remediation Program (see Section 2.9.3).

While not legally binding on their own, these types of instruments need to be reviewed and assessed as part of environmental compliance. They can illustrate an agency's position toward a particular situation. If incorporated into the terms of a license, permit, or other approval, or referred to in a regulation, these types of instruments can be legally binding on that specific operation.

This approach is substantially different than that used in the United States where most requirements are contained within legally binding instruments (i.e. acts or regulations). Policies, guidelines and voluntary compliance programs play important roles in environmental management in Canada. These types of instruments present industry with the opportunity to engage in cooperative discussions with government agencies and influence regulatory developments.

2.4 IDENTIFYING REGULATORY REQUIREMENTS

One of the first steps in developing an EMS is to identify all of the pertinent regulatory requirements (see Section 1.3). This task can be onerous and confusing. In some situations, more than one level of government will have regulatory requirements for the same discharge. For example, the results of effluent monitoring from pulp and paper mills in Ontario must be filed with the Ontario Ministry of Environment and Energy, Environment Canada, and Oceans and Fisheries Canada. Figure 2.1 presents an example of the regulatory requirements for a hypothetical facility in Ontario.

FIGURE 2.1
EXAMPLES OF PERTINENT LEGISLATION FOR ONTARIO INDUSTRY

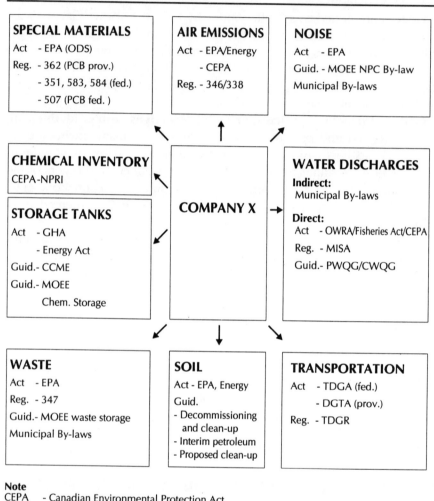

SPECIAL MATERIALS
Act - EPA (ODS)
Reg. - 362 (PCB prov.)
     - 351, 583, 584 (fed.)
     - 507 (PCB fed.)

AIR EMISSIONS
Act - EPA/Energy
     - CEPA
Reg. - 346/338

NOISE
Act - EPA
Guid. - MOEE NPC By-law
Municipal By-laws

CHEMICAL INVENTORY
CEPA-NPRI

STORAGE TANKS
Act - GHA
     - Energy Act
Guid.- CCME
Guid.- MOEE
       Chem. Storage

COMPANY X

WATER DISCHARGES
Indirect:
   Municipal By-laws

Direct:
Act   - OWRA/Fisheries Act/CEPA
Reg. - MISA
Guid.- PWQG/CWQG

WASTE
Act - EPA
Reg. - 347
Guid.- MOEE waste storage
Municipal By-laws

SOIL
Act - EPA, Energy
Guid.
- Decommissioning
  and clean-up
- Interim petroleum
- Proposed clean-up

TRANSPORTATION
Act - TDGA (fed.)
     - DGTA (prov.)
Reg. - TDGR

Note
CEPA   - Canadian Environmental Protection Act
CWQG - Clean Water Quality Guidelines
EPA   - Environmental Protection Act
GHA   - Gasoline Handling Act
MISA   - Municipal Industrial Strategy for Abatement
MOEE   - Ontario Ministry of Environment and Energy
NPC   - Noise Pollution Control
NPRI   - National Pollutant Release Inventory
ODS   - Ozone-depleting Substances
OWRA - Ontario Water Resources Act
PWQG - Provincial Water Quality Guidelines
TDGA   - Transportation of Dangerous Goods Act
fed.   - federal
prov.   - provincial
reg.   - regulation
guid.   - guidelines

In general, Canadian environmental legislation imposes four requirements on individuals, companies, and government agencies:

- discharges of materials that may "impair" or cause an "adverse effect" in the natural environment are prohibited
- appropriate permits, certificates, and/or licenses for discharges to the environment must be obtained
- agencies must be notified of a spill or unusual event, and
- the natural environment must be restored following a spill or damaging event.

A useful rule of thumb is that the following two questions should be asked prior to performing any new undertaking:

- Is a permit required for the release (air, water, soil and waste streams)?
- Are levels in the release acceptable (when examined in terms of toxicity, concentration, and loading)?

There are numerous ways for a company or organization to identify the legislation that pertains to its operations or activities:

- Copies of legislation can be obtained directly from federal, provincial, and municipal sources. It may take considerable effort to review these, find pertinent sections, develop a good understanding of the requirements, and critically review the pertinent sections.
- Experts (such as environmental engineers, scientists, or lawyers) can be retained to identify and describe pertinent sections of the legislation.
- In some cases, books that summarize legislation (e.g. Handbook of Environmental Compliance in Ontario, 1994) are available.
- Services are available that provide subscribers with copies of acts and regulations, and reviews of the highlighted sections.
- Computer software can be obtained that provides rapid access to legislation (federal, provincial, and municipal) and which can be customized to the user's needs (see Section 9.6).

2.5 AIR EMISSIONS

2.5.1 Federal Requirements

The Canadian Environmental Protection Act (CEPA) addresses air quality and atmospheric emissions at the national level. Key elements of CEPA include:

- provisions to control all aspects of the life cycle of toxic substances including emissions during development, manufacturing, storage, transportation, use, and disposal
- the regulation of fuels and the components of fuels
- provisions to create guidelines and environmentally safe codes of practice, and

- provisions to control sources of air pollution in Canada where a violation of an international agreement would otherwise result

For atmospheric emissions, the requirements of CEPA are most relevant to those impacting on the United States.

Sector- or chemical-specific federal regulations have been passed to regulate the import and export of Ozone-Depleting Substances (ODS), and emissions from asbestos mines and mills, secondary lead smelters, chloro-alkali mercury plants, and vinyl chloride and polyvinyl chloride plants.

Environment Canada has developed a **Management Plan for Nitrogen Oxides (NO$_X$) and Volatile Organic Compounds (VOCs)** to identify domestic environmental protection requirements and to ensure that Canada fulfils its international obligations. The objective of the plan is to reduce the one-hour ambient air concentration of ozone to below 82 parts per billion (ppb) across Canada. Both NO$_X$ and VOCs are precursors to ozone formation. The plan describes numerous initiatives aimed at NO$_X$/VOC emission sources:

- vehicle emission standards
- energy conservation measures
- gasoline vapour recovery for service stations
- industrial source control
- power generation source control
- urban transportation management plans
- product modifications

One recent outcome of this effort has been the preparation of a code of practice for dry-cleaning operations by the CCME.

2.5.2 Provincial Requirements

Table 2.3 identifies the provincial acts and general regulations related to air emissions. These regulations contain several common elements:

- permits must be obtained for most emissions
- allowable emission levels and/or ambient air concentrations are defined
- limits are established for the opacity (i.e. visibility) of emissions
- there are general prohibitions on causing adverse effects
- there are requirements placed on the storage and release of ODS

All provinces require that a **permit** (also called Certificate of Approval, Certificate of Authorization, license, etc.) be obtained for all new or modified air emissions sources. Exempted from the requirement to obtain a permit is routine maintenance and general heating for dwellings of three or fewer families. It is critical that the conditions stipulated in the permit be reviewed and disseminated to all parties involved in the management of air emissions. Normally, the details of a permit will include allowable emission levels, operating conditions, reporting, and maintenance requirements.

Table 2.3
PROVINCIAL LEGISLATION AFFECTING AIR EMISSIONS

Province	Permit	Allowable Levels	Opacity	General Prohibition	Control of ODS
Alberta	EPHA & Reg.110/93	Reg. 124/93	Reg. 124/93	None	Reg. 125/93
B.C.	WMA	None	None	WMA	ODSR
Manitoba	Env. Act	None	None	None	Reg. 103/94
N.B.	CEA & Reg. 208/83	Reg. 208/83	None	None	Reg. 208/83
Nfld.	Env. Lands Act	Reg. 26/81	Reg. 26/81	None	None
N.S.	EPA	None	None	None	Reg. 8/91
Ontario	EPA & Energy Act	Reg. 346/93 & 338/93	Reg. 346/93	EPA & Reg. 346/93	EPA & Reg. 189/94
Quebec	EQA & QAR	QAR	QAR	QAR	Reg. 812/93
Sask.	CAA	CAR	CAR	CAA	ODSCA

Note

* Regulations presented are for general air emissions and do not cover sector specific requirements

Definitions
CAA-Clean Air Act
CAR-Clean Air Regulation
CEA-Clean Environment Act
EPA-Environmental Protection Act
EPAEA-Environmental Protection & Enhancement Act
EQA-Environment and Quality Act
ODSR-Ozone-depleting Subtance Regulation
ODSCA-Ozone-depleting Substances Control Act
QAR-Quality of the Atmosphere Regulation
WMA-Waste Management Act

Allowable emission rates have been established in a few provinces and typically they are for specified industrial operations. Most jurisdictions have **allowable standards for ambient air concentrations** and some jurisdictions have allowable levels for point-of-impingement (POI) concentrations. POI concentrations often are based on short duration averaging times (e.g. 30 minutes to one hour), whereas ambient levels are typically for 24-hour periods. In some jurisdictions, algorithms for air dispersion modelling are provided in regulations dealing with emissions (e.g. the Ontario MOEE provides equations that can be used to calculate POI concentrations).

Opacity is a measure of the transparency of a visible emission. At 100% opacity, the emission is impervious to light. Several provinces have established the "acceptable" levels of opacity. Key factors when assessing opacity are the averaging time and the type of material that is the source of the emission (often a fuel).

General prohibitions typically prohibit the release of a "contaminant" into the "natural environment" which causes or is likely to cause an "adverse effect" or "impairment." The definition of adverse effect that appears in the Ontario Environmental Protection Act includes:

- impairment of the natural environment for any use that can be made of it
- injury or damage to property or plant or animal life
- harm or material discomfort to any person
- an adverse effect on the health of a person
- impairment of the safety of any person
- rendering any property or plant or animal life unfit for use by man
- loss of enjoyment of normal use of property, and
- interference with the normal conduct of business

This type of definition can also be used to control odours, nuisance dust, and noise.

There are also important **differences** between provinces in the management of air emissions. Some examples include:

- Exemption Dates — sources constructed before a prescribed date are exempt from requiring a permit if they have not been modified.
- Dual Permits — a permit is required for the construction of the device and another permit is required for the operation.
- Dispersion Modelling — in some jurisdictions dispersion models prescribed in regulations are to be employed in the assessment of compliance with POI concentrations.
- Combined Permit — in some jurisdictions a facility permit is obtained for all air emissions, water discharges, and waste storage.
- Renewable — in some jurisdictions, the permit has to be renewed within a specified time period.

2.5.3 Municipal Requirements

Three municipalities have developed by-laws specific to air emissions:

- Greater Vancouver Regional District (GVRD) By-law No. 725 covers all aspects of air emissions
- Montreal Urban Community (MUC) By-law 90 covers all aspects of air emissions including allowable emission limits, POI concentrations, and dispersion modelling (algorithms for single source and multiple source)
- City of Toronto By-law 279-93 covers management of ODS

2.6 WATER DISCHARGES

2.6.1 Federal Requirements

The Fisheries Act prohibits the carrying out of a work or undertaking that results in the harmful alteration, disruption, or destruction of fish habitat or the deposit or causing or permitting the deposit of material which is deleterious to fish in water frequented by fish. Section 14 of the Act forbids the depositing (or permitting the deposit) of a deleterious substance in any type of waters frequented by fish or in any other place under circumstances where the substance could enter the water. A deleterious substance is defined by the Act as:

- any substance that, if added to water, would degrade or alter the quality of that water so that it is rendered harmful to fish, and
- any water that contains a substance in which, quantity or concentration that it would, if added to water, degrade the quality of the water and, therefore, cause harm to fish

The CEPA authorizes the Minister of the Environment to set environmental quality objectives, codes of practice and guidelines, and to regulate the discharge of specific chemicals (e.g. dioxins, furans, PCBs, etc.). Section 34(1) of the CEPA allows for the regulation of releases of toxic substances (as defined in Schedule 1) in terms of:

- quantity or concentration
- places or areas where the substance may be released
- the commercial or processing activity which gives rise to the release of the substance
- the manner and conditions in which the substance may be released into the environment, either alone or in combination with any other substance
- the circumstances or conditions under which the minister may, for the proper administration of this Act, modify any requirement for sampling, analysis, testing, measurement, or monitoring, or the methods and procedures for conducting any required sampling, analysis, tests, measurements, or monitoring

The CEPA also covers the concentration of nutrients in products. Subsection 50(2) prohibits the manufacture for use or sale in Canada or import of any cleaning agent or water conditioner that have nutrient concentrations above those specified by regulations made under the Act. Part VI of the Act addresses ocean dumping, conditions, and terms of dumping permits, dumping to avert danger, and the granting of permits to dump.

Sector or chemical-specific regulations have been passed to control water discharges at the federal level, recent examples of which include regulations passed under the Fisheries Act and CEPA for pulp and paper mill discharges .

Several guidelines have also been developed by federal agencies for water quality, the most prominent being the Canadian Water Quality Guidelines which cover both ambient water and drinking water quality.

2.6.2 Provincial Requirements

Provincial legislation typically covers all direct discharges (i.e. discharges to an open water body and not to a municipal sewer system). An exception is Newfoundland where allowable limits for discharges to municipal sewer system are stipulated in provincial regulations. Table 2.4 presents the acts and general regulations for provincial water discharges. In general, provincial legislation stipulates:

- permits that must be obtained to operate sewage works and water works
- allowable discharge levels
- general prohibition on causing impairment

As indicated in Table 2.4, all jurisdictions require that a permit, certificate, or license be obtained for all new or modified sewage works. Most provinces also require a permit or license for the taking of water in excess of a specified amount from an open water body. In several provinces, a permit is also required for the alteration of a water course.

Copies of the permit should be disseminated to all permit parties as they typically contain the allowable discharge levels, monitoring and reporting requirements and, in some cases, requirements to prepare an operations manual and perform regular maintenance.

Few jurisdictions stipulate **allowable discharge levels** in a general act or regulation. Most either:

- develop industrial discharge quality limits on a case-by-case basis on numerical water quality values from provincial or federal guidelines, objectives, or criteria in conjunction with an appropriate mixing zone for the receiving water body. These values are added to the site-specific permit thereby making them legally binding on the operations. Or, they

- have sector-specific regulations such as the Ontario Municipal Industrial Strategy for Abatement (MISA) program and the Québec Depollution Attestation, which typically are based upon the concept of using the Best Available Technology Economically Achievable (BATEA).

Table 2.4
PROVINCIAL LEGISLATION AFFECTING WATER DISCHARGES

Province	Permit	Allowable Levels	General Prohibition
Alberta	EPAEA, Reg. 121/93 & 110/93	None	None
B.C.	WMA	None	WMA
Manitoba	Env. Act	None	None
N.B.	Reg. 82-126	None	None
Nfld.	Env. Lands Act & Reg. 406/78	Reg. 156/80	Env. Lands Act
N.S.	Water Act, Reg. 95/90, 16/92 & 73/78	None	Water Act
Ontario	OWRA	None	OWRA, EPA & GHA
Quebec	EQA	None	PPR
Sask.	EMPA	None	EMPA

Note
* Regulations presented are for general air emissions and do not cover sector specific requirements

Definitions
EMPA-Environmental Management and Protection Act
EPA-Environmental Protection Act
EPAEA-Environmental Protection & Enhancement Act
EQA-Environmental Quality Act
GHA-Gasoline Handling Act
OWRA-Ontario Water Resources Act
PPR-Petroleum Products Regulation
WMA-Waste Management Act

The Ontario MISA program is a major provincial initiative to reduce water pollution from industrial and municipal discharges. The overall objective of the program is the virtual elimination of persistent, toxic contaminants from all discharges into Ontario waterways. The MISA program divides all dischargers into two broad categories: indirect and direct dischargers. The latter are industries and municipalities that discharge effluents directly into surface waters. Regulations that specify effluent requirements for each sector are being developed in three phases:

Phase I   Effluent Monitoring Regulation

Phase II   Effluent Limits Regulation

Phase III   Abatement and Enforcement

The potential exists for other provinces to adopt portions of the MISA program to regulate discharges. The MISA regulations specify sample/laboratory containers, sample type (grab versus composite), material to be used in the sampler, minimum sample volumes, maximum sample storage time, sample preservatives, method detection limits, flow accuracies, quality assurance/quality control procedures, instrument measurement method principles, data storage and reporting procedures, and the retention time of records.

The indirect discharger portion of the MISA program has been delayed. It is anticipated that a new general sewer-use by-law may be available in draft form by the end of 1995.

Several acts contain a general prohibition against the discharge of any material into water that may cause impairment or an adverse effect. Typically, impairment/adverse effect refers to injury to any person, animal, bird, or other living thing as a result of the use or consumption of any plant, fish, or other living matter or thing in the water or in the soil in contact with the water.

Methods that can be used to assess compliance with this general prohibition include i) comparing concentrations of chemicals in the discharge to provincial or federal water quality guidelines/objectives allowing for some dilution (i.e. mixing) depending upon the assimilation capacity of the receiving water body; or ii) performing aquatic toxicity tests (e.g. using aquatic species such as rainbow trout or Daphnia magna) on samples collected of the discharge.

Regulatory requirements vary from province to province. Some examples include:

- Exemption Dates — sources constructed before a prescribed date are exempt in some provinces from requiring a permit if they have not been modified.
- Dual Permits — some provinces require one permit for the construction of the device and another permit is required for the operation.

- Combined Permit — in some jurisdictions, a facility permit can be obtained for all air emissions, water discharges, and waste storage.
- Renewable — in some jurisdictions the permit has to be renewed within a specified time period.
- Abandonment — some provinces are developing legislation for the abandonment of sewage works.

2.6.3 Municipal Requirements

Municipal by-laws for liquid effluents generally contain the following five elements:

- stipulate the allowable concentrations for discharges to storm, sanitary, and/or combined sewers
- expressly prohibit dilution to achieve those limits
- prohibit the discharge of specified substances and/or waste to storm, sanitary, and/or combined sewers
- prohibit the discharge of types of water to specific sewer lines (e.g. discharge of storm water to a sanitary sewer line is usually prohibited)
- express the option for a discharger to enter into agreements with local municipality for overstrength discharges (typically for very few parameters), compliance issues, or water surcharge situations

Note that discharges from waste water treatment facilities (including those operated by municipal agencies) are considered to be "direct" discharges and hence fall under both provincial and federal agreements.

2.7 WASTE HANDLING AND DISPOSAL

2.7.1 Federal Requirements

The major piece of federal legislation that influences waste management is the Canadian Environmental Protection Act (CEPA) which includes provisions for the control of all aspects of the life cycle of toxic substances, including their importation, transport, distribution, and ultimate disposal as waste. CEPA has the following elements related to waste management:

- authority to regulate waste handling elements and disposal practices of federal departments, boards, agencies, and Crown corporations
- provisions to create guidelines and codes of environmentally sound practices as well as objectives setting desirable levels of environmental quality, and
- provisions to issue permits to control dumping at sea from ships, barges, aircraft, and man-made structures (excluding normal discharges from off-shore facilities involved in the exploration for, and exploitation and processing of, seabed mineral resources)

Several regulations have been promulgated under CEPA to control the movement or storage of waste. Key regulations include the Import and Export of Hazardous Waste Regulation and PCB Material Storage Regulation.

A second piece of federal legislation that influences waste management activities in Canada is the Transportation of Dangerous Goods Act.
The TDGA and associated regulations govern the classification, handling,
and shipment of dangerous goods, including most hazardous waste (see
Section 2.8).

Table 2.5
PROVINCIAL LEGISLATION AFFECTING WASTE
HANDLING AND DISPOSAL

Province	Properly Classify	Permit & License	Manifests
Alberta	EPAEA	EPAEA & PHA Reg. 250/85	EPAEA Reg. 129/93
B.C.	WMA & SWR	WMA	WMA & SWR
Manitoba	DGHTA	DGHTA	DGHTA
N.B.	None	None	None
Nfld.	None	None	None
N.S.	None	Reg. 97/89	None
Ontario	EPA, WMA & Reg. 347	EPA	Reg. 347
Quebec	LQE, RDD OL674-88 & RRSW	1000-85	1000-85
Sask.	None	HSWDGR	None

Note
   *   Regulations presented are for general discharges and do not cover sector
        specific requirements
  **   Management of municipal waste facilities

Definitions
EPA-Environmental Protection Act
EPAEA-Environmental Protection & Enhancement Act
LQE-Environmental Quality Act
PHA-Public Health Act
RDD-Hazardous Waste Regulation (Rëglement sur les Déchets Dangereux)
RRSW-Regulation Respecting Solid Waste
SWR-Special Waste Regulation

2.7.2   Provincial Requirements
Table 2.5 presents the pertinent provincial acts or general regulations
related to waste storage, handling, and disposal. These include the following requirements:

- proper classification of waste according to legislation
- a permit/license for waste management facilities (includes carriers, processing locations, and disposal sites)
- use of manifest for movement of hazardous waste and liquid industrial waste, and special waste (the latter including materials from the other two categories)

All jurisdictions require that generators **classify** waste according to provincial criteria. Ontario uses a system based upon a three-digit waste class number and letter for waste category. Waste is divided into hazardous waste (ten categories), liquid industrial waste, registerable solid waste, and non-registerable waste. In most other provinces, waste is classified using classes and groups prescribed by the Transportation of Dangerous Goods Act with additional categories for waste oil and asbestos.

Most provinces require that carriers be **licensed** to transport waste and that all processing and disposal sites and waste processing or transfer stations have a valid permit, certificate, or license.

Unlike the United States where generators are responsible for their wastes forever, the responsibility for disposal of waste may be transferred in Canada to a third party (a disposal site operation, the owner of a disposal site, or the owner of a transfer station) provided that the license and permit requirements are met and that the facility is within Canada. However, most provinces consider both the generator and the carrier to be responsible during the transportation of the waste to the disposal or processing site.

In some provinces, an environmental assessment is required for the siting of new waste management facilities (e.g. landfill and hazardous waste treatment facilities). Section 2.10 presents additional information on environmental assessments.

Manifest systems are used to track for the transport of hazardous, liquid industrial, special waste, etc. in most jurisdictions. They often consist of six copies that are distributed as follows:

- provincial environmental agency is sent a copy shortly after waste shipment
- generator retains a copy for two years
- carrier sends provincial agency a copy
- carrier retains a copy for two years
- disposal site retains a copy for two years
- disposal site sends a copy back to the generator

If the generator does not receive the copy from the disposal site (the completion of the circle), then the generator is usually required to notify the provincial agency.

Regulatory requirements vary from province to province. Some examples include:

- Exemption Dates — waste management facilities constructed before a prescribed date are exempt in some provinces from requiring a permit if they have not been modified.
- Combined Permit — in some jurisdictions, a facility permit can be obtained for all air emissions, water discharges, and waste storage.
- Generator Number — some jurisdictions require that a waste generator register and obtain a generator if it produces specific types of waste.
- Notification of Storage — in some provinces, the environmental ministry or department must be notified if hazardous waste or liquid industrial waste is stored for more than a specified period, while in other provinces an annual report and weekly inspections are required for hazardous waste.

In some of the provinces requiring the generator to be registered, it is an offence to store, dispose, and transport waste unless a generator number has been obtained. An out-of-province waste generator that transports or disposes of hazardous or liquid industrial wastes in these provinces must register with the relevant provincial ministries. Any changes to processes or the types of wastes that are generated must be reported to the government agencies in writing.

2.8 TRANSPORTATION OF DANGEROUS GOODS

2.8.1 Federal Requirements

The Transport of Dangerous Goods Act (TDGA) pertains to marine, air, rail, and interprovincial and international road transportation.

2.8.2 Provincial Requirements

The TDGA is administered by Transport Canada. Environment Canada provides technical advice and recommendations for regulatory initiatives or matters related to hazardous waste. When radioactive materials are involved, conditions of the Transport Packaging of Radioactive Materials Regulation must also be met.

Part IV of the TDGA requires all shipments of dangerous goods to be accompanied by a **shipping document** providing information on the substance, companies involved in its shipment, etc. The consignor, carrier (excluding a roll-on/roll-off), and consignee must retain a copy of the document for a period of two years.

If the dangerous goods are being transferred by road vehicle, a copy of the document must be kept in the cab within the driver's reach.

All dangerous goods must be **properly packaged** and marked with

proper safety marks, labels, signs, and placards. Part V and Schedule V of the TDGA describes the proper markings required for dangerous goods. Marking involves the use of dangerous good labels and safety marks on small containers and the use of placards on large transport units. It is the generator's responsibility to ensure that the appropriate placards are in place prior to shipment. The carrier, however, is responsible during the transportation of the dangerous good.

If the dangerous good is a waste, the consignor (i.e. the shipper) must insert the word "waste" immediately preceding the shipping name.

The shipping document for a hazardous waste is called a "manifest" and is compatible with most provincial manifests. A manifest must provide:

- detailed information on the types and amounts of hazardous waste being shipped
- a record of various firms or individuals involved in the shipment
- information on the treatment, storage, and/or disposal of the hazardous waste when it reaches its final destination

For some dangerous substances specified in Schedule XII of the TDGA regulation including infectious wastes, explosives, certain gases, and radioactive wastes, the generator or consignor must file an **emergency response plan** with the Director General of the TDGA regulation. The documents for each shipment must show the emergency response plan number and the telephone number for activating the plan. The plan must outline the assistance that can be provided in the event of an emergency.

Some industrial associations have established regional response centres to respond to emergencies. One example is the Canadian Chemical Producers' Transportation Emergency Assistance Program (TEAP).

Any person who handles, offers for transport, or transports dangerous goods must be **trained or be directly supervised by a trained person.** The training must be relevant for the types of duties performed. A trained person may be required to produce a certificate of TDGA training upon request by an inspector.

If a **"dangerous occurrence"** takes place, notification of certain government agencies by the person in charge at the time must occur immediately. Several provinces (e.g. Ontario Spills Action Centre) have established 24-hour response centres. At the federal level, the National Environmental Emergencies Centre in Hull, Quebec will respond to inquiries and provide technical assistance 24 hours a day, seven days a week.

Classification involves assigning dangerous goods into classes and divisions based on criteria that are described in Part III of the TDGA regulation. Classification involves picking the substance from a comprehensive list given in the regulation, or comparing the properties of the substance to criteria given in the regulation. There are nine different classes of dangerous goods:

1) Explosives
2) Gases
3) Flammable and Combustible Liquids
4) Flammable Solids
5) Oxidizing Substances and Organic Peroxides
6) Poisonous (toxic) and Infectious Substances
7) Radioactive Material
8) Corrosives
9) Miscellaneous Dangerous Goods

Each type of dangerous good is assigned one of the nine classes as its primary classification. In addition, one or more subsidiary classifications may be assigned. The primary classification describes the main hazardous properties of a particular dangerous good. A subsidiary classification describes other hazardous properties.

The following materials are **exceptions** to the TDGA:

- gasoline for use in vehicles
- retail purchases
- movement of less than one kilometre between plants or properties of the same owner
- service truck exemption for material being used in repair
- limited quantity exemptions

Recyclable material was previously exempted from the regulation if it was transferred by a generator and destined for a site where it would be wholly utilized (this does not include combustion or land application), promptly packaged for retail sale, or offered for retail sale. However, materials going for recycling must now have a shipping document as per Schedules 8 and 12 of the TDGA.

The provincial acts pertaining to the transportation of dangerous goods (including hazardous waste) regulate movement within a province using roads. Typically, the provincial acts are little more than an administrative formality in that they essentially defer to the federal TDGA.

2.9   SOIL CONTAMINATION

2.9.1 Provincial Requirements

In Canada, issues such as property contamination (and therefore reme-diation) largely fall within provincial jurisdiction; however, due to its rela-tively recent emergence as an issue of widespread concern, the remedia-tion of contaminated property is not addressed in the statutes (acts) or regulations of most provinces. Provincial acts typically address soil quality in general terms (i.e. soil or land will be identified as part of the environ-ment, and the act will prohibit impairing the environment or causing "adverse effects"). In some provinces, there are regulations that identify the parties that can be held responsible for the clean-up of contaminated sites. A few of the provinces also have developed definitions for various categories of waste which may apply to soil depending on the types and concentrations of contaminants that are present (i.e. hazardous waste, inert fill, etc.). Table 2.6 presents a partial listing of provincial regulations and related documents that address the assessment and management of contaminated land.

The provinces that have directed the most attention to soil quality and remediation to date include British Columbia, Alberta, Ontario, and Quebec. These provinces have relatively large environmental ministries and the resources to examine emerging environmental issues. They also have relatively more situations where environmental concerns about redevelopment proposals arise. Other provinces often pattern their environmental requirements after those of one or more of those four provinces or the efforts of joint federal-provincial agencies (such as the CCME which is discussed in Section 2.9.5). This is also the case for remediation of contaminated property.

Several provinces have established numerical guidelines or criteria for selected chemicals in soil or ground water that can be used to determine when remediation is necessary. There is considerable variability from province to province as to the number of parameters addressed, the actual concentrations assigned to specific parameters, and the ways in which the guidelines are intended to be used.

Until the late 1980s, numerical guidelines most often addressed various metals (such as copper, cadmium, lead, nickel, mercury, and zinc) and a few general indicators such as pH, conductivity, and total oil and grease. In the 1990s, organic contaminants have proven to be just as troublesome (if not more so), and several provinces have recommended clean-up guidelines for some of the volatile components of gasoline (usually benzene, toluene, ethylbenzene, and xylenes); chlorinated organic compounds including solvents such as trichlorethylene and tetrachlorethylene; polychlorinated biphenyls (PCBs); dioxins and furans; and a dozen or more of the polycyclic aromatic hydrocarbons (PAHs).

Despite recent efforts to develop guidelines for more parameters, the proper use and interpretation of clean-up guidelines continue to be a source of confusion and delay for those who design and implement remediation and redevelopment programs. For most types of sites and most types of contaminants, remediation efforts must contend with numerical guidelines (often prefaced by qualifiers such as "draft," "interim," or "provisional"), and a patchwork of regulatory policies and philosophy (sometimes sparingly distributed or unwritten). Seldom are the numerical guidelines or policies legally enforceable, but they can be if incorporated into environmental orders or permits issued by regulatory agencies to specific sites or activities.

Table 2.6
PARTIAL LISTING OF REGULATIONS AND DOCUMENTS RELEVANT TO THE ASSESSMENT OF CONTAMINATED SITES

ALBERTA
- Environmental Protection and Enhancement Act
- Tier I Criteria for Contaminated Soil Assessment and Remediation (DRAFT)
- Remediation Guidelines for Petroleum Storage Tank Sites

BRITISH COLUMBIA
- Special Waste Regulation
- Waste Management Act
- Criteria for Managing Contaminated Sites in British Columbia
- Developing Criteria and Objectives for Managing Contaminated Sites in British Columbia

ONTARIO
- Environmental Protection Act
- Energy Act
- Guidelines for the Decommissioning and Clean-up of Sites in Ontario
- Interim Guideline for the Assessment and Management of Petroleum Contaminated Sites in Ontario
- Proposed Guidelines for the Clean-up of Contaminated Sites in Ontario

NEW BRUNSWICK
- Guidelines for the Assessment and Remediation of Contaminated Sites

QUEBEC
- Environmental Quality Act
- Contaminated Sites Rehabilitation Policy

SASKATCHEWAN
- Environmental Spill Control Regulation
- Hazardous Substances Regulation
- Interim Guidelines for the Decommissioning of Petroleum Storage Facilities

FEDERAL
- CCME Canadian "Interim" Environmental Quality Criteria
- CCME Interim Guidelines for PCBs in Soil
- Guidelines for managing radioactive materials

2.9.2 Federal Requirements

There are many instances when federal regulations, legislation, or policies must be taken into account during the remediation or redevelopment of contaminated property. Federal agencies are directly responsible for remediating federal properties such as international airports, harbours, defence facilities, prisons, research facilities, parks, reserves, etc. Federal legislation has been enacted for specific materials (i.e. radioactive materials and PCBs) that establishes clean-up criteria that apply across Canada (except in cases where specific provinces have established more stringent requirements).

2.9.3 Joint Federal-Provincial Initiatives

In 1989, a joint federal-provincial agency, the Canadian Council of Ministers of the Environment (CCME) initiated the National Contaminated Sites Remediation Program (NCSRP). The focus of the NCSRP is to ensure that appropriate remediation occurs at sites where contamination poses a serious threat to human health or environmental quality. A guiding principle of the NCSRP is that of **polluter pays** (i.e. the party responsible for site contamination will be held liable for its remediation.) There also is an **orphan site** component that comes into play where a polluter cannot be found, identified, or charged with the task of remediation.

In 1991, the CCME introduced "interim" environmental criteria for more than 80 substances that could be applied at federal and orphan sites across Canada. In July 1994, the CCME released a "final draft" document that proposes how soil quality criteria should be derived by considering the potential to adversely affect the environment and human health. If adopted, this protocol will be used to replace the "interim" criteria with scientifically defensible remediation criteria.

Various changes in provincial regulations and policies are occurring in response to the CCME efforts. The interim criteria are being used in provinces that have not established criteria for the contaminants addressed by the CCME. Several provincial governments are reviewing and are, as necessary, incorporating the polluter pays principle into regulations so that the liabilities of those responsible for contaminating property are clearly identified. Several provinces are considering adopting, in whole or in part, the CCME protocol for determining remediation criteria.

2.9.4 Municipal Requirements

The role of municipal governments is focused more on redevelopment than remediation. Municipal agencies are responsible for planning and approving land uses, and all proposals to redevelop properties must be submitted to municipal authorities. When proposals to redevelop property also have a remediation component (or when it is suspected that contamination on the property may not be compatible with a proposed use of the property), municipal agencies will often consult with provincial agencies. Because of numerous situations where municipal governments have allowed redevelopment of property that subsequently was found to be contaminated, municipal governments of several cities have recently established offices that review remediation plans and comment on other environmental aspects of property redevelopment.

2.10 ENVIRONMENTAL ASSESSMENTS

Most provinces have enacted legislation that requires the preparation of an environmental assessment (EA) for projects of certain types and scale. For example, facilities for the treatment and/or disposal of waste usually have an EA prepared as a prerequisite for receiving approval. The main components of an EA document typically include:

- the purpose for the undertaking
- a statement and description of the reasons behind the project and its alternatives
- a description of how the project and its alternatives will affect the environment
- a description of the environmental effects and actions necessary to prevent, change, mitigate, or remedy environmental effects
- evaluation of advantage/disadvantage to the environment of the project and its alternatives

The rationale for the undertaking should not only identify reasons for pursuing the undertaking but also provide an explanation of why the other options were considered less acceptable in terms of environmental effects and fulfilling the intended purpose. The evaluation of options is considered to be the cornerstone of the environmental assessment process. One must assess a "reasonable range" of possibilities. The same philosophy applies to the rationale for the selection of the technology and site.

2.11 RECENT TRENDS IN REGULATORY PHILOSOPHY

Government agencies are shifting towards pollution prevention as opposed to end-of-pipe controls. Examples include the Canadian/United States Pollution Prevention agreement and the Ontario Waste Reduction Strategy. Key components of these programs are the identification of toxic chemicals pertinent to a particular industrial section and the subsequent development of reduction strategies.

As part of the "Pollution Prevention" approach, government agencies also are shifting from "command and control" to "voluntary" programs. A recent review of these voluntary types of programs by government agencies and industrial associations indicates that there are approximately 100 of these programs being proposed or already in place.

An example of a voluntary program is the **Accelerated Reduction/ Elimination of Toxics (ARET)** program. The purpose of the ARET program is to reduce the potential adverse impacts of toxic substances on health and the environment by the accelerated reduction/elimination of selected toxic substance emissions. Members of the ARET committee include representatives from industry, health and academic associations, and governments (both federal and provincial).

The basic premise behind ARET is that voluntary action on the part of users and emitters of toxic substances may work more quickly and effectively than the traditional regulatory approach. It also has the potential of being less costly for both industry and government. It is anticipated that the ARET process may alleviate the need for some regulations to the extent that environmental goals are achieved through a voluntary approach. It also provides an opportunity to improve corporate image and gain public support.

To date, a prioritized list of candidate toxic substances for action has been developed based on the work of a multi-stakeholder technical subcommittee. Emitters participating in the ARET program were required to submit action plans to reduce/eliminate emissions of these substances by the fall of 1994.

REFERENCES

Templegate Information Services Inc. 1994. Canada's Environmental Legislation, 1994/95 edition. Toronto.

3

The Legal Framework

---

by
Roger Cotton
Tory Tory Deslauriers & Binnington

3.1 RECENT TRENDS IN ENVIRONMENTAL JURISPRUDENCE

Canadian environmental jurisprudence has evolved dramatically over the past 15 years. Emerging from relative obscurity, environmental decisions are increasingly finding their way into headlines across the country. The widespread publicity surrounding the decision in and the attendant implications of *R. v. Bata Industries Limited* (infra) is an example of this development.

Canadian case law with respect to the environmental legal regime includes hundreds of cases covering many environmental subjects. While it is not possible to present a complete overview, some of the more significant jurisprudential developments, and their implications for environmental management, are reviewed in this chapter. Emphasis is placed on what the courts are looking for when judging cases and passing sentences, and the protection that can be gained from having a sound EMS in place.

3.2 DUE DILIGENCE

One of the leading Canadian cases in the area of environmental law (and, indeed, criminal and quasi-criminal law) is *R. v. Sault Ste. Marie.*[1] The city of Sault Ste. Marie had entered into an agreement with a company for the disposal of all garbage generated in the city. The company was supposed to provide a site, labour, and equipment for this purpose. The site bordered a creek which ran into a river. As a result of dumping city garbage, both of these watercourses became polluted and the city was charged under what was then s.32(1) of the Ontario Water Resources Act (OWRA).[2]

Writing on behalf of the unanimous nine-member Supreme Court of Canada, Mr. Justice Dickson thoroughly reviewed the law with respect to what were until that point the only two types of offenses in the field of criminal law: (i) those offenses which are truly criminal and for which the Crown must establish a mental element of intent, or *mens rea;* and (ii) absolute liability offenses which entailed conviction on proof merely that the defendant committed the actual prohibited act constituting the *actus reus* of the offence.

After a thorough review of the law, Mr. Justice Dickson concluded that there were "compelling grounds for the recognition of three categories of offenses rather than the traditional two"[3]:

- offenses which require a full *mens rea;*
- offenses of absolute liability; and
- **offenses of strict liability, in which it will be open to the accused to show that they exercised due diligence even though the offence occurred.**[4]

Thus, since the Sault Ste. Marie decision, it has been open to an accused charged with violating a public welfare offence to prove, on the balance of probabilities, that they exercised due diligence to prevent the occurrence of the incident(s). While some might question the appropriateness of requiring the defendant to prove innocence by establishing due diligence, the Supreme Court of Canada has held that putting such an onus on an accused is permissible under the *Canadian Charter of Rights and Freedoms* (the *Charter*), notwithstanding the *Charter* provision that any person charged with an offence has the right to be presumed innocent until proven guilty according to law in a fair and public hearing by an independent and impartial tribunal.[5] It is the need to satisfy this onus that causes lawyers to attach such importance to the development of an EMS. If such a system is in place and is effective, then the person or company is well on the way to establishing its due diligence defence.

3.3 SENTENCING IN ENVIRONMENTAL CASES

Implementing an effective and comprehensive EMS makes not only good business sense, but it also affords corporations, officers, and directors protection from liability under environmental statutes and regulations. The need for such protection has grown markedly in the recent past, as courts have turned their attention to the necessity of punishing those responsible for environmental damage. To fully appreciate sentencing considerations and the potential penal and financial liabilities, it is useful to examine a few of the more seminal environmental cases addressing sentencing issues.

R. v. United Keno Hill Mines Limited (1980)

One of the earliest environmental court cases which visited the issue of environmental management is that of *R. v. United Keno Hill Mines Limited*,[6] a leading Canadian court case with respect to sentencing in Canada. The case involved a mining company which pleaded guilty to an offence of depositing waste in Yukon waters contrary to the Northern Inland Waters Act.[7] Accordingly, it was only necessary for the judge to determine the appropriate sentence. The ensuing judgment of Chief Justice Stuart is one of the most thoroughly reasoned reviews of the factors which should be considered when sentencing an accused in respect of environmental offenses.[8] Although it was written in 1980, the decision is still widely referred to today by judges across Canada.

Based on a review of Canadian and American case law and authorities, Chief Justice Stuart noted that there are (i) unique considerations to bear in mind in sentencing for environmental offenses, and (ii) sentencing principles peculiar to sentencing a corporation as opposed to an individual offender.[9] The court established the following list of considerations for sentencing corporations charged with pollution offenses.

1) Nature of the environment affected
2) Extent of damage inflicted
3) Wealth and size of the corporation
4) Criminality of conduct
5) Extent of attempts to comply
6) Remorse
7) Profits realized by the offence
8) Prior criminal record

One of the points which the judge discussed at length was the ineffectiveness of corporate fines in ensuring environmental compliance by corporations. He firmly believed that "fines alone will not mold law abiding corporate behaviour"[10] and that the corporate managers should also be prosecuted. According to the judge:

> Sentencing, to be effective, must reach the guiding mind — the corporate managers — be they directors or supervisors. They are the instigators of illegality either through wilfulness, wilful blindness, or incompetent supervisory practices.[11]

> After a few corporate presidents are prosecuted, it is likely senior executives will make it their business to know what all subordinates are doing and effective policies and checks against illegal activities will be implemented.[12]

From this decision it can be seen that, as early as 1980, judges were examining the role of management in environmental offenses and beginning to question the traditional shield afforded by the corporate veil.

Crowe v. R. (1991)

More recently, the sentence imposed by the decision of the Ontario Court of Justice (Provincial Division) in *Crowe v. R.*[13] made history in Canada. It marked the first time that a polluter was imprisoned for having committed an environmental offense.[14]

The accused individual (the president of the company) and his company were convicted of burying 185 barrels of liquid industrial waste on the lands of the accused. The drums had leaked into and impaired the ground water of the surrounding natural environment. At the trial, the individual was sentenced to six months in jail (the maximum time available) and the corporation was ordered to pay a fine of $90,000. On appeal, the sentences were reduced to 15 days in jail and $30,000 respectively.

Nevertheless, in rendering its decision on the appeal, the court expressed the current view of the courts with respect to environmental offenders:

> This is a serious matter and it is viewed as being increasingly serious by the society in which we live. . . . [T]he act complained of in this matter seriously impaired the quality of life which ought to have been enjoyed by Mr. Crowe and his neighbours. This impairment was done in a calculating and totally irresponsible manner. This type of behaviour cannot be condoned. In the interests of general deterrence, potential polluters must clearly receive the message that to engage in this type of behaviour, either out of laziness or for financial gain, will involve clear and severe penalties if uncovered.[15]

R. v. Varnicolor Chemical (1992)

In the case of *R. v. Varnicolor Chemical*,[16] a company officer and director were sentenced to eight months in jail for causing or permitting an unlawful discharge of contaminants into the environment. Varnicolor operated a plant in Elmira, Ontario involving the recycling of waste paint manufacturing solvents using a continuous distillation process to regenerate the solvents.

Over time, the accused company began to accept all types of hazardous waste. The company failed to comply with many of the requirements of the Certificate of Approval (C of A) issued by the Ministry of Environment and Energy (MOEE),[17] and environmental sampling of the property and ground water in the area revealed the presence of contaminants exceeding applicable guidelines.[18] A hydrogeological report prepared by the MOEE concluded that these contaminants would migrate with the ground water and may eventually discharge into an adjacent creek.

The environment in issue was not of "unique significance," although the contaminants would eventually find their way into a river which was used for a municipal water supply. It was estimated that it would cost more than $2.5 million to clean up the site. The court held that the defendant individual, who took an active part in the operations and management of the company, had acted in defiance of a C of A he had obtained, and that he had done so deliberately, or at least recklessly. The court further found that the defendant had not been co-operative or helpful to the MOEE, and nothing had been done to rectify problems at the site or to initiate a clean-up.

Although it can be argued that it is only in the most egregious of fact situations that officers and/or directors will be sentenced to jail, it is doubtful that this is the culmination of what appears to be a continuing trend. Undoubtedly, we will continue to see environmental prosecutors asking for stiffer sentences in the future against both corporations and individuals. The response of the courts to these requests will be keenly reviewed by business, individuals, and all other groups interested in the environment. In this context, the *Bata* decision (described in Section 3.4) will serve as one of the cases where the parameters of sentencing for environmental offenses will be set.

The clear message from these three cases is that the courts are willing to punish polluters and the officers and directors of polluting companies for their misdeeds. In addition to the increased penalties for committing offenses, provisions were added to Ontario's Environmental Protection Act (EPA)[19] and OWRA in 1988 requiring every officer and director of a corporation that engages in an activity that may result in the discharge of a contaminant contrary to the legislation to take all reasonable care to prevent the corporation from causing or permitting such unlawful discharge.[20] These changes have placed a positive duty upon officers and directors to manage the affairs of the company so that due diligence can be shown and liability for environmental offenses, both personal and corporate, can be avoided.[21]

3.4 CASES WITH LESSONS FOR EMS

3.4.1 *R. v. Bata Industries Limited*

Bata Industries Limited (BIL) is an Ontario corporation. In the late 1980s, BIL had four operating divisions. One of the divisions was known as Bata Footwear, which operated a footwear manufacturing plant in Batawa, Ontario.

During the 1980s, it became increasingly difficult throughout Ontario to remove and dispose of liquid wastes. The passage of legislation further regulating waste disposal found a waste disposal industry ill-prepared for the demands which were being placed upon it. It was a "seller's market" and BIL found it increasingly difficult to dispose of its liquid wastes.

As a result, drums of liquid waste accumulated at the Batawa plant awaiting removal. BIL tried to store the drums properly while it continued to try to find a waste hauler to remove the drums from the plant. By August 1989, the drums had still not been removed. The drums had rusted and deteriorated with time. One drum was later proved to have leaked its contents into the ground.

In addition to six charges against BIL, the MOEE charged Thomas G. Bata, Jr. (chairman of the board and a director), Douglas Marchant (president and a director) and Keith Weston (vice-president responsible for Bata Footwear and a director), with failing to take all reasonable care to prevent an unlawful discharge into the environment or the ground water, contrary to s.147a (now s.194) of the EPA and s.75 (now s.116) of the OWRA.[22]

The trial judge acquitted the company of all but one of the charges, the exception being the discharge offense (s.s.16(1) of the OWRA). Thomas G. Bata Jr. was acquitted of all charges. The court convicted Douglas Marchant and Keith Weston of failing to take all reasonable care to prevent the discharge (s.s.75(1) of the OWRA).

The trial judge concluded that Thomas G. Bata, Jr. was aware of his environmental responsibilities and had personally approved written directions in a company *Technical Advisory Circular* published in 1986 which addressed environmental matters, including liquid wastes. The court held that Mr. Bata responded to the matters that were brought to his attention promptly and appropriately and had placed an experienced director on site. The court found that "Mr. Bata was entitled to assume that Mr. Weston was addressing environmental concerns at the facility and that he (Mr. Bata) was entitled to rely upon the system in place, unless he became aware the system was defective." The trial judge concluded that Mr. Bata had met his obligations under the legislation, and had met the onus of proving due diligence.

The president of BIL, Douglas Marchant, was required, according to the trial judge, to exercise a higher degree of supervision and control, one that demonstrated that he was exhorting those whom he may be normally expected to influence or control to an accepted standard of behaviour. Although Mr. Bata was entitled to rely on Mr. Weston, who was "an experienced Director," Mr. Marchant could not. While there was evidence of some activity to direct the removal of the waste when the matter was brought to his attention, the level of activity was not enough, in the trial judge's view, and, therefore, his conduct fell below the appropriate standard.

The vice-president responsible for Bata Footwear, Keith Weston, had the highest degree of responsibility since he was the on-site manager. While he delegated responsibility to a subordinate in environmental matters, he did not give the subordinate the financial resources to take and implement decisions on his own. When he took on the job, Mr. Weston demanded and received complete authority to manage. Having received that authority, the court concluded he was not entitled to rely on delegation unless the delegate was properly trained and had all the resources at his disposal to do the job. While the company was in financial difficulties, that in itself was no excuse not to treat environmental matters as a priority.

Of the three, Mr. Weston had the highest duty to regularly view the condition of the site so as to ensure that environmental damage did not occur. In the court's view, Mr. Weston's conduct fell below the appropriate standard.

The trial judge acknowledged that there was very little judicial guidance available to him when he had to define the **standard of care** to be imposed upon directors for environmental matters. By its very nature, the standard will always be a constantly evolving one. The Bata directors were judged using 1991 standards on conduct which occurred in the late 1980s. Given the rapidly changing and ever-heightening concerns for the environment, it is to be expected that the standard established by the trial judge will also evolve with time. However, for the time being, the standard can be summarized as follows:

a) **Responsibility** The board of directors is ultimately responsible for environmental compliance.

b) **Delegation** If the board chooses to delegate its responsibilities to officers of the corporation, it must ensure that a system of adequate and effective supervision is in place, such that the board is kept regularly informed of environmental matters affecting the corporation. Directors must ensure that delegates are properly educated in environmental matters and have the resources to deal with environmental problems. It is important that information and enquiries flow up from the field and down from management.

c) **Reliance** The board of directors is entitled to place reasonable reliance upon delegates, and reports provided to them by such delegates, including corporate officers, consultants, or counsel.

d) **Policy** There should be a corporate environmental policy, which has been approved by the board of directors, dealing with the prevention of pollution, and including waste management and disposal. The board should regularly ensure that the policy is being complied with. This is likely to involve conducting an environmental compliance review (audit).

e) **Standards** The board of directors should be aware of the standards in its own industry, as well as other industries that may deal with similar environmental concerns, such as chemicals.

f) **Records** For now, the onus is on directors to prove they were duly diligent (as opposed to the onus being on the Crown to prove a lack of due diligence). Directors should ensure that the minutes of board meetings reflect adequate consideration of environmental matters.

g) **Action** The board of directors should be informed of and must react to environmental concerns which affect the company as quickly as possible.

The trial judge stated that, depending upon the nature and structure of the corporate activity, one would hope to find remedial and contingency plans for spills, a system of ongoing environmental compliance reviews (audits), training programs, sufficient authority to take action, and other indications of a proactive environmental policy.

The trial judge fined BIL $60,000, and imposed a probation order against BIL which required (a) two payments of $30,000 each to the local household hazardous-waste program; (b) the facts of the case and the conviction be published by the Bata Shoe Organization (not a defendant before the Court) in its worldwide newsletter; (c) a caution be placed on title against the Bata property; and (d) the company publish an advisory circular with respect to Ontario standards for toxic waste storage for distribution to its companies worldwide. The trial judge also ordered BIL to make environmental issues a mandatory agenda item at all board meetings during the term of the order.[23]

One of the more interesting aspects of the sentence was a term of the probation order that the company must not indemnify the directors for the fines imposed against them. As this was not a case where the accused deliberately and intentionally set out to damage the environment, and on a "first case" basis, each director was fined $12,000. Although there were differences in length of service and relative position and control, each director was treated equally from a sentencing standpoint.

BIL and Messrs. Weston and Marchant appealed their sentences.[24] Mr. Justice Cosgrove delivered his decision on 31 May 1993 and concluded that the trial judge had not given enough credit to BIL and the individuals in determining the appropriate financial penalty. Accordingly, His Honour reduced BIL's financial penalty from $120,000 to $90,000 ($60,000 fine and $30,000 to a local household hazardous-waste program). The directors' fines were each cut in half (from $12,000 to $6,000).

The most important issue for the corporate community is Mr. Justice Cosgrove's ruling on indemnification.[25] His Honour stated that the roles of the company and individual defendants were intertwined, and that if the court did not prevent indemnification by BIL, the fines imposed against the individuals would effectively be "wasted." For Mr. Justice Cosgrove, indemnification would allow corporate officials to "turn a blind eye" to their responsibilities.

The MOEE argued that if corporate officials could be indemnified, they would not feel the "sting" of the penalty. The fines would be absorbed by the company, and could be regarded as a cost of doing business. By exposing individuals to potentially large personal fines, directors and officers will be compelled to ensure that their companies comply with the law.

Conclusions from the *Bata* Case

- Every company should have an environmental policy and procedures for implementation, as well as an enforcement procedure for the policy. These are the basics of an EMS. Information must flow down from and up to the most senior levels of management. Written records are essential to prove you are "doing the right thing."
- Every company should consider conducting an environmental compliance review (audit) of its operations. Deficiencies reported in such reviews must be rectified.
- Company management must be properly trained in environmental issues, through attendance at environmental seminars or other educational activities. Delegation by the board is acceptable, but it should be done properly, with good communication to and from the board.
- Be aware of industry standards. While these standards will evolve with time, they are at least a guide as to what is expected of corporate directors.

It is readily apparent from the *Bata* decision that the development of an EMS — a way of doing business that recognizes the possible impacts of a company's operation on the natural environment — is an ideal way to prepare oneself for the possibility of a prosecution. The procedures developed through this system (and the documentation associated with it) will form useful evidence to meet the burden that a defendant faces (i.e. that it was duly diligent in attempting to prevent the occurrence that is the subject of the prosecution).

3.4.2 *R. v. Courtaulds Fibres Canada Inc.*

In a recent case in Cornwall, Ontario,[26] the defendant corporation was charged with 13 counts of spilling acid and zinc on its property, which then discharged into the St. Lawrence River. The spills occurred because of human error and faulty equipment.

The court acquitted the defendant on all charges, finding that the company had been making "an earnest effort to address environmental concerns, and was engaged in a continuous dialogue with the Ministry's [MOEE] officials to that end."[27]

Further, the judge stated that after a worker is properly trained, it would be unreasonable to conclude that the employer should be held responsible for an employee's error, which neither training nor anticipation could prevent or foresee. The company had arranged seminars for management, and engaged counsel experienced in environmental law to provide such seminars. Specific attention was given by the company to the EPA and OWRA, and all employees attended meetings and received instructions and directions with respect to their responsibilities and duties when dealing with environmental problems such as spills.

The court found it significant that, as early as 1985, representatives of both the MOEE and the company had been engaged in continuing and detailed discussions as to the MOEE's requirements for the company. It is clear that although a new control order was contemplated, the terms of such an order were never determined by the MOEE.

The judge concluded that the vice-president of operations, the most senior company executive at the plant, was highly skilled, highly trained, and highly motivated, and did not allow the consideration of profit to interfere with what he determined had to be done with respect to environmental matters. The court concluded that given the continuing earnest and widespread efforts of the company to address its environmental problems, the company had proved it was duly diligent with reference to the spills. The judge stated that *"reasonable care and due diligence do not mean superhuman efforts. They mean a high standard of awareness and decisive, prompt and continuing action"*[28] (emphasis added).

The judge went on to outline the criteria to be examined in determining whether a valid defence of due diligence was available.

The question of how long a company must prove that it was duly diligent before it can become a valid defence cannot be clearly answered by considering only how long the company was so engaged. The state of the facility, the age of the facility, the problems to be addressed, and the scope of the actions taken to deal with them, as well as the time the company was engaged in remedial action, must all be weighed and balanced.

3.4.3 *R. v. Commander Business Furniture Inc.*

Activities at Commander Business Furniture Inc. included spray painting office furniture. The company was charged and convicted of discharging a contaminant, namely odour, into a neighbouring residential area.[29] Mr. Hanson, the company's vice-president and general manager in charge of operations during the offense period, was also charged.

Mr. Hanson, together with his wife, had purchased the company in 1985. At that time, there had been odour complaints and the new management began to work closely with MOEE to resolve the problem. Company representatives and the MOEE met repeatedly in 1988 and 1989 to discuss steps which could be taken to reduce the odour emanating from the company's facility. However, the proposed solution of thermal incineration was, in the company's opinion, too expensive. Discussions continued over the next few years and the company retained a consultant to review its operations and recommended process changes which would reduce fugitive emissions. The consultant issued a number of reports, most of which also recommended incineration as a solution.

Upon reviewing the facts, the court found that the act required for a conviction had been proved and moved to consider the company's claim of due diligence. Her Honour Justice Hackett identified several factors which must be weighed in assessing due diligence. These include:

1) The nature and gravity of the adverse effect
2) The foreseeability of the effect, including abnormal sensitivities
3) The alternative solutions available
4) Legislative or regulatory compliance
5) Industry standards
6) The character of the neighbourhood
7) What efforts have been made to address the problem
8) Over what period of time, and promptness of response
9) Matters beyond the control of the accused, including technological limitations
10) Skill level expected of the accused
11) The complexities involved
12) Preventative systems
13) Economic considerations
14) Actions of officials

In this case, the court reviewed in particular economic considerations and the actions of officials.

The court held that the cost of various alternative solutions alone is not determinative of due diligence, but is one consideration to be weighed in assessing due diligence. This is because the degree of control a defendant can exercise over a problem must have an air of reality about it. In addition, the advice, actions, and opinions of government officials are factors to consider in assessing the defendants' knowledge of the problem and the solutions, as are the advice, actions, and opinions of the defendants' own consultants. *But the defendant alone must acquire knowledge and act with due diligence, and cannot hide behind one opinion that conflicts with the weight of reliable evidence* (emphasis added). The court concluded that the defendants acted with due diligence by pursuing "before end of the pipe" solutions for four and a half years, up until May of 1989. At that point, the defendants knew thermal incineration was the most effective solution, but they attempted to delay implementation because they prioritized their own economic interests over the need to balance their interests with their neighbours' interests. The balance of competing interests shifted with that knowledge, and the defendants should have acted more aggressively to solve the problem. As a result, a conviction was entered against the company.

Ministry officials, however, acted appropriately throughout. Their failure to use alternative actions to prosecution did not relieve the defendants from their duty to act reasonably.

3.5 THE RELATIONSHIP BETWEEN AN EMS AND THE BOARD OF DIRECTORS

3.5.1 Matters to Report to the Board

The cases discussed above reflect two main thrusts adopted by the courts:

- corporations (and individuals) will continue to be taken to task by the courts if they do not abide by the legislation designed to protect the environment; and
- the primary tool available to corporations to avoid environmental liability is an efficient and effective EMS

Although the cases are clear that the board of directors have ultimate responsibility over environmental matters, many of the guidelines outlining the duties and responsibilities of a duly diligent board of directors discussed in these cases are general in nature and fail to provide the specific mechanisms to meet these court-defined guidelines. However, experience allows the following observations to be made with respect to reports to the board.

Environmental subjects to be reported to the board usually cover three distinct areas:

- matters which indicate non-compliance with environmental laws and regulations
- environmental "incidents," including spills and discharges, which could give rise to substantial fines, personal liability, or publicity; and
- anticipated initiatives by the company, governments, or other organizations which could significantly affect the company and/or its business activities

A board needs to discuss these "significant" issues; however, to leave "significant" undefined runs the risk that matters will be either over- or underreported. Often, an arbitrary threshold is established by the board defining which matters should be brought before them and which matters should be dealt with by management. This threshold might include one or more of the following components:

(a) matters, including spills and discharges, resulting in potential liability exposure over a specified dollar amount in fines must be reported to the board

(b) matters which involve potential personal liability must be reported to the board, and

(c) environmental matters which may raise potential public concern must be reported to the board

Clearly, the threshold established by a board of directors should reflect the nature of that company's business and the level to which the board has delegated responsibility for environmental matters. In other words, environmental issues only come to the board if any exist above the threshold.

3.5.2 Frequency of Hearing Environmental Reports

It is clear from the *Bata* decision that environmental reporting must be a regular feature of board meetings. It is difficult to state conclusively that all companies should have environmental reporting at every directors' meeting. The need to discuss environmental matters and the frequency of those discussions will depend on the nature of a company's business.

3.5.3 Periodic EMS Review

The EMS established by a company should be reviewed on an ongoing basis, usually annually, by the board or by a committee of the board with the delegated power to perform such a review. The requirements and specifics of an EMS will change over time, and the board should be able to respond appropriately.

It is anticipated that future cases will help delineate the requirements of an effective EMS. In the meantime, companies should ensure that matters which require the involvement of the company's directors arrive before the board promptly, and that any decision reached by the board is implemented in a timely manner.

3.6 ENVIRONMENTAL COMPLIANCE REVIEWS AND SOLICITOR-CLIENT PRIVILEGE

One critical element of an EMS is the regular performance of environmental compliance reviews or audits. A key aspect of any audit is the actual process involved (see Chapter 11 for a detailed discussion of environmental audits). As the audit report will summarize compliance with environmental laws and regulations, it is often necessary to have an environmental lawyer involved. The involvement of a lawyer accomplishes two things: the lawyer is able to opine as to legal matters; and the audit can be done under solicitor-client privilege.

Solicitor-client privilege arises when written or oral communications are made to a lawyer for the purpose of seeking legal advice. It is not necessary that litigation be contemplated for the privilege to arise. The law recognizes this privilege because of the importance attached to the belief that citizens should be able to seek legal advice without fear that the information they disclose to their lawyers could be used against them.[30] Significantly, other types of communications, such as those between a client and an accounting firm, a management consultant firm, or an engineering firm are not recognized in their own right by the courts as having any privilege attached to them. Accordingly, one should bear in mind that when compliance advice is sought from one of these types of professionals, a claim for privilege and protection from disclosure cannot be made.

Government inspectors and investigators, armed with the powers provided to them by law to investigate alleged offenses, are not entitled to seize privileged documents. If an investigation is taking place, one should inform the officer when a document is privileged; envelopes marked "Privileged and Confidential" should be kept on hand and the documents should be placed in such an envelope, and sealed if there is disagreement with the investigator on the privilege claim. They will then be placed in the custody of the court until a judge rules on whether the documents are indeed privileged.

The issue of privilege in environmental matters has assumed importance recently because companies are, as part of their EMSs, carrying out audits of their facilities to determine their level of compliance with laws and regulations. In the course of these audits or other communications, lawyers are retained to advise companies on the legality of the company's operations *vis-à-vis* the current state of environmental law. Not surprisingly, some government investigators have been showing interest in obtaining these reports for use in prosecutions.[31]

It is becoming increasingly obvious that companies should take the appropriate steps to meet the tests laid down by the courts to establish the privilege and keep these documents from investigators. These steps do not include merely sending a lawyer to sit in on a meeting and take notes of what a consultant discovered in the audit. The lawyer should be actively involved in giving legal advice — the consultant should be used by the lawyer to gather technical information which the lawyer needs to give that advice. Simply sending the environmental consultant's audit report to a lawyer for the lawyer to send to the company will, in all likelihood, not be viewed as having established the privilege.

When faced with an application by a company to prevent documents seized by investigators from being used by those investigators on the basis that they are privileged, a court will embark on an inquiry as to the nature of the role played by the company's counsel in the generation of those documents. Do the documents constitute or form part and parcel of legal advice given to the company? If not, then they will not be protected from disclosure to the prosecutors. Merely that a lawyer has spoken to the company (in writing or otherwise) is insufficient to establish the privilege. The communication must be for the purpose of giving legal advice. Lawyers, on occasion, speak to their clients without providing them with legal advice. Similarly, if the lawyer's role is to just act as a "scribe" and keep a record of the discussions during an environmental audit, no privilege will attach. The communications between the lawyer and the client must be either for the giving of legal advice by the lawyer to the client, or for the provision of information from the client to the lawyer so that the lawyer may give that advice. If the communication between the lawyer and the client is not within these contexts, it is doubtful that the court will uphold the privilege.

Creating the conditions to establish a claim for privilege should not be done for the purpose of hiding anything, but rather to achieve the best level of environmental compliance without fear that regulators will use the company's own efforts in this regard against it. It is accepted that there is more for society to gain from encouraging proactive environmental activities by businesses than there is from gaining disclosure of information to merely increase the number of convictions for environmental offenses.

3.7 CONCLUSION

Clearly, persons carrying on business in Canada would be remiss if they did not devote sufficient attention to all applicable environmental laws. In today's society, environmental law touches almost all aspects of life. From a legal point of view, environmental law considerations are found in such diverse fields as real estate transactions, administrative hearings, litigation, and corporate law. When the legal issues are combined with other factors such as the scientific aspects of the environment, public opinion, and interest groups, it is easy to understand why the field is a complicated one.

One positive result of the growing environmental awareness among corporations is the growing importance being assigned to environmental compliance. As recently as five or ten years ago, many corporations would only contact their lawyers with respect to an environmental matter if they were being charged by the government for an environmental violation, or sued by a private party. Today, numerous companies have changed their corporate philosophy toward the environment from a reactionary to a proactive one.

More and more, companies are retaining full-time environmental counsel to keep them up to date on current environmental issues and legislative developments. Indeed, knowing what the proposed changes to a certain law are *before* they come into effect is one of the most effective ways to plan for change and to be prepared for such change at the time of implementation.

Perhaps the most effective way for a company to ensure that environmental standards are being complied with is to conduct an environmental compliance review within the framework of an EMS. Compliance reviews involve the use of environmental consultants to go through a corporation's premises and comprehensively review all environmental issues from manufacturing processes and mechanisms for dealing with emergencies such as spills, to management awareness of environmental laws and an in-house policy on the environment (if any) for employees.

Other elements of an effective EMS are also gaining prominence, put in place to reduce the liability and exposure of employees, management, officers, and directors of companies in the environmental spotlight, particularly with respect to the positive obligations on directors and officers to take all reasonable care to prevent discharges. Some of the issues currently being addressed by corporations include the threshold levels at which environmental matters are to be reported to the board, the threshold levels at which environmental matters are to be brought to the attention of regulators, follow-up procedures from the board to ensure that matters brought to their attention are dealt with, and ensuring the documentation necessary to establish a defence of due diligence is in place.

There are no magic formulas. It is not enough simply to set up an environmental committee of the board of directors to discharge these obligations. Each corporation must address the issues on its own, with the assistance of outside advisers, including legal counsel where appropriate. However, while the issues are still being debated in the courts, it is clear that some form of EMS is a minimum requirement for due diligence in the courts and, more importantly, that it is possible for a corporation to defend itself from charges resulting from a spill or environmental incident by establishing a successful defence of due diligence aided by its EMS. There is a growing sense that the courts are beginning to recognize the practicalities of carrying on business in assessing due diligence. As a result, the successful defence of environmental charges remains difficult, but it is not impossible.

ENDNOTES

1. *R. v. Sault Ste. Marie,* [1978] 2 S.C.R. 1299, 85 D.L.R. (3d) 161.
2. R.S.O. 1970, c. 332, s.32(1). Section 32(1) provided, *inter alia,* that every municipality or person that discharges or deposits or causes or permits the discharge or deposit of any material of any kind into any river or other watercourse is guilty of an offense. The section has been replaced by s.16(1) of the current Ontario Water Resources Act, R.S.O. 1990, c. 0-40.
3. "Public welfare offenses obviously lie in a field of conflicting values. It is essential for society to maintain, through effective enforcement, high standards of public health and safety. Potential victims of those who carry on latently pernicious activities have a strong claim to consideration. On the other hand, there is a generally held revulsion against punishment of the morally innocent." *R. v. Sault Ste. Marie* (1978).
4. Mr. Justice Dickson described the strict liability offenses as follows: "Offenses in which there is no necessity for the prosecution to prove the existence of *mens rea;* the doing of the prohibited act *prima facie* imports the offense, leaving it open to the accused to avoid liability by proving that he took all reasonable care. This involves consideration of what a reasonable man would have done in the circumstances. The defence will be available if the accused reasonably believed in a mistaken set of facts which, if true, would render the act or omission innocent, or if he took all reasonable steps to avoid the particular event. These offenses may be properly called offenses of strict liability." *R. v. Sault Ste. Marie* (1978). For an analysis of the decision in *Sault Ste. Marie,* see M. Jeffery, "Environmental Enforcement and Regulation in the 1980s: *Regina v. Sault Ste. Marie* Revisited" (1984), 10 *Queen's Law Journal* 43; A. Hutchinson, "*Sault Ste. Marie, Mens Rea* and the Halfway House: Public Welfare Offenses Get a Home of Their Own" (1979), 17 *Osgoode Hall Law Journal* 415.
5. *R. v. Wholesale Travel* (1991), 67 C.C.C. (3d) 193 (S.C.C.).
6. *R. v. United Keno Mines Limited* (1980), 10 C.E.L.R. 43 (Y.T. Terr. Ct.).
7. Northern Inland Waters Act, R.S.C. 1970 (1st Supp.), c. 28, s.6(1).
8. See also *R. v. New Brunswick Electric Power Commission* (1991), 10 C.E.L.R. (N.S.) 184 (N.B. Prov. Ct.).
9. *United Keno Hill Mines* at 45. See also *R. v. Kenaston Drilling (Arctic) Ltd.* (1973), 12 C.C.C. (2d) 383 (N.W.T.S.C.) which also explicitly acknowledges a special approach to corporate environmental offenders.

10. "Fines are only one part of a necessary sentencing arsenal to foster responsible corporate behaviour. A greater spectrum of sentencing options is required to ensure effective deterrence and prevent illegal economic advantages accruing to corporations willing to risk apprehension and swallow harsh fines as operating costs. Fines are inadequate principally because they are easily displaced and rarely affect the source of illegal behaviour. Usually fines can be ultimately passed on in the form of higher prices to either the consumer or the taxpayer." *R. v. Kenaston Drilling (Arctic) Ltd.* at 52.

11. *R. v. Kenaston Drilling (Arctic) Ltd.* at 52.

12. *R. v. Kenaston Drilling (Arctic) Ltd.* at 53-54.

13. Released May 7, 1991, Ont. Ct. Prov. Div., Mr. Justice Anderson.

14. Prior to this decision, environmental offenders had been jailed, but only for contempt of court after they failed to comply with court orders requiring them to stop polluting or to undertake a clean-up of their sites.

15. *Crowe* at 17-18.

16. *R. v. Varnicolor Chemical,* unreported decision released September 3, 1992 (Ont. Ct. Prov. Div., Woodworth, J.P.).

17. The Ontario Ministry of the Environment merged with the Ministry of Energy in February 1993. It is referred to as the MOEE throughout this chapter.

18. Ontario Drinking Water guidelines (existing and draft) for vinyl chloride, trichloroethylene, benzene, toluene, and total xylenes.

19. R.S.O. 1990, c. E-19.

20. Subsections 194 and 116 of the EPA and OWRA, respectively. For an interesting discussion of the intent and application of s.194 of the EPA, the diverging decisions in *Bata* and *R. v. Commander Business Furniture Inc.* (infra) should be examined.

21. See also *R. v. United Keno Hill Mines* at 56.

22. See note 20.

23. The trial judge did not have an order with respect to the clean-up of the property, as it was being dealt with by the company and the MOEE under a Director's Order.

24. The appeal was heard in early 1993 and the decision released on 31 May 1993.

25. On 4 August 1993, the Ontario Court of Appeal granted BIL leave to appeal on the issue of indemnification. The appeal is expected to be heard late in the spring of 1994.

26. *R. v. Cortaulds Fibres Canada Inc.* (1992), 9 C.E.L.R. (N.S.) 304 (Ont. Ct. Prov. Div.).

27. *R. v. Cortaulds Fibres Canada Inc.* (1992) at 309-310. Dialogue with government authorities will not always be determinative of whether due diligence has been shown. (See *R. v. Commander Business Furniture Inc.*)
28. *R. v. Cortaulds Fibres Canada Inc.* (1992) at 313.
29. *R. v. Commander Business Furniture Inc. and Raymond Hanson* (1992), 9 C.E.L.R. (N.S.) 185 (Ont. Ct. Prov. Div.).
30. For an excellent and in-depth discussion of the development of solicitor-client privilege and confidential information, see "Privilege and Confidential Information in Litigation," CBA-O Conference, October 19, 1991.
31. *MOE v. McCarthy Tetrault, Lafarge Canada, and David Stafford,* [1992] O.J. 31680. 13 August 1992 (Ont. Ct. Prov. Div.; MacDonnell J.). Some jurisdictions in the United States and the Canadian federal government have established policies in respect of their approach to the seizure of environmental audits. See also *Gregory v. Minister of National Revenue,* [1992] F.C.J. No. 854, 21 September 1992, Fed. Ct. T.D., where an environmental audit was held not to be privileged.

4

Environmental Accounting and Reporting Practices

by
Greg Judd
Deloitte & Touche

4.1 EVOLVING IMPORTANCE AND EXPECTATIONS

Financial practices are identified in Chapter 1 as one of the **external factors** that influence an EMS. Some of the ways this occurs are familiar and direct. A piece of pollution control equipment has a capital cost and its value can be depreciated following generally accepted accounting principles. Similarly, the cost of disposing of a waste can be quantified and reported as a cost of doing business.

But increasingly, the traditional methods used to assess financial aspects of a company or organization are proving to be poorly suited to addressing environmental aspects. In quick order, new issues seem to have emerged to challenge financial practices. If a site requires extensive remediation before it can be sold or redeveloped, when and how should the costs be reported? Should the manufacturer of a product also be responsible for the ultimate disposal or re-use of the product? Should users of natural resources such as air or water pay to do so?

Environmental issues also are becoming more important to financial concerns such as the ability to raise debt and equity financing. Businesses are finding that credit is much more difficult to obtain if they have practices or conditions that lenders feel pose a high level of environmental risk. And there is the growing presence of government involvement in environmental management that takes on financial forms that range from so-called "Green Taxes" in the form of tax incentives to the fines and penalties of not complying with environmental laws and regulations.

There also are growing expectations among the public that financial reports will describe how environmental issues are being identified, measured, and disclosed. Given that scrutinizers of financial reports can include investors, creditors, employees, government agencies, suppliers, customers, and special-interest groups, better methods of communication that the conventional financial statement are needed to meet the needs of these groups.

These issues illustrate the growing recognition that environmental management and financial policies are inextricably linked to one another. They also reflect the growing expectation that responsible corporations will take steps to act in ways that promote long-term sustainability, recognize the full costs of compliance, and report on environmental goals and achievements.

4.2 RECOGNITION, VALUATION, AND DISCLOSURE OF ENVIRONMENTAL COSTS AND LIABILITIES

4.2.1 Generally Accepted Accounting Principles (GAAP)

A company's financial statements and annual report present information about revenues, costs, and risks. External auditors attest to the reasonableness and fairness of those representations by ensuring that the information is presented according to the standards of GAAP.

GAAP allows for financial information to be compared between companies and sectors on a basis which is consistent from year to year. In addition, it incorporates specific rules, practices, and procedures which form the basis on which financial statements are prepared. In the absence of specific guidelines, professional judgement is required.

Preparers of financial information have traditionally held the view that the impact of a company's operation on the environment was not financially material. That view is beginning to change as growing numbers of companies try to become accountable for environmental liabilities and costs. At the same time, users of financial statements are asking for criteria that can be used to evaluate a company's environmental performance.

It will take considerable time before the accounting and reporting of environmental costs and liabilities are standardized and incorporated into GAAP. In the interim, guidance is being provided by professional accounting organizations and capital market regulators, as well as some government agencies as illustrated in the following sections.

4.2.2 Definition of an Environmental Cost

Environmental accounting requires agreement as to what costs and expenditures should be categorized as environmental in nature.

The CICA research report, *Environmental Costs and Liabilities: Accounting and Financial Reporting Issues* (1993), separates environmental expenditures into two categories: Environmental Measures and Environmental Losses.

Environmental Measures are defined as the steps taken (i.e. costs incurred) to "prevent, abate, or remediate damage to the environment or to deal with the conservation of renewable and non-renewable resources."

Environmental Losses are defined as environmental costs "for which there are no return or benefit." Examples include fines or penalties for not complying with environmental regulations, damages paid to others for environmental damage, or assets of the entity that have to be written off because their costs cannot be recovered due to environmental concerns.

In using the above definitions, the preparer of a company's financial statements must apply the appropriate accounting and financial reporting standards. Environmental reporting issues that arise can include:

- expensing in the current period vs. capitalizing the environmental cost and amortizing over a reasonable period of time
- recognition in the financial statements that an environmental liability exists followed by determining an appropriate method of measurement
- determining if an asset such as land should have its book value reduced as a result of an environmental impairment
- meeting the required disclosure requirements for environmental concerns as set out by regulatory authorities

4.2.3 Site Clean-up and Removal Costs

The CICA handbook specifically addresses the issue of environmental obligations by requiring companies to provide in their financial statements the cost of future site clean-up and restorations costs (Section 3060, "Capital Assets"). This provision should be made when the costs, net of expected recoveries such as salvage values, are reasonably determinable. The cost of clean-up for past environmental damage together with the current obligation for site restoration should be recognized in the financial statements and amortized by a charge to the income statement in a rational and systematic manner. In the case of a mining operation this would be over the useful life of the site.

In practice, calculation of the liability is not easily performed. The liability is calculated using the work of specialists such as engineers or environmental consultants to help in the identification of contamination and the extent of remediation work required. The results of negotiations with various regulatory agencies may also impact the extent of clean-up work required. If there is a reasonable probability that a liability exists, but its amount cannot be estimated, a contingent liability may exist which should be disclosed in the notes to the financial statements. In its 1992 annual report, Inco Limited disclosed that "The estimation of future removal and site restoration costs depends on the development of environmentally acceptable closure plans which, in some cases, may not be implemented for several decades."

Crown corporations such as Atomic Energy Canada Ltd. (AECL) are being forced to come to terms with accounting for site restoration costs. In an article from The Canadian Press, published in *The Globe and Mail*, it was noted that AECL failed to make provisions in its 1994 financial statements for future clean-up costs of its decommissioned reactors. The Auditor General qualified his certification of the AECL 1994 annual report by stating that the AECL balance sheet, without annual provisions for future clean-up of old reactors, doesn't fully measure up to GAAP. Estimates of the clean-up costs by AECL were quoted as potentially amounting to as much as $200 to $300 million, to be incurred into the next century. The article went on to state that the AECL was of the opinion that "it was too early to come up with an amount precise enough to budget on financial statements. In addition, such costs have traditionally been born by the federal treasury — not AECL — with some of the cost offset by sale of salvageable assets at the site."

A 1993 survey of environmental reporting practices concluded that companies have considerable information on costs, accounting treatments, emission data, etc., but that the information is not "consistently or aggressively reported" (KPMG, 1993). Environmental disclosure was found to result from a need to ensure compliance with legislative and accounting requirements.

The survey also concluded that companies resist establishing sophisticated methods to verify environmental data. Survey respondents were found to be disclosing only the costs of investments or fines as indicators of environmental performance, and that "overall, there is a lack of statistical data" in environmental reports.

4.2.4 Contingent Liabilities

Companies that incur site restoration and related costs on an ongoing basis may substantially reduce the future costs that would otherwise be incurred following the site closure; however, where restoration costs cannot be reasonably determined, a contingent liability may exist and should be disclosed in the financial statements, if material.

Guidance for the recognition of the environmental costs and liabilities is found in Section 3290 of the CICA handbook, *Contingent Gains and Losses*. That section provides for the recognition of obligations and commitments of a company, such as for site restoration costs, in the financial statements, if they are likely to exist. The amount of the loss should be measured at management's best estimate. The definition of likely is, "the probability of incurring the loss is greater then 50%." Contingent losses determined to be other than remote (>15%) should be disclosed in a company's financial statements. Where a contingent loss is accrued under Section 3290, the accrued loss should be shown as a liability and should be distinguished from other liabilities.

In practice, disclosure of a contingent environmental liability in the notes to the financial statements is much more common than recognition of the liability in the balance sheet. This is due in part to the difficulty of accurately quantifying the amounts from within a range of estimates. For example, in the Inco annual report for 1992, the notes to the financial statements on future site restoration costs included the following narrative: "It is currently not possible to reasonably estimate the ultimate liability for future site removal and site restoration costs or to indicate definitively whether or not the ultimate liability will have a material adverse effect on the Company's operating results or financial condition."

Greater disclosure of environmental costs can adversely affect a company's value and prospects. Companies are aware of the potential negative impact on earnings per share that disclosure can cause, and some have argued that future environmental expenses, capital investments, or site restoration costs do not have a material effect on operations or the financial health of the company.

4.2.5 Write-Down of Long-Term Investments

If a long-term investment is impaired in value as a result of environmental concerns, its carrying value on the financial statements should be reviewed for possible impairment. Section 3050 of the CICA handbook, "Long-term Investments," provides that where "a loss in value of an investment that is other than a temporary decline, the investment should be written down to recognize the loss." Where a reduction in carrying value is declared or "booked," it can have a snowball effect on a company's financial stability. The lower asset base as a result of the write-down will affect the company's ability to meet debt/equity covenants on existing loans and its ability to borrow new funds. It also may increase the borrowing rate and impose new borrowing constraints.

4.2.6 Commitments and Contractual Obligations

Recognition of environmental expenditures in the current year's operating results provides financial statement users with information as to the effect on the company's current cash flows. Where a commitment exists affecting future operating periods, it should be disclosed (CICA handbook, Section 3280, "Contractual Obligations") in the current financial statements if the future capital expenditures are "abnormal in relation to the financial position or usual business operations." The need for capital expenditures for assets required to ensure compliance with new environmental legislation would, therefore, have to be disclosed under Section 3280.

4.3 STANDARDS FOR REPORTING

4.3.1 Canadian Institute of Chartered Accountants (CICA)

The CICA plays a major role in establishing accounting and disclosure standards for the reporting of environmental liabilities. Accordingly, the CICA has taken steps to address the growing gap between what audited financial statements provide and what stakeholders and users of the statements believe should be communicated regarding environmental costs, liabilities, and risks. A 1993 CICA research report, *Environmental Cost and Liabilities: Accounting and Financial Reporting Issues*, recommends that "all clean-up obligations relating to environmental damage that has occurred and that are probable and reasonably estimable should be recognized in financial statements." The report also suggests that there is a need for new recognition, measurement, and disclosure standards for environmental concerns.

Environmental reporting, on the other hand, relies on comparing established indicators of performance to declared environmental targets. These indicators form a framework for measurement which can be consistently applied in accordance with industry standards. In selecting suitable criteria, consideration should be given to how well stakeholders will understand the criteria, a company's environmental objectives, and the availability of data collection and reporting systems.

4.3.2 United States: Emerging Issues Task Force

Environmental accounting issues have been addressed in the U.S. by the EITF of the Financial Accounting Standards Board. The task force report entitled "Capitalization of Costs to Treat Environmental Contamination" can be used to classify expenditures on the treatment of environmental contamination as either a current expense of the business or as capital in nature, and should be matched against future revenue streams (FASB, 1990). There are three classes of environmental expenditures:

- The treatment extends the life, increases the capacity, or improves the safety or efficiency of an existing asset. However, the improvements are based on comparisons with the asset when it was originally constructed or acquired.
- The treatment mitigates or prevents environmental contamination that has yet to occur or that might result from future operations or activities. Again, the costs must improve the asset compared with its condition when constructed or acquired.

- The treatment is made in connection with an asset held for sale.

EITF standards require expenditures for pollution treatment which affect ongoing operations to be capitalized and matched against future revenue streams. Expenditures which are for liabilities arising from past operations should be accounted for in the period incurred.

4.3.3 Capital Market Regulations

Corporations finance their operations using a combination of equity and debt. Debt and equity holders, whether they are financial institutions with loans or mortgages or the shareholders of the company, are becoming increasingly concerned with the potential impact of environmental liabilities on their investments. Banks are now insisting that assessments be prepared on the probable environmental risk from operations and on the value of security provided. Consequently, there is an overall increase in the cost of capital, especially to companies with operations considered to be likely sources of contamination or environmental impacts.

The Ontario and Quebec Securities Commissions require listed companies to disclose as part of their Management Discussion and Analysis section of the annual report, information about the "financial or operational effect of environmental protection requirements on the capital expenditures, earnings, and competitive position" for the current year and expected impact on future years.

The U.S. Securities and Exchange Commission requires publicly traded companies to complete forms requiring disclosure of:

- the financial or operational effect, if material, on the current year and future years on capital expenditures, earnings and competitive position for compliance with federal, state, and local environmental laws
- material environmental administrative or judicial proceedings of which the company may be aware, and
- material environmental contingent liabilities or problems which should be quantified by management as far as is reasonably practical

4.4 METHODS OF REPORTING ENVIRONMENTAL PERFORMANCE

4.4.1 Financial Statements

Traditional financial statements are designed for general use by shareholders and creditors. Increasingly, preparers of financial statements are finding there is a wider range of users requesting specific and complete information on environmental issues. These new users include groups who are seeking information on a company's compliance with environmental laws and its intended course of action to help manage, restore, reduce, or eliminate environmental concerns.

In analyzing requests for additional environmental disclosure, companies are finding that they often are faced with the prospect of including items which are relatively immaterial, and so warrant no special disclosure.

Companies such as BC Hydro have tackled this problem by looking at how an environmental expenditure is defined. Taking into account such things as what should be reported, how it should measured, and current reporting mechanisms, it has adopted the following definition for an environmental expenditure:

> Expenditures [must be] specifically incurred to maintain or enhance the quality of the natural and social environment, or to minimize adverse impacts therein.

Although BC Hydro has developed guidelines to identify qualifying expenditures and categorization within this definition, it has found that "the reporting of environmental expenditures is a process of estimation that requires continual refinement."

4.4.2 Management Discussion and Analysis (MDA)

Within a company's annual report, the MDA section has the highest level of auditor involvement outside of the financial statements. It is here where a discussion is normally made of environmental concerns requiring disclosure in a company's annual information form for securities commissions. A qualitative review is often included of the company's environmental initiatives, management of resources, and progress against specific targets that may have been set.

4.4.3 Separate Environmental Reports

In issuing separate environmental reports, companies are looking outside of the constraints of GAAP to produce meaningful, environmentally focused, supplemental information which is primarily qualitative in nature. These reports are more popular from a management assessment standpoint and are useful for meeting the demands of the widening external audience. However, for the most part, special-purpose environmental reports have little application to private companies or non-profit organizations as there is not normally a reporting requirement. In addition, these types of organizations do not have the financial resources or reporting systems to prepare them.

Internally, an environmental report can be used for the measurement of an operation's performance, from which management can make current and future operating decisions and monitor the implementation of policies and strategies.

Outside users of environmental reports may use the information to evaluate corporate performance, make investment decisions, and hold directors and senior management of the company accountable for achieving financial, social, and environmental objectives. These reports may also be used by various government agencies to evaluate compliance with regulations.

Separate environmental reports have currently utilized a wide range of formats without a standardized framework for disclosure of subjective information. This includes data of a financial, scientific, and statistical nature which are difficult to integrate into the structure of present financial statements. The reports, although not currently required to be externally verified, are increasingly incorporating quantitative data of a financial nature. As a method of accountability to stakeholders, the separate environmental report runs the danger of being one-sided as it is not subject to independent audit attestation as is the annual report. What is needed is a framework for disclosure where companies set measurable targets and tell the bad news as well as the good.

4.4.4 Industry Practice

Corporate disclosure continues to change over the years. A survey of 1988 and 1989 annual reports concluded that "few companies described how they accounted for environmental costs" (Hawkshaw, 1991). A subsequent study of 1990 annual reports found there had been an increase in the environmental information disclosed (Coopers & Lybrand, 1991); however, there were large differences between the information provided in the reports.

A review of the 1992 annual and environmental reports of 37 large Canadian companies found that approximately 76% of the companies surveyed were making environmental liability disclosures. In addition, six of the companies were issuing separate environmental reports: Noranda Minerals Inc., Noranda Forest Inc., Canfor Corporation, Falconbridge Gold Corporation, Shell Canada Limited, and Dow Canada (Heuston, 1993).

The types of disclosures which companies are making include the cost of future site restorations and contingent claims for environmental lawsuits. Where a company has operations in the United States, disclosure is made if it has been identified as a potentially responsible party as defined by the Comprehensive Environmental Response Compensation and Liability Act (also known as the "Superfund" act). These types of disclosures were found most likely to be quantified in the financial statements and notes to the financial statements. Very little quantitative information was found in the separate environmental reports except as to how well the company was meeting government emission and effluent standards.

Companies which operate in industries such as mining or oil and gas are more likely to be disclosing environmental liabilities as they have more clearly defined guidance on future removal and site restoration costs. The oil and gas sector is required to disclose the cost of site restoration and clean-up under guidelines issued by the Canadian Petroleum Association. Specific guidance for these sectors is also provided by the CICA. The likelihood of a provision being required for this type of liability is dependent on the need for the company to comply with environmental regulations, contractual obligations entered into, and company policy in regards to specific accounting treatment.

The 1993 review of annual reports concluded that environmental liabilities were being reported in 15% more reports than in 1990. Of the 51 types of environmental disclosures noted in the study, only three types were used more then 5% of the time, indicating that there continues to be a wide divergence in the reporting standards which companies are using to disclose these types of issues. A noted weakness was the sparseness of quantitative information, which has been attributed to the lack of accounting systems necessary to support this kind of disclosure (Heuston, 1993).

Guidance for a company in determining an acceptable framework for reporting on its environmental responsibilities has come from the CICA, which in association with the Canadian Standards Association (CSA) and several other groups, prepared a 1993 discussion paper titled *Reporting on Environmental Performance*. This paper proposes a five-stage process to preparing a report on environmental performance. The stages included defining the objectives and target audience of the report, defining what is significant for reporting purposes, and soliciting feedback from the target audience to identify areas of the report for improvement (CICA *et al.*, 1993).

4.4.5 Outlook

A recent survey of the motives and views of more than 70 companies from around the world concluded that "Corporate environmental reporting provides an excellent means of ensuring that a company is in touch with — and responding to — the evolving needs of the main environmental stakeholders" (Deloitte Touche Tohmatsu International, *et al.* 1993).

Corporate reporting of environmental liabilities and costs will improve with the continued development of environmental management and reporting systems. These systems must be able to provide quantifiable information which can be used to assess progress towards legal and corporate objectives including financial reporting. The subjectivity of the results and medium used to communicate to stakeholders will also require greater involvement by independent bodies to give credibility to the information.

4.5 "GREEN" TAXES AND INCENTIVES

4.5.1 Federal Income Tax Act

The Income Tax Act (ITA) has only general provisions which specifically address environmental related expenses and issues. The ITA focuses on granting allowances based on expenditures of a capital nature that can be deducted at an accelerated rate against taxable income. It also gives recognition through investment tax credits for expenditures on scientific research and development projects by a business for the purpose of developing new methods of cleaning up or conserving our limited resources through greater efficiencies in use or developing alternative resources.

The focus of the ITA appears to be providing tax incentives to companies to update their facilities to meet modern standards. There are few tax incentives designed to encourage environmental protection.

4.5.2 Federal Tax Incentives — Accelerated Depreciation

Capital Cost Allowance (CCA) classes 24 and 27 allow for an accelerated three-year write-off of water and air pollution control equipment based upon rates of a 25%, 50%, and 25%. To be eligible for inclusion in the above two classes, the assets must first be approved by Environment Canada. The equipment (in addition to meeting specific capital asset requirements) must be used for the prevention, reduction, or elimination of water pollution (class 24) and air pollution (class 27) caused by operations carried on by the same taxpayer from a time prior to 1974. New production facilities are excluded.

Class 34 provides for accelerated CCA at the same rates as above for energy efficient equipment and equipment which utilizes alternative energy sources. Included in this class would be windmills and solar heating equipment. Each class 34 asset must be included in a separate class for CCA purposes and is subject to specific restrictions including approval of Environment Canada before its inclusion in the class.

4.5.3 Provincial Tax Incentives

In Ontario, businesses which acquire new equipment are allowed a special onetime deduction for environmental equipment which is included in classes 27 or 24. For qualified pollution-control equipment, the allowance is phased in over three years with equipment acquired subsequent to 1991 allowed a 30% deduction based upon the eligible cost.

4.5.4 Scientific Research and Development Credits

Companies that engage in environmental R&D such as new energy technology or pollution clean-up may be eligible to earn tax credits and be able to claim a tax deduction for qualifying capital expenditures.

Scientific research conducted by a company must include "a systematic investigation or search carried out in a field of science or technology by means of experiment or analysis." The research must fall under one of the three following categories:

1) Basic research, namely work undertaken for the advancement of scientific knowledge without a specific practical application in view.
2) Applied research, namely work undertaken for the advancement of scientific knowledge with a specific practical application in view.
3) Development, namely use of the results of basic or applied research for the purpose of creating new, or improving existing materials, devices, products, or processes.

To obtain the investment tax credit, a company must maintain extensive project information records and file a prescribed form. Circular 86-4R2 should be reviewed for specific information on qualifying R&D costs.

This incentive is particularly beneficial to Canadian Controlled Private Companies (CCPC) which are granted a 35% investment tax credit on qualifying R&D, subject to certain limitations. In addition, a CCPC may be eligible for a refundable investment tax credit to the extent that the credit cannot be used to offset Part I tax payable.

4.5.5 Ontario Research and Development Superallowance

An R&D Superallowance is available for qualifying expenditures on pollution control incurred in Ontario after April 20, 1988. This super allowance provides for write-offs of 37.5% or 52.5%, depending on the size of the company, for expenditures in excess of the average of the corporation's expenditures over the three previous years. A deduction of 25% or 35% is also allowed on the lesser of the company's net eligible qualifying expenditures incurred in the year and its expenditure base.

4.5.6 Quebec Incentives

In Quebec, qualifying R&D expenditures on pollution control are 100% deductible in the year acquired. In addition, tax credits are available at the rate of 20% for wages, fringe benefits, and subcontracted wages incurred in Quebec as part of R&D projects.

If the corporation is controlled by Canadian residents and the associated companies have a combined asset base of less than $25 million and equity of less than $10 million, then it is eligible for a tax credit at the rate of 40% on the first $2 million of R&D wages paid in Quebec.

4.5.7 Nova Scotia Incentives

In Nova Scotia, non-refundable tax credits are available of up to 10% of the eligible R&D expenditures on pollution control made by a business resident in the province. These credits can be used to reduce current provincial taxes payable or carried back three years and forward seven years to reduce taxes otherwise due.

4.5.8 Site Reclamation Costs

The cost of restoring land to a re-usable state, such as in the case of a lumber or mining company, is often not incurred until the end of operations. Section 3060, "Capital Assets," of the CICA handbook requires that "when reasonably determinable, provisions should be made for future removal and site restoration costs, net of expected recoveries." In estimating these costs, a company sets up a reserve against current income for the future cost in its financial statements.

The ITA does not specifically address site reclamation and shutdown costs. Reserves of this nature have been denied a deduction for tax purpose as they have been held to be of a contingent nature in that the liability to incur such future expenditures is said to be not certain.

A secondary factor which impacts upon the tax treatment of site reclamation and shutdown costs is whether the costs are incurred in the ordinary course of business or as a betterment to an existing asset. Capital expenditures are not deductible for tax purposes in the year incurred. However, expenditures which are for ordinary or extraordinary repairs and maintenance may be deductible as incurred. Interpretation Bulletin IT-128R from Revenue Canada provides guidance on distinguishing between a deductible expense and an expenditure which is capital in nature:

> Maintenance or Betterment — Where an expenditure made in respect of property serves only to restore it to its original condition, that fact is one indication that the expenditure is of a current nature. This is often the case where a floor or roof is replaced. Where, however, the result of the expenditure is to materially improve the property beyond its original condition, such as when a new floor or a new roof clearly is of better quality and greater durability than the replaced one, then the expenditure is regarded as capital in nature. Whether or not the market value of the property is increased as a result of the expenditure is not a major factor in reaching a decision. In the event that the expenditure includes both current and capital elements and these can be identified, an appropriate allocation of the expenditure is necessary.

4.5.9 Fines and Penalties

Fines and penalties which may be levied under environmental legislation, although not specifically addressed by the ITA, will normally not be deductible under the ITA (paragraph 18(1)(a)). Expenditures of this nature are generally not considered by Revenue Canada to have been incurred for the purposes of producing income.

There are, however, some cases where a deduction in computing income is allowed for fines. It is advisable to consult Interpretation Bulletin IT-104R for guidance. Professional fees such as legal and accounting costs which are incurred to defend against environmental penalties and fines currently are deductible.

4.5.10 Emission Trading

Emission trading is not practised in Canada but has been used for several years in the United States. Maximum amounts of atmospheric emissions are determined for specific sources. If an emitter does not need to use all of its allotted amount, the difference can be transferred to another source in the same "airshed." In principle, this concept encourages the most cost-effective reductions to be made first.

The trading of emission allowances "has been praised by both environmental groups and utilities as an innovative solution to a costly problem" (Dao, 1993). A possible disadvantage of emission trading is that "utilities might be encouraged to buy credits, rather than to install pollution control devices, or scrubbers." This can be described as another form of "asset management."

4.6 LENDER LIABILITY AND BANKRUPTCY ISSUES

4.6.1 The Growing Importance of Environmental Issues

When environmental concerns are raised by banks and other lending institutions as part of loan portfolio reviews, companies are finding that the consequences can be dramatic. Viable businesses are learning that property provided to lenders for security is now being rejected due to its being classified as "environmentally risky." The underlying security for loans and equity base of companies can be effectively diminished.

As noted in Section 4.2, environmental concerns are often not fully recorded or disclosed in a company's financial statements. A company issued a clean-up order from a government agency may need to have the resources to face a possible prosecution for non-compliance in addition to the actual cost of clean-up and the possible cost of lost production time if the operation is ordered to close until the environmental problem is resolved. A business that is unable to absorb the costs of complying with a government order may be putting itself into a position of insolvency.

The general nature of audited financial statements is also a barrier to being able to predict if environmental liabilities will affect the viability of a company. Financial statements do not reflect the adequacy of the company's insurance policy against environmental spills or accidents. There is also no recognition if the costs of clean-up or future compliance cannot be reasonably measured. Stakeholders must look beyond the traditional financial statements to evaluate a company's environmental risk.

In addition, environmental legislation is forcing lenders to be more circumspect in their enforcement of security when a debtor goes into default. The impact of environmental issues in an insolvency situation is clearly illustrated by the case of Kemtec Petrochemical Corp. When it was reported that the Kemtec refinery in Montreal required an estimated $50 to $100 million to clean up soil and groundwater at the site, the lender banks, owed a reported $125 million, did not seize control (McKenna, 1991).

4.6.2 Liability Based upon Control

The Ontario Environmental Protection Act prohibits the discharging of any contaminant into the natural environment in an amount, concentration, or level in excess of that prescribed by regulations.

Where there has been a breach of this prohibition, control orders or stop orders may be issued to:

1) an owner who is or was in occupation of the source of the contaminant

2) a person who is or was in occupation of the source of the contaminant, or

3) a person who has or had the charge, management, or control of the source of the contaminant

Consequently, the lender that is closely involved with the day-to-day operations of the debtor, and wishes to realize on its security, may find itself liable for compliance costs, bills for clean-up, or penalties which may exceed the value of the property.

Before taking control of a debtor's business, or any assets where environmental concerns have been raised, the lender should review the operations and history of the site. A typical review consists of seeking professional advice on identifying potential environmental issues, determining the extent of the actual and potential contamination, and estimating costs of clean-up. The initial review can be performed to meet the standards for a Phase I Environmental Site Assessment (ESA) as described in the Canadian Standards Association document CSA Z768-94. To improve the confidence of clean-up cost estimates, it may be necessary to conduct a Phase II ESA.

The information reported in the ESA is incorporated in to an evaluation of the ability of the debtor to carry on the business and repay the loan. Appraisals would normally be obtained, where practical, of the net realizable value of the assets. There have been cases where secured creditors have elected to walk away from a security rather than risk incurring unknown clean-up costs.

The liability of a financial institution for the environmental problems of its customers pivots upon the lender's control over or possession of a customer's property. This has been determined in the Ontario Divisional Court case, *Canadian National Railway Co. v. Ontario (Director, Minister of Environment)*, [1991] O.J. No. 684 ("Northern Wood Preservers"), wherein the court concluded that Abitibi-Price, as lender, even if it was aware of a contravention of environmental laws by the borrower, cannot be held responsible for that contravention if it has taken no active steps to obtain control of the actual source of contaminant.

A lender's exposure appears to be limited to the value of its security interest if the lender was not in possession and has exercised no control. Courts have also taken into account the lender's capacity to influence the financial operation and management of the borrower when considering the issue of control.

Lenders are now looking for ways to protect themselves from environmental liabilities as the legal cases on this issue reveal the courts' tendency to try to find a solvent responsible party at any cost. To give lenders a greater sense of security, The Bankruptcy and Insolvency Act was amended in 1992 to limit the direct financial liability of trustees (and indirectly petitioning creditors who may have provided indemnification agreements). Subsections 14.06(2) and (3) read:

(2) Notwithstanding any provision of federal or provincial legislation respecting the protection or rehabilitation of the environment, a trustee is not personally liable under any such provision, in relation to the trustee's position as trustee of a bankrupt's estate, in respect of any environmental condition that arose, or any environmental damage that occurred,

(a)   before the trustee's appointment as a trustee of the estate; or

(b)   after that appointment, except where the condition arose or the damage occurred as a result of the trustee's failure to exercise due diligence.

(3) Nothing in subsection (2) exempts a trustee from any duty to report or make disclosure imposed by a provision referred to in that subsection.

These revisions may provide some encouragement to government agencies to enter into agreements with receivers/trustees to limit the receiver/trustee's exposure to environmental risks.

4.6.3 Default by Debtor

Before enforcement of security, the lender should consider the use of professionals: trustee/receivers, lawyers, and others who have experience dealing with environmental issues and who can assess the expected realizations of security under the various opportunities available. If the possibility of environmental exposure exists, a Phase I ESA report from an environmental site assessor may be requested. Having received this report, the lender is able to make decisions on the risk of continuing to extend financing or alternatives available to recovering on funds currently provided.

Environmental liabilities can arise primarily from two areas:

1) those liabilities already existing at the time of the default, and

2) those liabilities arising from the continued operation or shutdown of the operations by the receiver/trustee

If the liabilities arose from prior operations, it may be in the interest of the secured creditors to petition for bankruptcy. Bankruptcy sets out the ranking of creditors in accordance with the Bankruptcy and Insolvency Act. Legal precedents for this was established by the facts of *Panamerica de Bienes y Servicos, S.A. v. Northern Badger Oil & Gas Limited*. In this case, the Energy Resources Conservation Board of Alberta had issued an order to the receiver to abandon seven oil wells at an estimated cost of abandonment of approximately $200,000. The issue in this case was whether the Board could order the cost of the abandonment to be paid out of funds held by the receiver for the secured creditors or out of excess funds payable to the trustee in bankruptcy.

Although the order had been issued prior to the bankruptcy, the court ruled that due to the bankruptcy, all creditors were subject to the provisions of the Bankruptcy Act. Consequently, the Board claim would rank as preferred behind secured creditor interests. The Alberta Court of Appeal subsequently ruled that the cost of the abandonment ranked ahead of the secured creditors and that the order was not subject to the scheme of distribution set out in the Bankruptcy Act.

Environmental liabilities arising as a result of the receiver/trustee taking control of the business either to continue operations or close it down are the responsibility of the receiver/trustee. It is now common for a receiver/trustee to obtain an indemnity from the secured creditor for the risk of any liability arising during the administration. Negotiating with government regulators prior to taking possession is also being done to limit liabilities to the extent of assets recovered from the estate.

Problems can arise quickly if a company has not set up an effective EMS to monitor compliance. The receiver/trustee must, upon appointment, assess the systems of the debtor company and ensure their continuance during operation. If there are no systems or if they are inadequate, then the cost of improving or setting them up must be born by the estate.

An example of this can be derived from the 1989 decision of *R. v. Bata Industries Inc.*, a case in which corporate officers were accused of failing to fulfil their statutory environmental duties as part of their responsibility for managing the business and affairs of the company.

Consequently, the company and two officers were fined for improperly storing barrels that were leaking industrial solvents. Although management was aware of the problem since 1983, cost-cutting restraints resulted in the delay of any action being taken until 1989 when the plant was investigated by the Ministry of the Environment. It was also found during the investigation that the plant manager lacked special environmental training and that inadequate systems had been put in place to deal with environmental issues (see Section 3.4.1).

4.6.4 Sale of Assets

A company's liability for outstanding work orders will affect the net realization of security held by the lender. Potential purchasers should also have adequate disclosure made to them of the existence, production, or storage of hazardous materials and wastes. Where operations have not continued and the property is to be redeveloped or rezoned, or is releasing contaminants into the environment, legislative requirements for cleanup likely will need to be met. This may fall to the receiver/trustee.

4.6.5 Prevention at the Outset

Lenders can help minimize their exposure to environmental problems by conducting a full review of the applicant's operations. Lending policy should include the completion of a questionnaire or checklist to help identify possible environmental risks. Warranties should be obtained from the debtor that all relevant environmental legislation is being complied with. Subsequent to the loan being granted, there should be continued monitoring of any changes in operating methods by the company and proposed changes in environmental legislation which may impact on the business. Loans staff with appropriate experience with environmental issues should be utilized in conducting such assessments.

4.7 SUSTAINABLE DEVELOPMENT AND SIMILAR CONCEPTS

4.7.1 Accounting for Sustainable Development

Companies are beginning to address the notion that we live on a "small" planet with finite quantities of living space and natural resources by adopting policies that incorporate the concept of sustainable development.

Sustainable development has been defined as "adopting business strategies and activities that meet the needs of the enterprise and its stakeholders today while protecting, sustaining, and enhancing the human and natural resources that will be needed in the future" (International Institute for Sustainable Development, 1992).

For the most part, this is an extension of what many companies have traditionally done in efforts to reduce operating costs and ensure compliance with governing laws. Sustainable development embraces these objectives and focuses on linking each activity of the company to its impacts on ecosystems and communities, and traditional financial measurement criteria. As an example, a company about to implement a policy of recycling traditionally would consider the cost of purchasing a shredder or the cost of segregating the recyclable waste. Sustainable development requires the decision to be considered in terms of a cost-effective and overall net benefit to the company.

Sustainable development involves changes in every level of an organization if it is to be successful. It requires the setting of broad environmental principles that are then broken down into corporate policies. Information systems must be designed to measure how these policies are applied using performance standards. These systems must be designed to monitor and measure the impact of environmental expenditures on the company's income as well as changes to assets and liabilities. The Conference Board of Canada has reported that between 30% and 60% of corporate environmental expenditures in the U.S. are legal expenses (Conference Board of Canada, 1993). Environmental groups, many of which are consumer or social advocates, are lobbying for more detailed breakdowns of environmental costs in financial statements. This information would help to identify the impacts of environmental issues on the bottom-line profitability of the company. Some argue that the disclosure of this type of information will improve environmental stewardship and management accountability.

The movement towards sustainable development is also being shaped by companies that see the environment as another marketing opportunity and are using market-based mechanisms such as linking specific products with environmentally concerned consumers. Some companies are restructuring their operations to ensure compliance with tougher regulatory standards and policies.

An example of how regulation can have a positive impact on a business involves the packaging industry in Canada. According to Robert Slater, senior assistant deputy minister with Environment Canada, "In return for leniency from federal regulators, the industry promised to cut its waste to half 1988 levels by 2000 and to meet other targets along the way. Not only is it meeting with interim goals, but it has developed products and methods that are being sold internationally" (Mahood, 1993).

Companies that set environmental objectives such as reduced emissions or incorporating more recycled material into their products, recognize that they have a responsibility to stakeholders. When they report on progress towards these objectives, it provides information on how the company is managing its environmental risk and the results of initiatives taken to date. A possible drawback to reporting is that companies risk not only raising legal concerns over compliance, but loss of competitive advantage. Sustainable development requires the setting in place of a process which balances environmental and other organizational objectives.

A company that adopts a policy of sustainable development does so at the request of its stakeholders, and to remain competitive in the face of higher input costs. From a purely economic standpoint, those organizations that do not comply face a) a higher cost of capital, as there is greater risk to the lender; b) higher production costs, as operating lines will not minimize resource and energy inputs; c) increased insurance premiums; and d) greater restrictive legislation.

Sustainable development issues are often multidisciplinary in nature. Consequently, it requires the combined efforts of managers, environmental advisors, lawyers, and public accountants, as well as others, to calculate the financial effects on the company, impact of operations on the environment, and the legal ramifications of non-compliance. An environmental management team uses environmental performance measures to evaluate progress in attaining performance goals set by the company. The goals need to be set using viable, realistic objectives to support the continual improvement toward sustainable development. Procedures and progress require monitoring at each step and periodic assessments on the headway being made. Based upon the review and investigation carried out, a report is prepared of environmental performance. Where shortfalls in attaining goals are identified, corrective action is needed to refocus the commitment of people, facilities, and financial resources.

A fundamental accounting concept is that financial information must be quantifiable, using the dollar as the unit of measure. Once the effect has been measured in terms of dollars, it can be readily used as a benchmark for decision-making. When this is applied, for example, to the decision of how to allocate a company's resources, it can sometimes be found that recycling may sound good, but reducing waste generation or energy needs may make more economic sense.

Although there has been a great deal of interest in having industry conform to the idea of sustainable development, its concepts are only slowly being adopted. The effects of past environmental damage also remains a challenge to stakeholders. For example, it has been estimated that "Canadian industry now faces a $20-billion pollution bill" but that "the health benefits of these clean-ups are thought to be modest. There is, however, a high level of uncertainty in valuing benefits, as most accrue to the unborn who are at risk as a consequence of possible future soil contamination or leaks into groundwater" (Lorinc, 1992).

The obligation of companies to clean up their past environmental damage will continue and, therefore, businesses are going to bear a large portion of this cost. Consequently, companies burdened with environmental liabilities and cost are experiencing a reduction in their market value as calculated by earnings per share, debt-equity ratios, and share price.

The magnitude of this adjustment can be seen from an estimate of the impact on the G.N.P. growth rate in the United States which was estimated as being reduced 0.19% per year between 1973 and 1985 as a consequence of mandated pollution control systems.

The Conference Board of Canada, in its report entitled *Valuing the Environment: Full-Cost Pricing — An Inquiry and a Goal*, reviewed the issues involved with environmental management and concluded the following:

- Environmental values are not currently reflected in market prices.
- The accounting approach to valuing the environment is based on the principle that what can be measured can be managed.
- The decision-making approach involves setting charges, fees, or taxes that bring market prices into line with full-cost prices consistent with sustainable management of the environment.

The report suggests possible alternatives for incorporating environmental costs in the financial model to allow for comparability between alternatives.

4.7.2 Full-Cost Accounting

Full-cost environmental accounting involves incorporating the cost of environmental compliance (i.e. fines and penalties, clean-up costs, and the cost of modifying operating system to ensure compliance) to production and operating costs.

Standard costing systems for most companies disguise material and waste losses by including them under the heading as production variances. When greater emphasis is placed on pinpointing how these losses occur and taking corrective action, there is an opportunity for savings. Dupont Chemicals in the U.S. "found that by adjusting their production process to use less of one raw material, they were able to slash the plant's waste by two-thirds. Yields went up and costs went down. The savings was $1 million a year" (Rooney, 1992).

4.7.3 Product-Cycle Analysis

Product-cycle analysis has recently been adopted as a "cradle to grave" method of tracking the resource use, production, consumption, and disposal cost during a product's life cycle. Various cost factors are incorporated including by-products and the ability to recycle. This process allows for comparability between alternative products and for monitoring the effects of changes made to a particular stage of a product's life. The results, when analyzed, may lead to improved efficiencies. An example of this would be analyzing the costs between a newspaper chain utilizing a higher degree of recycled paper versus switching suppliers to a mill which utilizes a chlorine-free production process.

4.7.4 Project Evaluation Approach

Another method of costing is to use a Project Evaluation Approach. The importance of various objectives in terms of their potential impact on the environment are first classified and then prioritized. Based upon this ranking, decisions are made on the cost of environmental protection versus expected results from both an environmental standpoint and financial effect on the project's bottom line. A zero tolerance for environmental impact is impossible as it is open to a wide range of interpretation and bears a high cost. Sustainable development attempts to take a middle ground seeking the best use of resources with minimal cost to the environment.

The Project Evaluation Approach is an effective tool when utilized for evaluating large-scale undertakings such as hydro-electric projects or as part of environmental impact assessments. The data used and results obtained can be very subjective. Economists and public opinion polls are often drawn upon to help establish the criteria used in calculating social costs and benefits of the projects. There is, however, little standardization in the methods of measurement which leads to different conclusions being reached by the various interest groups involved.

4.8 CONCLUSION

Environmental laws, regulations, and legal decisions in Canada and the United States are changing the way companies incorporate environmental issues into accounting and reporting practices. Guidance for these changes is coming from professional organizations, government, and capital markets which have recognized that traditional practices are not properly addressing the needs of companies or their stakeholders.

Communicating the interrelationship between the environment and economics is in the early stages of development. Environmental management systems are being linked to traditional financial reporting systems to develop new accounting models for the environment. The costs of pollution prevention and waste reduction, and the methods used to measure progress in attaining environmental objectives are being disclosed by companies in their annual reports with greater frequency. Some companies are going so far as to issue special stand-alone environmental reports.

Past environmental damage and the continued releases of contaminants affect us all. The capital costs of clean-up have been estimated to be enormous and procedures must be put in place to encourage progress on these fronts. So-called "Green Taxes" can act as incentives both to reward successes and discourage unsound environmental practices from continuing. Also, companies which are not in compliance with environmental standards are finding that it is becoming increasingly difficult to find and afford financing.

The concept of sustainable development offers a method for integrating environmental policies and economic considerations. It has the potential to make businesses more responsible and accountable for their activities, yet at the same time minimizing the financial cost to an organization where possible. When the full cost of operating — including environmental costs — is factored into the business plan, it is expected that the company and its stakeholders will be able to make informed and superior decisions.

New cost-effective environmental management strategies need to be developed together with an acceptable method for quantifying and disclosing unrecorded liabilities. This will require the work of many specialists to help measure, interpret, and communicate financial and other economic information. As a consequence, environmental accounting and reporting will be undergoing many changes to meet the information requirements of its users.

REFERENCES

Canadian Institute of Chartered Accountants. "Capital Assets." *CICA Handbook*, Section 3060.

_____. "Long-Term Investments." Section 3050.

_____. "Financial Statement Concepts." Section 1000.

_____. "Contractual Obligations." Section 3280.

_____. "Contingent Gains and Losses." Section 3290.

_____. "Research and Development Costs." Section 3450.

_____. Research Report 1993. "Environmental Costs and Liabilities: Accounting and Financial Reporting Issues."

_____. In association with Canadian Standards Association, Financial Executives Institute, Canada. International Institute for Sustainable Development. July 1993. "A Discussion Paper: Reporting on Environmental Performance."

Canadian Insolvency Practitioners Association, Advanced Topics Module 3. "Insolvency and Environmental Issues."

Conference Board of Canada. Report 103-93, 1993. "Valuing the Environment: Full-Cost Pricing — An Inquiry and a Goal."

Coopers & Lybrand. 1991. *Environmental Disclosure: The Accountant's Role.*

Dao, J. "Will the Trading of Pollution Credits Improve Air Quality?" *Miami Herald.* February 7, 1993.

Deloitte Touche Tohmatsu International and the Institute for Sustainable Development and Sustainability Ltd. 1993. "Coming Clean: Corporate Environmental Reporting: Opening Up for Sustainable Development."

Dao, J. "Will the Trading of Pollution Credits Improve Air Quality?" *Miami Herald.* February 7, 1993.

Financial Accounting Standards Board (FASB). 1990. *Capitalization of Costs to Treat Environmental Contamination.* FASB Report 90-8.

Hawkshaw, Anthony. March 1991. "Status Quo Vadis." *CA Magazine.*

Heuston, Krista. Spring 1993. "An Examination of Current Environmental Liability Disclosure Practices and of the Degree of Auditor Involvement with Those Disclosures."

The Income Tax Act, R.S.C. 1952, c. 148 (am. S.C. 1970-71-72, c. 63), as amended.

International Institute for Sustainable Development. 1992. *Business Strategy for Sustainable Development. Leadership and Accountability in the 1990s.* In conjunction with Deloitte & Touche with the participation of the Business Council for Sustainable Development.

KPMG Peat Marwick Thorne. 1993. "International Survey of Environmental Reporting."

Lorinc, J. September 1992. "The Reckoning: The Crunch has Come". *Canadian Business.*

Mahood, C. "Canada Falls Behind U.S. American Demands for Green Technology Outstrips Ours." *The Globe and Mail.* June 8, 1993.

McKenna, B. "Toxic Shock for Taxpayers." *The Globe and Mail.* December 7, 1991.

Rooney, C. Spring 1992. "Waste—Not Just an Environmental Issue." *Business Quarterly.*

5

Public Involvement and Consultation

by
Thomas Rahn
LURA Group

5.1 PUBLIC INVOLVEMENT: PERCEPTIONS AND TRENDS

5.1.1 The Challenge

One of the common images associated with the term "public involvement" is the public meeting. The proponent of an initiative and various experts and advisors sit before an audience that is angry and opposed to the project. Those at the front make presentations; some catcalls come from the audience, and then questions are posed that are often more statements of pointed opinion than attempts to seek information.

Once the public meeting is concluded, the proponent and advisors feel relieved if some semblance of order was maintained; the public consultation requirements have been fulfilled. Members of the audience leave largely confirmed and strengthened in their opinions that the proponent did not listen to their views, answered their questions evasively, and played down their concerns. The whole event was frustrating and justifies the opposition of the local citizens' group.

Is this the best public involvement can do? Numerous examples suggest that another route is possible. Indeed, far from being an onerous requirement, public consultation can improve the project and the climate around its implementation.

5.1.2 A Short History of Public Involvement

The history of public involvement has been described as a steady evolution from public relations, through public education to consultation, leading finally to public participation in making the decisions. Within this broad sweep, earlier developments may not necessarily be discarded, but serve as building blocks for new approaches. Thus, all the past stages can be found in the present, and even as complementary components of a single public involvement program. At the same time, the focus and the expectation, especially in controversial situations, has clearly shifted to favouring some degree of public participation in the actual decision-making.

A useful way of understanding the evolution of public involvement is to see each new stage as a response to the failings of the previous stage. While the actual history is far more complex, this perspective does bring out the salient characteristics of each approach.

For a given project, when it became apparent that the public relations effort put forward by the proponent was failing in its attempt to convince enough people to take the proponent's view, it seemed beneficial to then "educate" the public. It was assumed that once the public understood the relative risks and the technical safeguards, they would share the certainty of the technical experts that the project should proceed. But the public had an uncanny ability to find the glitches in the technical arguments, and in any case remained unimpressed by the risk assessments. That led to the idea that the public actually had something to contribute, and that the education should go both ways. Thus the emphasis shifted to public consultation, where public comment and input were sought at various stages in the planning of the project. Unfortunately, public anger only seemed to increase when, after their comment had been requested, the "experts" subsequently gave the public input a different relevance than the public had suggested. It became apparent that the public wanted to do more than comment — they wanted to share in the decision-making. The focus shifted again to developing processes that incorporate the public in the actual decision-making.

5.1.3 An Example of the Leading Edge

Inviting the public to assist in the decision-making may at first seem an impossible proposition. However, the example of a wood products company in northern Ontario serves to illustrate how the process can work. Logging practices in many parts of Canada have become controversial. This particular company decided to involve the public in the development of a new five-year timber management plan for its license area on Crown Land.

The company put out an invitation to various groups to participate in a committee it called the "Allocations Working Group." Eleven groups accepted. Their interests covered a broad range: First Nations, unions, trappers, business, recreation, tourism, and naturalists. Two company representatives and two members of the general public joined with the other representatives to form a working group. The goals of the working group were to develop a harvest allocation proposal that represented the range of interests and concerns around the table, and to provide a forum for non-members to comment on the proposal. Members agreed to work toward consensus on all issues. The company committed to providing the group with the information it requested and to consulting with the group before communicating with the media or the general public.

The group also helped to plan other public information and consultation activity. The meetings of the group, open to the public, were supplemented by two open houses in the communities closest to the license area. A workshop, attended by company and ministry staff and some members of the working group, developed the first draft of harvest plan for each of the five years (Lajambe, 1993).

Processes such as this one represent a profound change in the way companies and governments go about involving the public in making decisions about the environment. It has not been the norm to give others the credit for being able to work together or to make intelligent choices jointly with those who may be regarded as adversaries. Nor has it always been easy, or for that matter successful. However, its proliferation in the last years, as well as the satisfaction participants derive from honest and fair processes, are signs that this way of involving the public needs to be taken seriously and applied more widely.

5.2 WHY INVOLVE THE PUBLIC?

5.2.1 The Mythological Landscape

It remains a common perception that public involvement means delay, changes to the project, the prospect of bad publicity, and angry confrontation. The viewpoint of public involvement as a public nuisance draws on the mythology of the entrepreneur as the modern-day cowboy. An American cable TV magnate, writing as Yankee Jones (1981), expresses it best:

I'm an entrepreneur,

Why do I feel like a gunslinger,

Or a dinosaur,

Here, on what was the unfettered frontier,

Of free enterprise?

The entrepreneur is portrayed as the modern-day successor to the frontiersman, surviving on a mixture of boldness and business smarts. The entrepreneur is interested in making things happen — not wasting time at public meetings.

Did that frontier ever exist, or were the constraints just different? Whatever the reality, the ideal of unfettered action, bolstered by appeals to efficiency and cutting red tape, continues as one of the forces shaping the landscape through which public involvement evolves.

Other ideals compete for attention in decision-making:
- the value of law and order
- inherited ethical values around regard for the needs of the neighbours
- democratic ideals that see public issues resolved through discussion and dialogue
- the value of community as a home for the family and the individual

The competing ideals surface in any debate over the role and usefulness of public involvement. They also shape the variations in expectations that individuals will bring to any process in which they participate. From a positive perspective, public involvement is the way in which representational democracy allows a great many more to participate than the few who are elected.

Although involving others in making decisions can add an unpredictable complexity to the process, the alternative is to stifle debate and to allow a chosen few to decide and act as they deem fit. Given that choice, the frustrations of complexity may start to appear more favourable.

5.2.2 Larger Trends

The larger place of public involvement can be best understood against the background of a number of continuing trends. These trends will not disappear by belittling public involvement. It is rather the opposite that is true — good public involvement programs have the chance to give new vigour to democratic systems.

Public trust in politicians, governments, and corporations is not particularly high. Recent examples are numerous: low voter turnout, the success of protest movements such as the Reform Party, boycotts of companies for marketing infant formula to the poor, or the controversy surrounding the logging practices in British Columbia.

Contributing to the erosion of trust is a wide range of developments where promises and rhetoric have not matched the results. Examples abound: layoffs despite profits, government cutbacks while politicians' perks increase, and promises of programs that never materialize. Perhaps most fundamental is a loss of faith in continuing economic growth to provide all with a bigger slice of the pie, and a questioning of the belief that all technological progress is for the best. As a result, the public has become more skeptical of the claims of anyone proposing a new project. Consequently, a major focus and goal of any public involvement strategy becomes the creation — and fostering — of trust.

Another trend with important ramifications for public involvement is a general sense of loss of involvement and control. With the increase in the complexity of technology and organizations, in the speed of change and the global span of interdependencies, the ability of a community to influence its own fate seems to shrink.

While the connections of individuals to the community remain strong, the ongoing migration to the cities weakens rural communities. In the cites and their suburbs, a number of factors serve to reduce the connection and sense of identity of individuals with the community. These include the mobility of individuals and the increased tendency of people to live but not work in the same neighbourhood.

As people no longer identify with the problems facing the community, they naturally expect others, such as the government, to take responsibility. In not feeling responsible, they also resent having to bear any impact of any proposed solution. At the same time, both communities and individuals feel less able to influence decisions that affect them. The sense of powerlessness raises the fear of change and promotes the adoption of strong inflexible positions as a way of rallying the community. Negotiation and discussion become difficult because the community does not have a strong sense of its own identity outside of the position taken, or the resources and ability to evaluate proposals and negotiate effectively, or the sense that it bears any responsibility for solving the problem. Paradoxically, the lack of trust and the feeling of powerlessness creates a very difficult situation for a proponent. A public involvement strategy that builds trust and gives the community some power and the resources to exercise it makes it easier for the community to accept change.

Concern about environmental issues also accounts for the interest in public involvement. Over and above the fluctuations of environmental concerns in opinion polls, a new and heightened sensitivity to the environment has developed. Whether measured by the participation in recycling programs, the boom in bicycle sales, or the continued existence of hundreds of environmental groups, and indeed the existence of this chapter in this book, it is difficult to see it all as just another fad. Furthermore, despite some progress, most environmental issues have not been resolved and new ones continue to appear. Addressing environmental concerns will remain a prime reason for engaging the public in decision-making.

The quality of the engagement is also an issue. As various groups gain experience with public-involvement programs, they are more interested in ensuring that programs meet their needs. The Canadian Environment Network paper *Proceeding with Process* (Mausberg and Coffey, 1993) is a recent and formal expression of a heightened awareness about the process itself. Various issues are at play; groups have put a large amount of effort into stakeholder meetings, only to see the results ignored, or have felt forced to participate in processes that they felt were not fair and open, that left the sense that the major decisions had been made regardless of their contribution. In other words, while groups once simply asked to be consulted, the request now is for involvement in a meaningful manner.

5.2.3 Why Involve the Public?

For those who have implemented meaningful public involvement programs, the factors influencing their decision have usually revolved around the direct requirements and benefits to the organization. Three reasons stand out:

- to satisfy regulatory requirements for obtaining a desired approval or permit
- to improve the proposal by incorporating other viewpoints
- to create a proposal that will win community acceptance

Regulatory Requirements

The expectation of meaningful involvement has been reinforced by requirements or recommendations for public consultation in a wide range of regulatory and approval processes. These include:

- provincial environmental assessment processes
- provincial land use planning requirements
- Ontario Environmental Bill of Rights
- Canadian Environmental Assessment Act
- federal and provincial Decommissioning Guidelines
- statutes governing licensing of water use, pesticide use, forest management plans, waste-management facilities, discharges into air and water, etc., and
- policy statements by governments at all levels

The specific requirements of these statutes and guidelines vary widely. The types of requirements generally fall into the following categories:

- notice of an application for a permit, or other approval
- opportunity for public comment, usually with some time limit
- response to concerns or objection, either by the proponent applicant or the permitting agency
- public hearing

Public notice is the most basic requirement; the others may then follow with changes and omissions.

In some cases, the statutory requirements for public involvement are supplemented by hearing decision precedents, tradition, and policy. A good example is the Ontario Environmental Assessment Act which formally requires only very minimal public involvement, primarily through the public notice and a public hearing. However, hearing decisions and policy have added much to those requirements including the following (Patterson, 1993):

- preparation of an environmental assessment proposal showing the process the proponent will use in proceeding with the Environmental Assessment (EA)
- specifically, the EA Proposal should include a public consultation strategy indicating methods, opportunities for input, and how concerns will be addressed
- the proponent should involve the Ministry of Environment and Energy and the public from the outset
- affected parties help plan the undertaking through consultation prior to the submission of the formal EA document, and
- documentation of the history of the consultation is required

---

Ontario's Environmental Bill of Rights (EBR): What Consequences for Public Involvement?

The Bill of Rights contains several provisions that may affect proponents and operators of facilities in Ontario. For certain approvals ("instruments"), the EBR requires notification through a listing in a central computer registry and gives the public 30 days to comment on the proposed instrument. The ministry responsible must then consider and respond to public comments. After an instrument has been issued, the public may seek leave to appeal the decision to a relevant board. Which approvals or instruments are subject to the EBR is set out in regulations that accompany the Act.

For existing approvals or instruments subject to the EBR, the public can ask the Minister for a review. If the Minister agrees with the review request, the Minister then carries out the review and announces the results.

Finally, the public also has the right to request an investigation of anyone believed to be violating an Act, regulation or instrument subject to the EBR. The Minister then decides whether or not to investigate, and reports any findings. If the concerned parties are not satisfied with the response, they may take the matter to court (Government of Ontario, 1993).

Any proponent or operator who believes that the public may use the EBR to press their concerns is free to initiate some measure of dialogue or public involvement with the concerned parties. This can happen long before any action under the EBR takes place. In other words, a meaningful public involvement program is the best prevention against actions under the EBR.

In the Ontario EA process, the original requirements for "meaningful public consultation" have been presented in greater detail primarily to assist proponents to resolve as many issues as possible prior to the hearing, and to ensure a fair consideration of concerns, rather than having to put worthwhile projects in jeopardy because of flawed processes. The detail was intended to give some reassurance to the proponent of what is adequate, while ensuring that public concerns are integrated early in the process. The realization that the minimal formal requirements do not meet the needs of effective public consultation in controversial situations is also the driving force behind initiatives, such as that of the British Columbia Round Table on the Environment and the Economy, to have government agencies encourage pre-decision and pre-hearing collaborative problem-solving stages in the permitting processes.

Whatever the formal public involvement requirements are, doing only what the requirements explicitly call for will generally result in an unsatisfactory program. The problem is not so much that the formal requirements are ill-founded, but that the situations vary too greatly for one prescription to be effective every time.

Benefits to the Proponent

Thus, although any public involvement program should meet whatever regulatory requirements apply, these requirements themselves should not be the only reason for engaging the public. To engage the public only because it is a requirement is to have the pain without any of the gain of a public-involvement program. If public involvement is to be of benefit to the community and the proponent, it needs to be driven by goals other than meeting legal requirements. What might those other benefits be?

Community Expertise

Perhaps the most difficult advantage to accept is that public involvement can improve the action being planned. Accepting this conversely means that the in-house staff and outside consultants will usually not come up with the optimal solution. However, time and again, people reviewing proposals have been able to find flaws and suggest real improvements, based on a combination of local knowledge, insights from other, seemingly unrelated fields and what can be best described as common sense. A public-involvement program can be designed in the awareness of this potential and seek to encourage the expression of this expertise into fruitful and positive channels.

An example of the benefits of participation in the improvement of a decision is the involvement of the Tahlton Tribal Council in the planning and construction stage of the access road to the Golden Bear Mine in British Columbia. The route initially proposed by the mining company was rejected by provincial and federal government agencies. An alternative route, and one that significantly reduced the impact on wildlife, that was proposed by the Tahltons was eventually chosen. For their contribution to the process, the Tahltons received the Environmental Award from the British Columbia Minister of Mines (B.C. Round Table, 1991).

Reliance on community knowledge about local conditions has become commonplace in a variety of situations. Other examples include the reliance on residents' knowledge of local geography in landfill siting, and the development of wildlife-management plans using traditional native ecological knowledge.

Community Goodwill

In many cases, the proponent needs the goodwill of the community to implement the proposed project. Often the goodwill of neighbours is also beneficial to the day-to-day operation of the project and even the success of the organization itself. Good relations with the community makes it easier to plan and implement other projects in the future.

The reverse is also true if the lack of community support becomes community opposition. The project can be delayed or even turned down through political and legal channels. Examples abound. Consider a subset of examples such as dams:

- Rafferty Alameda Dam
- the Alcan Aluminum Dam on the Kemano River
- the Oldman River Dam
- Hydro Quebec's James Bay II project

All have experienced delay and some may never be built because the public involvement program failed to deal with the concerns of interested parties. A similar list can be drawn up for waste-management facilities, where opposition has halted or significantly delayed many projects including the following:

- two municipal waste incinerators in Toronto
- a new municipal waste landfill for Metropolitan Halifax
- a new municipal waste incinerator in Montreal
- a hazardous-waste treatment facility in Ontario

Where opposition runs high, costs include not only the delay or loss of the project, but also the negative publicity and loss of credibility of the proponent.

On the other hand, creating a positive climate around a proposal not only allows the project to proceed, but puts credibility "in the bank" where it can benefit future projects by reducing uncertainty and shortening planning and approval processes. Thus, a public involvement program that seeks to understand and address community concerns needs to play a central role in the planning of a project, especially if the project is controversial. The principal motivation for such programs are:

- legal requirements for public consultation
- improvements to the proposed action through the contribution of participants, and

- the generation of community goodwill and public trust toward the project and the proponent

5.3 WHAT IS PUBLIC INVOLVEMENT?

Public involvement programs range from a few informal phone calls to a complex program of newsletters, cable phone-in shows, open forums, public meetings, and advisory or joint-planning committees. Usually, a program integrates informing, educating, consulting, and joint problem-solving, rather than relying on any one of these in isolation. The nature of a program suitable to any given situation depends on a number of variables including the level of awareness and concern, the budget, who is affected, and geographical scope.

As the term "public involvement" suggests, two questions arise: Who are the public? and How should they be involved? Indeed, these are the central questions; once they have been resolved the rest falls largely into place.

The public are more usefully regarded as several or many publics with different interests in the issue. This differentiation led to the term "stake-holder" or "multi-sectoral" consultation. A stakeholder is any person or organization that has an interest in or will be affected by the outcome of a decision. In essence, any proposed action that will affect, attract the interest of, or fall under the jurisdiction of one or more of the following groups is a candidate for public consultation:

- federal and provincial government agencies
- municipal governments
- customers or clients
- business and business associations
- local citizens or environmental groups
- national or provincial environmental organizations
- other institutions and non-governmental organizations
- the general public, and
- technical specialists

Not only may these various publics desire different outcomes, but their ability and interest in being involved will vary. Thus, the first step in designing a public consultation program is to establish who the publics are and what type of interaction will suit each public best.

The other major question to be resolved is how the publics are to be involved. Essentially, this is a question of how much control will be given to the stakeholders and how much is retained by the proponent. The ladder in Figure 5.1 shows the range from manipulation or public relations to citizen control at the other end. A complex program will have several different levels of involvement.

Most programs in Canada stay in the realms of consultation and placation. Landfill siting is a typical example of a process that would have a better chance of succeeding at a higher level of public control, but which generally remains at the placation level. Typically, the municipal public works department recognizes that the landfill is almost full. A consultant is hired to do the technical work involved in reviewing the options and planning for the waste-management system. To manage the process, a steering committee is created of works department staff, provincial staff, consultants, and sometimes token members from the general public. A parallel public advisory committee is set up to represent further publics. The steering committee controls the process: commissioning and releasing studies for public comment and choosing how to use the comment that comes back. Decisions are made by a small group of experts who define what is in the public interest. The usual recommendation of a new landfill site creates controversy and an impression that the process was flawed and inaccessible.

FIGURE 5.1
THE LADDER OF CITIZEN PARTICIPATION

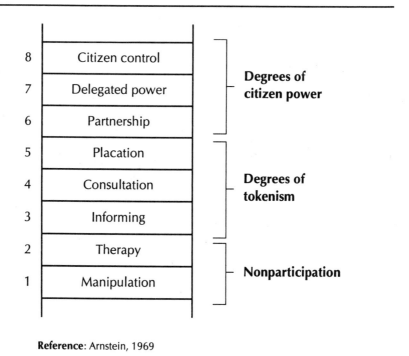

Reference: Arnstein, 1969

While such a process may be entirely adequate for taking action on a basic consensus about a problem and the need for a certain type of solution, for more controversial proposals more appropriate processes have been developed. These are found higher up the ladder of public participation and involve greater public control over the decision.

5.4 WHERE IS PUBLIC INVOLVEMENT LIKELY TO BE USEFUL OR NECESSARY?

Generally, interest in a decision is a function of the political nature of that decision. "Political" in this sense does not refer to political parties, but to decisions about the distribution of costs and benefits that are not captured by the economic system. For instance, siting a waste-disposal facility presumably results in a small, individual benefit to all those who will be served by the facility because it is cheaper than transporting waste elsewhere, and provides some security into the future. The many small benefits to individuals add to a large benefit to the region. However, the facility imposes costs on the neighbours by impacting on property values, traffic loads, pollution, and levels of increased anxiety. Although comparatively few people are affected, the cost to each individual is high. The overall cost to all individuals may well be lower than the overall gain, but the cost distribution is uneven. As long as some individuals perceive the costs to themselves to be higher than their benefits from the facility, concern — and thus controversy — can be expected.

Many of these costs and benefits are intangible, and the controversy is often over how to value them rather than compensation. Those arguing that higher values should be ascribed to the costs — such as the logging of old-growth forest — consequently argue that the forest is more valuable as old growth than as lumber and pulp. The cost-benefit perspective loses its usefulness at this point, because differences in value are rooted in differing deeply held beliefs about the world and the place of humans in the world. Reaching some accommodation of these values to make decisions about practical matters is clearly a political process.

Forests are but one of many examples of public goods whose uses are determined by political decisions. Other examples include the use of air, water, and land to discharge industrial wastes, the disruption of a river system by building a dam, and the benefits that go with a favourable zoning change on a property.

Three different kinds of situations can lead to public involvement for a proponent. In the first situation, the ongoing activities of the proponent become a matter of public concern, either through some incident such as a spill that draws attention, or because public awareness has heightened or developed a new focus.

Increasing concern about toxic chemicals in the Great Lakes combined with the publicity surrounding the discovery of the "toxic blob" in the St. Clair River led to increased public scrutiny of the chemical plants in the Sarnia, Ontario area. One consequence has been the development of a spills communication guideline by the Lambton Industrial Society for the use of its members. Because the community felt communication about spills had not been adequate in the past, the industrial society consulted with the community in the preparation of the guideline. Other examples of increased concern about ongoing activities include Inco's reduction of emissions of acid gases from its Sudbury, Ontario operations after acid rain became a public issue, or the development of the National Packaging Protocol (NAPP) which set waste recycling and reduction targets for packaging in response to concerns about waste generation. In all of these situations, business as usual became controversial enough to warrant some level of public consultation.

The second type of situation involves new undertakings or changes to existing practices. Examples include the siting of new facilities — landfills, transmission lines, electrical generating stations, roads, ski runs, and so on, where the term "proponent" is conventionally used. Changes to existing facilities, whether through expansion or decommissioning, can also become a source of public concern. When governments propose changes to legislation, regulation, or policy, or indeed new legislation altogether, they create this type of situation. Two examples of extensive consultation around new regulations are the Clean Air Strategy for Alberta (CASA) and the Municipal, Industrial Strategy for Abatement (MISA) program for effluent management in Ontario. Also included in this type of situation are proposals for resource use or extraction such as logging operations, mining, or fishing. In all of these cases, the proponent initiates the proposal for change that gives rise to public concern.

The third type of public involvement activity arises out of one of the first two situations but finds the "proponent" in a very different role. In this case, companies and government agencies join with other sectors to find a consensus-solution to a particular problem. Rather than being initiators of the consultation, they have become participants. Often the roles are blurred because the participants are active in initiating and shaping the program they are involved in — both the process around the table as well as further programs to inform and involve other publics. Relatively rare only five years ago, such stakeholder consultations are proliferating as the value of their consensus-based decisions becomes widely recognized. Examples include the following:

- the national, provincial, and local Round Tables on the Environment and the Economy
- the federal Pesticide Registration Review

- the National Task Force on Packaging
- the clean-up plans being developed by coastal communities under the Atlantic Coastal Action Program, and
- the B.C. Stakeholder Forum on Sapstain Control

In many of these stakeholder consultations, companies and government agencies have been included because a resolution of the issues will require some changes or action on the part of those participating. In many ways, participation in such a forum is an outgrowth of the situations more typically defined by the proponent-public relationship. Accordingly, it can be guided by many of the same principles.

5.5   WHAT TO TALK ABOUT WITH THE PUBLIC

5.5.1 The Three Basic Types of Issues

The question as to the topic of dialogue is intimately bound up with who the publics are, and the content and level of their concerns. It is useful to be aware of the range of possibilities.

A common assumption on the part of proponents is that consultation is about the substantive issues. This brought much grief to public-involvement programs as the public persist in raising non-substantive — and thus seemingly irrelevant — issues. To avoid this confusion a two-fold shift in perspective is necessary.

First, communicating with the public implies a two-way flow of information. While it may be possible to steer the subject matter to some degree, it is inevitable, and desirable, that the public will give some responses and raise some questions that do not suit the proponent. The credibility of the process and the proponent are enhanced if the process can accommodate and address such concerns, even if their relevance or appropriateness are questionable.

Second, it helps to understand that accompanying any substantive issue are procedural and psychological concerns. Only by addressing all three areas can a satisfactory solution be found. The satisfaction triangle in Figure 5.2 shows this graphically: when only substantive issues are discussed, only outcomes close to the substantive axis are possible (e.g. Point B), while the optimal outcome (e.g. Point A) lies somewhere in the multidimensional region (Priscoli, 1990).

5.5.2 Procedural Issues

The procedural issue is the public-involvement program itself. In other words, not only is the proposed project or action uncertain to the degree that it can be changed by public input, but the program to discuss that project is subject to some uncertainty. The process issues that need to be addressed, whether or not with public input, are the following:

- timeline and deadline for the process
- decision-making structure
- decision-making process
- membership and participants in any meetings or committees
- resources for public participants
- responsibilities of participants
- accessibility and openness, and
- information issues

These issues are discussed in greater detail in Section 5.6.3

FIGURE 5.2
SATISFACTION TRIANGLE

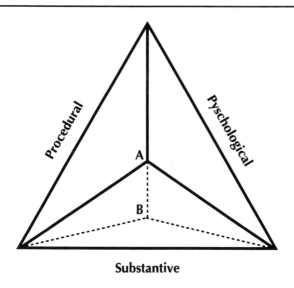

Substantive

Reference: Priscoli, 1990

5.5.3 Psychological Issues

Recognition and satisfaction of psychological needs have less to do with formal structure than with the behaviour and attitudes of individuals in the process. There is no mystery here — just the giving of ordinary respect, acknowledgement of feelings, acceptance of differences, and the giving of trust and honesty. The inherent difficulties do not lie in all parties agreeing on the desirability of civility, but in actually practising it.

A major and unnecessary source of conflict forms around the relationships between people involved in the discussion of an issue. When relationship issues are not addressed, they spill over into substantive and procedural wrangles. Conversely, good relationships give participants the strength to continue to search for solutions when the obstacles seem particularly difficult.

The proponent can set the tone for good communications by striving to be open, forthcoming, and honest about problems, and by respecting the positions and acknowledging the feelings of those who do not share the proponent's standpoint. Even if it does not win over the opposition, setting the right tone helps to convince others of the proponent's sincerity, and thus credibility, and it is the first step in arresting the spiral of conflict toward a totally adversarial relationship.

Such conduct, especially admitting problems and weaknesses, flies in the face of convention, especially that of typical legal advice. However, legal advice stems from an adversarial system that leads to legal battles. In a public-involvement program, behaviour based on an adversarial model becomes self-fulfilling. Because an adversarial process tends to create caricatures of participants, personal differences are magnified and exaggerated to sustain the conflict. The psychological satisfaction of the winner is reflected in the distress of the loser. Such a situation does not lead to durable solutions. If the proponent, who wants the project to proceed, is not willing to risk non-confrontational behaviour, it is generally not in anyone else's interest to do so.

Opportunities for making people feel good about their participation can also be built into the structure of the programs. These range from the large to the small:

- Giving the public shared decision-making power indicates that their views, and thus they themselves are valued.
- Engaging a facilitator to steer a process that encourages collaborative problem-solving creates a positive atmosphere. Joint problem-solving creates win-win situations that make all participants feel good about the results.
- Setting up the room in a public meeting to place everyone on an equal footing conveys the message that everyone's opinion matters. A circle or hollow square works well.

5.5.4 Substantive Issues

Even without the burden of suppressed process and psychological issues, the substantive issues can remain difficult. Because the toughest issues often need to be addressed before it makes sense to talk about any of the other issues, the process can face difficult tests early on before working relationships have had time to gel. The needed practise in collaborative problem-solving can be had by addressing the procedural issues first.

The tough going begins with the definition of the problem. Generally, companies and governments want to define the problem more narrowly than environmental groups. In the Federal Pesticide Registration Review process, the industry felt the problem was the cumbersome regulatory process that delayed the registration of new pesticides. The environmental and union representatives in this multi-stakeholder process saw pesticides, and how to eliminate them, as the problem. Underlying each perspective is a set of values and assumptions that are fundamentally divergent. Yet both sides could agree that protecting the environment and minimizing unnecessary pesticide use were important. Their definitions of "unnecessary" differed as did their perception of the harm caused by pesticides, but their common values sufficed to enable them to work together. Each to some degree accepted the other's problem definition and the final agreement addressed both sides' concerns (Carrow, 1993). Without some recognition of each other's needs as expressed in the definition of the problem, further progress in a joint decision-making mode is hardly possible.

At some point, it will be necessary to evaluate the severity of the problem or the suitability of proposed solutions. By developing evaluation criteria first, the discussion is kept more objective. However, the criteria themselves may be controversial. A common area of disagreement is the acceptability of government standards. In Sarnia, Ont. a chemical company wanted to decommission several leachate ponds by treating the water to meet all applicable standards and then discharging it into the St. Clair River. However, the community insisted on zero discharge of contaminants and water — far stricter standards than were required by law. The company agreed to pursue a zero-discharge solution first because it hoped to avoid long and costly delays by finding a solution that the community supported.

In the development of remedial action plans (RAPs) for damaged aquatic ecosystems around the Great Lakes and on the Atlantic Coast, many RAP committees have developed a vision for their area which served as the foundation for clean-up objectives and evaluation criteria. Focusing on a common vision enabled criteria to grow from a positive source rather than being solely a reaction to past or existing problems.

Finally, the dialogue will shift to finding options that would meet the needs of the situation. The discussion around alternative solutions starts broadly and then becomes more specific to discuss items such as alternatives sites, routes, timing, mitigation measures, technology vendors, monitoring, and compensation. Especially during the broad consideration of alternatives, value differences come to the fore. For example, in energy planning, environmental groups have favoured demand-side management, while the suppliers looked to new energy sources.

Rather than ignoring one alternative or the other, a useful technique is to create scenarios that fit the values of the different parties. Each scenario is then evaluated using the criteria established previously. It may not lead to agreement, but it will give a thorough airing of the issues and the give all sides the recognition needed to continue the process. In the case of the chemical company in Sarnia, the creation of alternative scenarios proved unnecessary because the parties had agreed upfront on the preferred approach.

Throughout the process, disagreements about facts arise. Facts in dispute can include:

- costs of clean-up measures
- performance of technology
- impacts of proposed solutions
- where the safety level lies, and
- nature and extent of the problem

Such disagreements are usually reflections of assumptions and values. The facts are not value-free. Resolving such disputes is a matter of finding an acceptable process. That, and indeed the design of the whole process, is the subject of the next section.

5.6 DESIGNING THE PROCESS

5.6.1 Information Gathering

As soon as a proposed project or a problem sparks public interest or concern, the process of developing a public involvement strategy should begin. Again, the two central questions are who are the "publics" and how should they be involved? The answer to the second question will come in part from the answer to the first. Identifying the publics will require answering a number of secondary questions about each public:

- What is their level of awareness of the issues?
- What are their particular concerns?
- How does the public see the problem?
- What level of involvement would suit their abilities and interests?
- What are their values and needs?
- How credible does the public perceive the proponent to be?

This information can be gathered through informal consultation with community leaders and representatives of other organizations with a possible interest in the project and surrounding issues. Other sources are newspapers, newsletters, and other publications, and histories of what occurred elsewhere under similar circumstances. If a similar type of project has not been proposed in the community, an organized public may not yet exist, and indeed community leaders may not have enough information to formulate concerns. In this case, events elsewhere are a better guide as to what may surface, but the lack of awareness itself will be important in designing a strategy. The scope and effort put into such a baseline survey depends on the scope of and expected controversy arising out of the proposal. Where public concern about ongoing activities is the reason for engaging the public, the survey will generate information on the views of those who have not as yet been heard.

In thinking about an appropriate public involvement program, it may be helpful to position each of the publics on the graph shown in Figure 5.3. The level of concern, or the potential for controversy, increases with the size of the differences in problem definition and values between the proponent and the publics. To be of benefit to the proponent and the publics, the process will increasingly need mechanisms to discuss and deal with these differences as one moves to the right on this axis.

FIGURE 5.3
PUBLIC INVOLVEMENT STRATEGIES

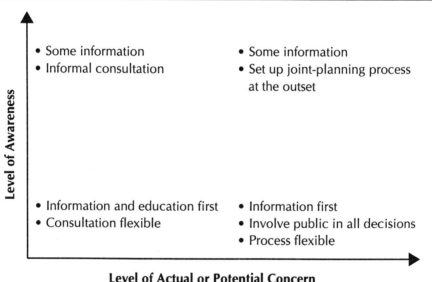

Level of Awareness (vertical axis) — Level of Actual or Potential Concern (horizontal axis)

- Some information
- Informal consultation

- Some information
- Set up joint-planning process at the outset

- Information and education first
- Consultation flexible

- Information first
- Involve public in all decisions
- Process flexible

Level of Actual or Potential Concern

The level of awareness determines to what degree the publics will need to become informed before much meaningful problem-solving can take place. In part, this information will come from the proponent. Its dissemination becomes the first major step in the strategy. A low level of awareness combined with high potential concern represents the longest possible process. Such a situation is also the most unpredictable and most difficult to plan for because public responses and needs are not yet formulated. On the other extreme is the case where awareness is high and concerns are low — process needs become minimal.

Because the various publics are usually at different points on the map, public involvement strategies usually include a variety of components. In keeping with the desire for two-way communication, most activities that are not joint decision-making at least have both an information and a response component. Examples of such information/response activities are:

- Newspaper ads/Clip out response forms
- Public service announcement/Telephone hotline
- Cable TV show/Phone-in segment
- Newsletters or reports/Response coupons
- Open house/Visitor survey
- Public meeting/Question and comment period; exit survey
- Information centre/Visitor survey
- Telephone survey/Responses

These are the traditional techniques of public consultation. Even if the public involvement strategy will include some form of joint decision-making, these techniques remain valuable to reach the general public who do not have time to become involved more actively. They also complement the work of planning committees by giving members a chance to revisit the public perspective — one that they can forget as they become immersed in the details of the project. The knowledge of the committee's work also helps to build support in the larger community as people identify with committee members.

To incorporate those publics who desire an active part in the decision-making, the possibilities range from one-time planning workshops through advisory committees to joint-planning committees that meet a number of times. Advisory and joint-planning committees require a high level of participation from their members. If the levels of concern and interest are low, such forums will not find the level of participation necessary to sustain them. On the other hand, when the level of concern is high, every aspect of the project — procedural and substantial — will be closely scrutinized. In that situation, a joint-planning forum facilitates the level of communication required. Similarly, low trust levels can best be countered by opening the decision-making process to the public.

5.6.2 Organizational Commitment

The survey of the public gives the initiating organization a good indication of what to expect from the public as well as what type of process will be appropriate. At this point, the organization decides whether it can accept and even benefit from the strategy and the response it will bring. The alternative is to risk the political and legal process.

If the organization commits to the public involvement process, then it is important that the process be supported at all levels of the organization, including senior management. Out of all the variables in such a process, the organization has the most control over its own conduct. Its conduct will largely determine its credibility. Without credibility, even the best projects will have trouble finding support.

For successful and credible public involvement, understanding and accepting the following is helpful:

- Public involvement is not an add-on feature. It works best when it is fully integrated into the planning process, even driving the process at key points. It will require a substantial time commitment of key people in the organization.
- Once the strategy has been publicly announced, cancelling or limiting it will diminish public trust.
- Involving the public creates uncertainty in project planning. Thus, timelines and outcomes cannot be guaranteed.
- Honest and forthright communication and respect for all opponents and supporters alike avoids embarrassing explanations later, and lay the foundation for productive working relationships.

The process will also benefit from an assessment of the organization's needs going into the process. This might entail revisiting the organization's mission statement or some creative brainstorming. By moving the focus away from the details of the initial proposed project, it will be easier to find new solutions that meet the needs of other parties as well. Early communication of those needs contributes to creating a problem-solving approach.

5.6.3 Process Questions

Once the organization has committed to an honest and open strategy, further questions do remain. To some extent the initiator of the consultation decides these issues; however, the more that can be decided jointly with other stakeholders, the greater the outside ownership, identification, and support for the process. In many instances, a neutral facilitator is hired to give the process an initial structure, initiate the process, and assist the group to design the remainder of the process.

The question of "what process will we follow?" is then doubly central to this chapter. The discussion around the main issues in designing a process provide an opportunity to develop relationships with the public before the substantive issues are tackled. In the following discussion of the main process issues, it becomes apparent that solutions will vary with the situation.

Timeline

A timeline, as in any venture, is a useful tool to set expectations and monitor progress. Setting out a timeline indicates the proponent's need to arrive at a final decision. Negotiating a timeline with the publics has the added benefit of encouraging some ownership and responsibility for the process on the part of others. Especially in joint-planning situations, external constraints such as budget decisions, new regulations coming into effect, or elections are helpful in giving the situation a desired urgency.

Decision-making Structure

The primary question around the decision-making structure is the level of participation by the public. Will the final decision on the inclusion of the public response rest with the proponent, a small select committee, or a larger joint-planning body? Will advisory bodies be created, either as relatively permanent entities for the duration of the planning effort, or as ad hoc creations, such as the participants in a single workshop?

Many projects require some regulatory approval before they can be implemented. The public involvement process must dovetail with the approval process. Usually, the intent of the public involvement is to resolve the problems before they receive a formal airing. Indeed, the hope and intent are often to remove the necessity for a formal hearing. Certainly this was the outcome in Sarnia, where neither the chemical company nor the joint-planning committee desired a hearing after developing a solution.

The process initiated by the forest company was also intended to resolve the issues before the official government consultation and review (Lajambe, 1993).

The regulatory outcome is often a source of uncertainty in the process because regulatory agencies have been reluctant to participate directly in collaborative-planning exercises. This was the case for both the wood products and the chemical company process and is repeated in one of the case studies that follow. When the agencies do not implement the consensus agreement, as was the case for the Canadian Environmental Protection Act, the agency loses credibility and the participants are less willing to be involved in similar processes. Consequently, every effort should be made to include the regulatory agency in the process, even if in an informal way. Understanding the needs and limitations of the regulatory process assists the planning committee. Similarly, the knowledge of the history of the decision gives the agency deeper understanding of the committee's decision.

The process by which both decision-making and advisory bodies arrive at decisions decisively shapes the process. Although majority rule is the dominant political process, various forms of consensus-building have been more prevalent in public involvement programs.

Majority rule has the disadvantage of creating winners and losers, and thus creating the adversarial situation that public involvement tries to bridge. It also makes the issue of membership more difficult. In the absence of elected representatives, it will not be possible to find a balance that finds acceptance. The minority has no great incentive to stay if it believes it will be outvoted on the important issues.

Consensus decision-making can range from unassisted negotiation through facilitation to mediation. All three can be regarded as forms of negotiation, with at least the assent, if not the support, of all parties required to reach decisions. In facilitation, a neutral third party directs the process, allowing the participants to focus on the issues. In mediation, the role of the neutral is stronger, asking questions, drawing the parties out and in some cases even suggesting solutions.

A consensus process usually requires some fall-back option that comes into effect when consensus cannot be achieved. Options include moving to majority vote; some form of arbitration, where an outsider makes the final decision; or, if the conflict seems very fundamental, pursuing adversarial political or legal options in the larger societal context. While the latter option always remains, it is helpful to agree before hand on the more cooperative forms of dispute resolution.

Some issues need conflict to increase the awareness of the general public and the political willingness of governments to make larger changes that will make room for a solution. After a period of conflict, there is often new willingness and incentive to try a negotiated process again.

Membership and Participation

Another question that can become very controversial is who should participate? The difficulties of finding a membership agreeable to all participants in a majority vote process have already been described. Clearly, the simplest principle is to open the membership to all who want to participate. Three issues arise with such an inclusive principle:

1) How to deal with latecomers
2) How to integrate those who are completely opposed to the project
3) What size is too large

The latter is the simplest to address: while working committees of fewer than 20 are the norm, a well-designed process and a good facilitator can assist groups of 50, and probably even 100, to work effectively. The Hamilton Harbour process, described in further detail below, made good progress with a stakeholder committee of 49 people (Leppard and Rahn, 1993), and a New Brunswick landfill search involved over 60 people (Turkstra, 1993).

Among some proponents and public consultation practitioners, concern has been expressed about groups and individuals who are opposed to the project and seem to misuse the process to pursue other goals. They are often labelled as fringe or radical groups.

The labelling itself is indicative of a public involvement process that has met its limits. When opponents receive dismissive labels, then it is highly likely that they are questioning some aspect of the project which the proponent is not willing to let go or which the proponent feels is beyond their mandate or power. At this point there are two options for the proponent: let go and agree to put the bone of contention on the table in exchange for an agreement to work together in good faith, or exclude the opponents and run a program that involves everybody but those opponents. Generally, the latter has been the favoured option.

Excluding opponents runs the risk of engendering a great amount of opposition when the "fringe" group proves it has more support than the proponent had calculated. Typical examples are the logging disputes in British Columbia such as the Stein Valley, South Moresby, Carmanah, Meares Island, and Clayoquot Sound. In each case, the opposition felt forced to use every available legal and political means, including civil disobedience. In the Clayoquot Sound case, the multi-stakeholder committee that had attempted to find a solution had included only minimal representation of those arguing for preservation of the old-growth forest, and even those representatives resigned after it became clear that the committee was tending toward a solution that in most respects favoured the logging company. The consensus reached by the committee was relatively easy, because it excluded those who would have made it difficult. In the months that followed, over 800 protestors were arrested and the issue gained national attention. The credibility of both the logging company and the provincial government suffered.

Inviting all who shared an interest in the forests of Clayoquot Sound to participate in making decisions on an equal basis would have required some initial willingness to talk about the issues central to those wanting to preserve the forest. Thus, who is included or excluded from the process is central to the whole process because inclusivity also carries with it a willingness to talk about everybody's issues.

Often this places the proponent in a very difficult situation, because issues are brought forward that can only be resolved at a higher level of government. Because no consensus has been reached at the higher level, the conflict is played out repeatedly on a local level. Forestry in British Columbia and landfill siting around urban areas provide typical examples. Characteristically, provincial or national environmental organizations become involved. Again, the inclusivity principle would welcome even these groups. In such situations some form of negotiation with the provincial or national groups would seem the only possibility to preserve a meaningful involvement program.

Another membership issue, similarly without much successful resolution, is that of latecomers. It occurs, predictably, during the siting process for controversial facilities. Before the preferred sites are announced, the public process to develop the system and its components does not attract much attention or participation. However, after the announcement of candidate sites, the attention of the public is very high, questioning not only the suitability of the sites, but the design of the entire system. Should those opposed to the decisions to-date be included on decision-making bodies, even if it means revisiting earlier decisions? Again, inclusivity would invite them to join the process.

Better yet would be a process that minimizes the number of latecomers. Several possibilities have been tried or suggested. The first would make an estimated guess of the facilities needed as early as possible, announce candidate site areas, and then invite the concerned public to jointly design the system and locate the resulting facilities (Coffey, 1993). This option has never been tried, and has the disadvantage of using people's fear of a new facility to motivate them to participate in a positive manner. Whether residents near candidate sites would participate as hoped for is not certain.

An alternative to the early announcement is the establishment of a multi-stakeholder committee of community leaders who represent the entire geographic area that will be considered when searching for sites. This committee would then ideally plan the system and choose the sites. A variation of this model was used to search for a landfill site in Guelph, Ont. and was successful in finding a landfill site in New Brunswick (Turkstra, 1993).

Yet a third possibility avoids the issue of membership to a large degree. This is the voluntary siting or willing host program which will be described in greater detail below using the example of the Alberta Hazardous Waste Treatment Facility.

Resources for Participants
The next process issue is that of resources for participants. Although funding possible opponents may seem counterproductive, it can work to the advantage of the process in several ways by:
- raising the credibility of the proponent
- recognizing the substantial time commitment required of the participants
- assisting concerned participants to educate themselves about the proposed project, and
- clarifying and focusing concerns

Typically, participants are reimbursed for expenses such as travel, photocopying, and mailings incurred while taking part. In some processes, such as the former Waste Reduction Advisory Committee to the Ontario Minister of the Environment, participants are paid an honorarium in recognition of the time they give. Honorariums are, however, rare, and generally involve situations where the participants are involved over long periods, the workload is large, and meetings are held during business hours.

Intervenor funding gives the participants funds to hire consultants to review the proponent's work, commission studies of relevance to the project, and to hire counsel to intervene at hearings. It is only provided to "intervenors" who are those persons or organizations wishing to express opinion at the public hearing. In some instances, funding for such purposes at the planning stage, prior to completion of an assessment, is called participant funding. The amount of funding requested and given out in both instances is usually a measure of the complexity of the issues and the degree of concern and opposition.

Finally, resources can be devoted to assisting advisory or joint-planning committees to do their work. The resources often come in the form of staff to facilitate, take minutes, and carry out tasks for the committee. In some cases, the committee may have a budget to commission needed research.

Participant Responsibilities

From the proponent's perspective, one of the most important needs is to have all the parties discussing the issues in a collaborative manner. Thus, any discussion about the process needs to resolve the issue of the responsibility of the participants. For a public meeting or a one-time workshop, it is not realistic to expect more than perhaps basic civility. However, when a stakeholder group meets regularly, especially in a joint-planning process, it will strengthen the decisions if participants are committed to informing and obtaining the agreement of their constituents or organizations as the process develops. Because stakeholder groups develop an identity and culture of their own, participants may find themselves estranged from their organizations, leading ultimately to a rejection of the position of the stakeholder committee.

Other responsibilities to discuss are commitment to attend meetings, a commitment to identify concerns as soon as they arise and to work in good faith with the other committee members.

Accessibility and Openness

The credibility of the process is closely bound up with its perceived accessibility and openness. Decisions made behind closed doors bring public suspicion. If the public and media are allowed to attend meetings, the question of public participation in those meetings will arise: Are questions allowed? Can deputations be made? Can new items be added to the agenda? Again, no best optimal answers exist — only a willingness to experiment and accept the advantages and disadvantages of whatever is chosen.

A general consensus does exist, however, with respect to sharing information: the earlier the better. Problems with the project or other information that might be of use to opponents are best shared early, at the initiative of the proponent. When information is not shared, but comes out later, it gives the appearance of a cover-up. Double damage results — the project is questioned and the credibility of the proponent suffers. It is easier to fix a project than to restore credibility, and thus better to share information about the project as early as possible. The news can be announced along with a commitment to resolve the problems, or better yet concrete steps to do so, as long as such commitments are subsequently honoured. Admitting problems and mistakes may not seem good for the project, but it does seem to raise the credibility of the proponent which is often more important in the long term.

Finally, those who are not part of the intensive public involvement activities need to know and feel that information is available and that their response would be treated with respect should they give one. Again, this is a matter of attending to the details, and is completely within the proponent's power to do well. All those who engage in the process and are satisfied will not create much, if any, news; it is those who feel they have been treated as outsiders who will generate the negative publicity. Consequently, attention to detail and a civil treatment of all are the key ingredients here.

Information Issues

Often disagreements about substantive issues turn out to be disputes about fact. Everyone can find an expert who will support their position. If the process aims to negotiate an agreement, then more studies commissioned independently by the disputing parties will not move the discussions forward. Instead, a useful strategy is to engage in joint fact-finding. By agreeing on the terms of reference, and the person to carry out the study, the chances of obtaining results that will be acceptable are much improved. If the process ends with a form of arbitration such as a hearing before an Environmental Assessment Panel, providing participants with funding to carry out their own studies will not necessarily lead to agreement, but does serve to give the process some credibility by giving participants an opportunity to participate meaningfully.

Confidentiality of information arises as an issue most often in joint-planning processes. To create a realistic plan or to convince participants of their position, some participants, especially from business and government, may need to share information which they do not want made public. If the level of trust among the participants is high, it may be enough to seek everyone's agreement to keep the information within the group. On the other hand, if the trust is not there, or participants feel that such a requirement creates an unacceptable conflict with the goal of keeping the process open, then another solution needs to be found. Possibilities include transforming the information in such a way that its public release no longer presents a problem, or having a neutral third party examine and verify the information, and provide only what is directly necessary for the group.

5.7 CASE STUDIES

5.7.1 Voluntary Siting Process

Alberta has been one of the few jurisdictions in North America to successfully site a hazardous waste treatment facility. In doing so, it pioneered the successful application of the voluntary siting strategy.

After initial private attempts to establish a hazardous-waste treatment facility met strong opposition, the government established a task force and convened hearings to examine the hazardous waste issue. The hearings identified the scope and nature of the problem and raised public awareness about the need for a solution. It found that a treatment facility was one necessary component of the solution. A siting team of respected individuals was established and committed itself to a voluntary siting strategy (McQuaid-Cook and Simpson, 1986).

The team first focused on developing and disseminating information. Those areas deemed unsuitable for a facility were identified on a map of the province. That map, the criteria used to develop it, and a description of the facility and its rationale formed the basis for the first public meeting presentation offered to local municipalities. In all, 120 counties, municipal districts and special areas requested and received this presentation. The presentations served to raise the general awareness around the issue and prompted 52 out of a possible 70 counties to request in writing the next level of analysis (Champion, 1989).

The next round of regional analyses examined the environmental suitability of each of the 52 counties at a greater level of detail than the initial provincial survey. The studies were carried out at no cost to the counties, with the proviso that the results be presented at a local public meeting. Local liaison committees were also established to keep each county up-to-date on the studies and other developments (McQuaid-Cook and Simpson, 1986).

The more detailed mapping eliminated some counties, as did local opposition to further participation in the program. Five communities emerged with invitations to the siting team to undertake detailed drilling: the next step in the program.

The activities of the local siting committees increased, and were supplemented by a seminar series in each community giving further detail on the hazardous waste program and the proposed facility. Finally, local plebiscites were held, showing the greatest support in Ryley and Swan Hills, where over 75% of the voters approved their community application. Formal requests for the facility were received from both communities.

After the selection of Swan Hills as the preferred site, a new liaison committee was formed in Swan Hills to act as the key link between the community and the Crown Corporation in the ongoing public information and involvement program.

The former director of communications for the siting team names six elements that were key to the success of the siting strategy:

- definitive environmental standards for facility siting
- freedom of choice remained with the communities
- an awareness program that emphasized personal contacts
- recognition of the value of "citizens" and informal community leaders in creating a positive climate
- a benefit to every community participating because the studies were useful for other areas of community planning such as waste management
- consistent provincial government commitment and support for the siting process (Champion, 1989)

This approach has also been applied to hazardous-waste facility siting in Manitoba (Brethour, 1990) and the siting of a low-level radioactive waste disposal facility in Ontario (Siting Process Task Force, n.d.). It represents a major departure from the conventional siting process, where experts determine the best site. Included in the expert assessment of "best" is a determination of where the least social and economic disruption will occur. The voluntary siting process relies on the communities themselves to determine whether the effects — both positive and negative — are acceptable and ultimately desirable. The difference is as subtle as being thrown from an airplane or choosing to go skydiving. Of course, the process accepts the risk that in the end there will be no volunteers — a clear indication that the perceived benefits of the project are too low.

While voluntary siting may not be directly applicable to most situations in which proponents find themselves, it illustrates how turning the process upside down can create a completely different dynamic. The freedom given the communities was in each case coupled to certain conditions about the process that communities were to follow in their decision-making: public meetings, liaison committees, plebiscites, council approval, and formal requests to be included in the next stage of the site search. The obligations of both sides were clearly laid out, including the next opportunity to opt out. At each step, the communities committed only to further clarification with the full knowledge that they could then choose freely based on the new information.

Thus, the very elements responsible for the not-in-my-backyard phenomena — lack of trust and the loss of control — were put squarely in the community's power. Only by winning and keeping the community's trust could the proponent obtain community consent — a very useful and direct incentive to keep the proponent and the community focused on what was critical, without imposing any process or action on any person or organization.

5.7.2 Collaborative Planning

Another approach for designing a process is the collaborative-planning model. A number of other names have been used to describe the process, each revealing a different aspect: joint planning, multi-stakeholder planning, and consensus decision-making. Both the Sarnia chemical company and the northern Ontario wood products company processes fit into this category.

Hamilton Harbour

One of the earliest applications of collaborative planning on a local level was the Remedial Action Plan (RAP) for Hamilton Harbour, Ont. Hamilton Harbour was one of a number of Great Lakes "hot spots" identified by the International Joint Commission for clean-up. Rather than one public agency preparing and attempting to implement a plan, it was decided to proceed with a joint-planning process. By involving all those who would be responsible for implementing the plan or interested in its outcome, it was hoped that the joint plan would be better than a plan coming from a lone source, and that the implementation would be quicker and more effective (Leppard and Rahn, 1993).

A facilitator was hired to design and implement a public- involvement process. The facilitator first identified and interviewed all the interested parties. Each stakeholder was asked to commit to participating fully, working with others to seek consensus on a clean-up plan, and inform and seek the consent of their constituency or organization. Forty-nine stakeholders took part representing large industries, other business interests, local and provincial environmental groups, unions, boating and recreations clubs, local governments, ratepayer groups, and a variety of provincial and federal agencies.

The stakeholder committee focused on the broad themes necessary for the plan such as:
- developing water quality goals for the harbour
- creating a vision for the harbour
- directing and reviewing studies on the issues and possible solutions for the harbour
- selecting the options to be implemented, and
- reviewing interim and final reports

The stakeholders formed subcommittees as necessary to address specific issues. Day-to-day management of the research and the process were carried by a RAP team composed of federal and provincial staff. Communication with the larger community through the members of the stakeholder committee was supplemented by a number of larger public meetings, newsletters, media advertising and reports, open houses, a phone line for questions and comments, and displays and presentations to local organizations (Rodgers, 1992).

The stakeholder committee met on an irregular basis over a period of six years. The committee operated in a consensus mode, often using facilitators to assist with the process. Through the consensus process, a relatively cohesive group emerged from a collection of individuals whose relations had often been adversarial. Differences were understood and respected. Members were able to focus on their common desire to improve the harbour. The group was able to withstand a challenge from a government agency as to its status. On at least one occasion when voting replaced consensus, members acted on their own initiative to restore the consensus process. The committee recently concluded its work and the plan is being implemented. The plan was accepted by all agencies and institutions required to implement it (Leppard and Rahn, 1993). Financial commitments are being negotiated.

The collaborative-planning model has also been used extensively at the provincial and national level to bring together competing interests on finding a consensus on contentious issues. Examples include:

- the National and Provincial Round Tables on the Environment and the Economy
- the National Task Force on Packaging
- the National Pollution Release Inventory (NPRI) Advisory Committee
- the Forest Round Table on Sustainable Development
- the Federal Pesticide Registration Review Committee
- the Clean Air Strategy for Alberta Advisory Committee
- the British Columbia Stakeholder Forum on Sapstain Control, and
- the Advisory Committee which developed the initial regulations to support the blue box program in Ontario

Sapstain Control Forum

The B.C. Stakeholder Forum on Sapstain Control is in many ways typical of such processes, with the twist that an industry association — the Council of Forest Industries (COFI) — took on the responsibility of developing a consensus process.

In 1989, a broad consensus existed that the anti-sapstain chemical pentachlorophenol (PCP) widely used to treat wood in British Columbia sawmills should be banned. However, there were similar concerns about some of the traditional alternatives, and all of the promising newly developed substitutes were missing one or more of the necessary studies for regulatory assessment. Agriculture Canada refused to register any of the new chemicals that the industry wanted until there was a consensus among industry, the provincial government, unions and the "public interest" on an acceptable course of action. Both the unions and the environmental groups were interested in more testing, monitoring, and greater safety. The provincial government had announced it would implement tougher regulations on the release of anti-sapstain chemicals from sawmills into the environment (B.C. Round Table, 1991).

COFI hired a neutral facilitator to design a process for reaching consensus among the stakeholders. The British Columbia Stakeholder Forum on Sapstain Control with 11 representatives was the result. The facilitator guided the group through six meetings. The stakeholders invited chemical manufacturers and other experts, and hired toxicologists to obtain a diversity of viewpoints.

In addition to the substantive issues, the group had to deal with a lack of trust between some parties and whether or not all the "confidential" information the group required would be forthcoming. The latter was essentially also a matter of trust, and was the substance of some tense negotiations. Ultimately, the matter could only be resolved indirectly, through the positive relationship fostered by engaging in the consensus process. The group was also concerned that neither Agriculture Canada nor any other federal agency participated directly. By keeping Agriculture Canada informed of the group's process, the facilitator was able to allay this concern. Through the facilitator, Agriculture Canada made it clear that they would only accept recommendations that fit in the existing regulatory framework. Thus, while not officially at the table, the informal communication through the facilitator served to make Agriculture Canada part of the process (B.C. Round Table, 1991).

In the end, one of the unions and both environmental organizations did not sign on to the final agreement. They could not endorse a sub-agreement that called for conditional registration of some of the newer chemicals.

The final agreement consisted of six sub-agreements that set out:
- an ongoing role and funding for the forum
- monitoring programs for health effects, and for markets for wood products
- recommendations on the review and registration process for various chemicals, and
- coordination of British Columbia sapstain regulations, Agriculture Canada initiatives and the work of the forum

Agriculture Canada responded to the agreement by implementing the recommendations that pertained to it, while acknowledging the reservations contained in the minority report.

The process of the forum resembled that of most other joint-planning exercises. The forum grew out of an issue that had developed to the point where a variety of sectors had seen the need for action. The forum process was developed and carried by a facilitator, it included a broad cross-section of interested parties, and strove for consensus in its decision-making. An indicator that the process has been productive is the agreement to keep meeting and working together, an outcome that also emerged from the Hamilton Harbour RAP.

Somewhat special to this process were the deadline set by the B.C. government through its intent to regulate unilaterally, and the failure to reach a consensus on the whole final agreement. Both elements are not unknown, and need not jeopardize the process. Consensus decision-making can work to a deadline. The lack of a final consensus need not render the effort in vain, if at least some needs are met, and the result does not represent a significant loss for the dissenters.

5.8 CONCLUSION

The dominant tendency in the management of public involvement has been to equate management with control. That meant identifying the goal and planning for every eventuality that might throw the process off-course. At its worst, it became what has been called the decide-announce-defend process, with public consultation little more than window-dressing. In effect, all effort went toward holding the fort on decisions that had been made. Even where the process was more open to change, the underlying assumption was still "us versus them," reflected in a very legal approach to wording and a reluctance to share any problems and difficulties with the public.

Involving the public in the decision-making shifts the focus of management to facilitation. The ideas and solutions come from the participants. Rather than trying to stymie new ideas, the process stimulates innovation. By requiring all to agree to decisions, the new ideas are tested against a broad range of experience. Those ideas that do become recommendations have the support of all involved; in other words, each participant has a personal stake and responsibility for the soundness of the decision.

The proponent can continue to influence the outcome through its participation in the process; however, the management of the process has been freed from the need to produce a predetermined project outcome and thus no longer needs to engage in manipulation. Instead, process management ensures that participants have the resources they need and that obstacles to communication are removed. The result is a process that participants feel good about; work is constructive and produces innovative results.

Key to deciding on a process is a sound assessment of the expectations of both the public and senior management. From an initial study of public concerns and expectations, an appropriate public involvement strategy can be outlined. The strategy indicates what mix of information/response activities and shared decision-making forums best suits the specific situation. It identifies public concerns, needs, and aspirations, thus indicating what direction the dialogue will likely take. It can also shed some light on the consequences of pursuing a confrontational approach instead.

In the end, the decision rests with senior management. Given the needs of the organization and the proposed action, does it make sense to exchange the uncertainty of an adversarial political-legal process for the uncertainty of sharing the decision-making? For numerous organizations, a meaningful public involvement program has been well worth the initial risk. To give the process the greatest chance of success, it needs to be integral to the project-planning process. That requires the commitment of the whole organization to communicating with integrity and to exploring alternative solutions with friend and foe alike.

REFERENCES

Arnstein, Sherry. 1969. "A Ladder of Citizen Participation." *Journal of the American Institute of Planners*. 35: 216-224.

Bethour, Ed. 1990. *Adapting a Siting Process to Fit a Rural Community*. Conference Proceedings: Hazardous Materials/Wastes: Social Aspects of Facility Planning and Management. Institute for Social Impact Assessment, Winnipeg, Man.

British Columbia Round Table on the Environment and the Economy. Dispute Resolution Core Group. 1991. "Reaching Agreement." In *Consensus Processes in British Columbia,* Volume I. "Appendices." In *Case Synopses and Case Studies*.

Carrow, Rod. 1993. *Developing Consensus on the Management of Pesticide Risk.* Presentation to Insight Conference, Toronto, Ont.

Champion, Jacqueline. 1989. *"Yes, in My Backyard": The Successful Siting of a Hazardous Waste Treatment Centre Near Swan Hills, Alberta.* Victoria, B.C.: Connor Development Services.

Coffey, Gerrard. 1993. *The Role of Community Planning in Waste Management: A Shared Power Model.* Credit Valley Coalition et al.

Government of Ontario. 1993. *Bill 26: An Act Respecting Environmental Rights in Ontario.* Queen's Printer for Ontario, Toronto.

ICI Canada Inc. 1993. *The Lambton Works Phosphate Decommissioning*

Project: How a Corporation and a Community Worked Together to Resolve a Major Environmental Problem. Sarnia, Ont.

Jones, Yankee. 1981. "That Sinking Feeling." *Briefcase Poetry,* Vol. 2.

Lajambe Forest Products. 1993. *A Harvesting Allocation Proposal Covering Lajambe Forest Products' Algoma Crown Management Unit License Area.* Sault Ste. Marie, Ont.

Leppard, S. and Rahn, T. 1993. "Consensus Decision-Making in Canadian Communities." *Municipal World* 103 (9): 20, 23.

Mausberg, B., and G. Coffey. 1993. *Proceeding with Process: Improving Consultations with Environment Canada.* Ottawa: Canadian Environment Network.

McQuaid-Cook, J., and K.J. Simpson. 1986. "Siting a Fully Integrated Waste Management Facility in Alberta." *Journal of the Air Pollution Control Association* 36 (9): 1031-1036.

Priscoli, J.D. 1990. "Public Involvement, Conflict Management, and Dispute Resolution in Water Resources and Environmental Decision Making." *Alternative Dispute Resolution Series,* Working Paper #2. Ft. Belvoir, Virginia: Institute for Water Resources, U.S. Army Corps of Engineers.

Rodgers, G.K. et al. 1992. *Remedial Action Plan for Hamilton Harbour: Goals, Options and Recommendations.* Volume 2: Main Report.

Siting Process Task Force on Low Level Radioactive Waste Disposal. n.d. *Opting for Co-operation.* Ottawa, Ont.: Energy, Mines and Resources Canada.

Turkstra, Herman. 1993. "Legislative Requirements for Public Consultation." *Conference Proceedings: Public Consultation: Critical Elements for a Winning Strategy.* Toronto, Ont.: Insight Information Inc.

6

Trade Barriers

by
Hugh Howson

6.1 RELATIONSHIP OF TRADE TO THE ENVIRONMENT

Over the past century, trading in goods has been the primary factor in the expansion of economies around the world. In 1990, the value of international trade was estimated to be $4.3 trillion.

Trade began as simple exchanges of raw materials and finished goods. As international trade volumes increased, countries began to institute measures such as import duties, production subsidies, and in extreme cases, sanctions to protect domestic production. It has only been in the last few decades that real strides have been made towards the systematic reduction of trade barriers through agreements such as the World Trade Organization (WTO, formerly known as GATT, the General Agreement on Tariffs and Trade), European Free Trade Area (EFT), the Canada/U.S. Free Trade Agreement (FTA), and most recently, the trilateral North America Free Trade Agreement (NAFTA).

As recently as a decade ago, little thought was given to the intertwined nature of trade and the environment. But changing attitudes were clearly signalled in 1987 when the World Commission on Environment and Development (WCED), better known as the Brundtland Commission, put forward the basic axiom that our essentially open economic system is pushing against an essentially closed ecological system.

Some experts feel the opening and expansion of trade through expanded trade agreements and the liberalization of existing agreements are inherently detrimental to the environment. They point to the evidence of global degradation such as the major trends reported in the 1992 *State of the World Report* by The Worldwatch Institute:

- The protective ozone layer in the heavily populated northern latitudes is thinning twice as fast as was postulated just a few years ago.

- Forested areas are vanishing at a rate of some 17 million hectares per year.
- A minimum of 140 plant and animal species are becoming extinct daily.
- Atmospheric levels of carbon dioxide are now more than 25% higher than pre-industrial concentrations, and are climbing.

Conversely, there are individuals involved in trade and environmental issues who see the interrelationship of trade and environment not as mutually exclusive or as counterproductive. A recent Organization for Economic Cooperation and Development (OECD) paper declared:

Trade and environmental policies should be seen as being mutually supportive rather than in terms of conflicting interests. Trade spurs economic growth and helps provide the technical and financial resources to protect the environment, while a healthy environment provides the ecological and natural resources needed to underpin long-run growth stimulated by trade.... It is therefore important that trade policies are sensitive to environmental concerns and that environmental policies take account of effects on trade. Unlike sustainable development, free trade is not an end in itself.

If the OECD paper is correct, the challenge is to determine how trade and environmental interests can be integrated to provide for sustainable development and management of resources. The concept of sustainable development was formally proposed in the Bruntland Commission report. Since then, more than 200 definitions have been offered for this term, but the majority of current thinking still falls in line with the Commission's concept that **sustainable development** is the ability to use the world's resources today in a way that does not detract from the availability of those resources to future generations.

A more precise and workable definition of sustainable development was presented in a position paper prepared in 1993 by Norway for the International Standards Organization:

Achieving sustainable development requires organizations to integrate environmental policies, objectives, and activities with their business growth and financial plans. Further, this requires the integration of these plans with the operational strategies and systems and procedures.

Another facet of the relationship between trade and the environment becomes evident when an importing country imposes environmental requirements on exporting nations that become non-tariff trade barriers.

Simply defined, a non-tariff trade barrier is a restriction applied to incoming goods through enacted laws or subsidies which treat those goods differently than domestically produced goods. In the case of environment, treaties such as the WTO and NAFTA recognize the sovereign right of countries to enact environmental rules to protect their environment; however, there is a fine line between these laws and additional elements which are disadvantageous or penalize imports.

An example of this is the German "blue angel" program. This program is one of the most comprehensive in the world with regard to solid packaging waste diversion from landfill. The legislation does not prohibit imported product, but instead imposes compliance requirements on the retail outlets. The retail outlets, in order not to be involved in taking back packaging material from everything they sell as mandated by the legislation, have only one option available to them. They have simply refused to stock anything without the "blue angel" logo. Therefore, out-of-country manufacturers must pay the very high fees to use the logo on their products or lose all sales in Germany. The law is consistent with the WTO, but has erected a non-tariff trade barrier to products moving into Germany.

Section 6.2 compares the emerging international environmental standards with the existing international quality standards. The potential exists for even more pervasive examples of non-tariff trade barriers, which have the capability to affect trade and business throughout the world.

6.2. INTERNATIONAL ORGANIZATION FOR STANDARDIZATION

The International Organization for Standardization (the ISO) is a world body which was formed for the specific purpose of creating international harmonization of standards. Its work is as diverse as the standardization of a global colour identification system to setting standards on quality and environmental matters.

Lessons can be learned from ISO efforts over the past few years in developing the international standard on quality, commonly known as ISO 9 000. This set of standards was developed through an ISO technical committee designated as TC 176 in the early 1980s. Canada is the secretariat for TC 176, which means that Canada, and specifically the Canadian Standards Association (CSA), administrates the technical committee including calling meetings, preparing minutes, and distributing paperwork.

North America has not been as proactive with regard to ISO 9 000 as European countries, and as a consequence, many European companies are certified under ISO 9 000 compared to only a handful in Canada and a similar small percentage in the U.S. Increasingly, ISO 9 000 certification has become a qualifier for business. When this is done on a large enough scale, the process of exclusion becomes a non-tariff trade barrier. This has prompted some North American businesses to become certified somewhat hastily, paying a premium to do so, and causing considerable disruption to their operations.

ISO is currently working on the 14 000 series of Environmental Standards through Technical Committee 207. (See Chapter 7 for a listing of the proposed standards.) The expected release date for several of the standards (i.e. environmental management and auditing) is early 1996. These standards have the potential to become the next major global non-tariff trade barrier.

By holding the secretariat for TC 176 (Quality) and TC 207 (Environment), Canada will play a major role in the development of future standards in these two areas.

The following are brief descriptions of the areas of concern for which standards are being developed.

A) ENVIRONMENTAL MANAGEMENT SYSTEMS — The establishment of formal procedures to be integrated into a company's management system in order that environmental considerations are taken into account when business decisions are made and that compliance or higher standards are maintained throughout the corporation.

A prescriptive document developed by the British Standard Institute (BS 7750) and a guidance document put forward by Canada (CSA Z750) were used to develop ISO documents. The attraction of the Canadian guidance document is that it is based on a generic management model, and this same model was reviewed for the ISO 9 000 quality standard. Given that a company cannot function with different management systems for different aspects of their operation, a unified quality/environment/general management system is the ultimate goal.

B) ENVIRONMENTAL AUDITING — Several standards are currently being developed to provide a high degree of standardization in the field of environmental auditing, as well as environmental initial reviews and assessments. Auditors will have to be certified. Reviews and assessments done by in-house personnel will need to follow standard protocols. Chapter 11 provides additional information on proposed ISO requirements for auditing and auditors.

C) ENVIRONMENTAL PERFORMANCE EVALUATION — The environmental performance evaluation subcommittee is comprised of two working groups. These groups are responsible for preparing a generic performance evaluation methodology standard and industry-specific environmental performance standards.

This area of standardization will have an extensive impact on environmental reporting to internal and external stakeholders. It has the potential to create a set of information that can be used to evaluate industries and products relative to their environmental impact and that of their competitors.

D) LIFE CYCLE ANALYSIS — Life cycle analysis is a technique for analyzing the total impact of a product on the environment. It is associated today with another environmentally related term, "full cost pricing." Life cycle analysis enables a company to evaluate all aspects of a product including raw material, production, packaging, and final disposal. With the evaluation, if done to the same protocol, comparisons can be made to other products' life cycle analysis results to determine relative environmental impact. Chapter 9 presents additional information about Life Cycle Analysis.

E) ENVIRONMENTAL LABELLING — The environmental labelling subgroup is developing a set of rules and definitions for what can and cannot be claimed on the label of a package. It is also defining terms such as "recyclable" in a uniform international format. The working groups within this subgroup will address terms and definitions for specific application in environmental labelling, environmental labelling symbols, environmental testing and verification methodologies, and guiding principles for type 1 environmental labelling (eco-labelling) schemes.

Environmental labelling can also lead to non-tariff trade barriers. The term "recycled material content" is currently creating barriers for Canadian newsprint manufacturers which traditionally have relied on raw material produced in Canada. To obtain sufficient amounts of post-consumer recycled material, they either have to backhaul newsprint from the U.S. or set up recycling operations close to major U.S. centres.

Environmental labelling programs identify those products whose full life cycle has least impact on the environment. In Canada, the Environmental Choice program features the "eco-logo." In Europe, the German "blue angel" was established in 1978. Together with Japan, these were the only countries that had eco-labelling schemes in place as of 1990. In 1991, more than a dozen countries, as well as the European Community, launched or were considering launching similar initiatives.

Early indications show that the flower symbolizing the EC eco-label has had a positive effect on the market share of those products displaying it. Importers who apply for an eco-label are submitted to the same test as European producers, including an evaluation of the environmental impact of processes and production methods.

6.3 NORTH AMERICAN FREE TRADE AGREEMENT

The years since the conclusion of the Canada-U.S. Free Trade Agreement (FTA) negotiations have witnessed a substantial growth of interest in the relationship between trade and the environment. The FTA encountered relatively little opposition from environmental groups. This may have been due to similarities between the two countries in terms of industrial structure, standard of living, and environmental policies.

The lack of enforcement of Mexican environmental standards was a major theme of the opposition to NAFTA. Environmental groups are campaigning for the inclusion of tight environmental rules within the trade pacts. Most environmental groups and citizens fear that without strong environmental rules and strict enforcement, investment could move to Mexico. Creating a "pollution haven" effect could not only transfer jobs to environmentally permissive jurisdictions, but also have a negative effect on the overall continental environment.

These concerns are reflected in the draft agreement, released on 7 October 1992, and remains virtually unchanged in the final ratified agreement. Compared to other trade agreements, the wording shows a high concern with environmental protection. Its approach is essentially five-pronged.

First, the agreement reaffirms, in language similar to that found in the GATT, the right of each country to determine its own level of environmental protection, even if it involves setting standards that are more stringent than international ones. This right is subject to requirements that such standards treat domestically produced and imported products similarly.

Second, the agreement commits the three parties to joint action to enhance environmental protection throughout the continent. Furthermore, NAFTA identifies "sustainable development" as a legitimate objective for introducing a standard-related measure.

Third, the impact on investment (the "pollution haven" effect) is addressed directly. Article 1114 discourages parties from waiving or derogating from an environmental measure as an encouragement to establish, acquire, expand, or retain an investment or an investor.

Fourth, provisions related to the dispute settlement mechanism explicitly allow panels to call scientific experts, if necessary, and rule on environmental matters. In the case of a dispute, the burden of proof is on the plaintiff; that is, environmental measures are allowable until shown to be inconsistent with NAFTA.

Finally, NAFTA obligations are subordinate to those of the trade provisions of international environmental treaties such as the Montreal Protocol in Substances that Deplete the Ozone Layer (1987), the Convention of International Trade in Endangered Species of Wild Fauna and Flora (1973), and the Basel Convention on the Control of Transboundry Movements of Hazardous Wastes and Their Disposal (1989).

On 13 September 1993, the governments of Mexico, the United States and Canada signed the **North American Agreement on Environmental Cooperation**. Under this agreement, a Commission on Environmental Cooperation is to be set up to foster and improve the environment in the three countries and to monitor the environmental effects of NAFTA.

The agreement has three main objectives:

- foster the protection and improvement of the environment in the territories of the three countries for the well-being of present and future generations
- promote sustainable development based on cooperation and mutually supportive environmental and economic policies
- increase cooperation between countries to better conserve, protect, and enhance the environment, including wild flora and fauna

The Commission on Environmental Cooperation will be structured with two levels of administration. The primary level is to be a council which is made up of equal representation from the three countries and manned by cabinet-level individuals. Also, there is to be a Joint Advisory Committee made up of 15 individuals, five from each country. The overall commission will be administered by a secretariat headed by a rotating three-year-term executive director. The secretariat will not be responsible to any one country, but will take its instruction only from the council.

The council and Joint Advisory Committee will meet concurrently at least once per year with additional meetings as required to deal with the business of the commission. The signatory countries may, at their discretion, form National Advisory Committees and/or Government Advisory Committees for their own benefit. It should be noted that although the Joint Advisory Committee is mandated by the agreement, there is no requirement for the council to seek its advice, nor does the secretariat have to consult it when preparing a factual record further to a complaint.

The secretariat will entertain a submission from any Non-Government Organization (NGO) or person asserting that a country is failing to effectively enforce its environmental laws, subject to the requirements set out in Article 14 (1)(a)-(f). A complaint must be in writing, properly documented, submitted by a resident of one of the countries, and already communicated to the country involved. Another important requirement is that the secretariat must accept that the submission is "aimed at promoting enforcement rather than at harassing industry." The secretariat can choose to pursue the submission in the same manner as a submission by government if the provisions in Article 14 are met.

One of the primary stumbling blocks of the negotiations was the enforcement measures that the commission can impose. Canada took a hard line in the negotiations prompted by the ramifications of some recent GATT rulings, and because of pressure brought to bear by industry and general-interest groups such as the National Round Table on the Economy and Environment. Canada would not accept, as Mexico did, trade sanctions as a potential tool for enforcing judgments of the commission.

Penalties in the form of fines can be assessed for failure to enforce environmental law. The commission is charged with the responsibility of producing a final report, whereupon the charged party has a chance to address the provisions set out in the "action plan." Where warranted, a "monetary enforcement assessment" can be imposed in accordance with Annex 34.

Annex 34 limits the fine to a value no greater than $20 million for the first year that the agreement is in force. After that, any fine shall be no greater than 0.007% of the total trade in goods between the countries. One of the areas which must be taken into account in assessing the fine shall be "the level of enforcement that could reasonably be expected of a Party given its resource restraints."

If the country fails to pay the fine, in the case of the United States and Mexico, trade sanctions can be used. Trade sanctions are limited to an amount no greater than that sufficient to collect the monetary enforcement assessment (i.e. essentially the amount of the fine). This may be done by increasing the rates of duty on originating goods of the country against which the complaint is lodged, limited to pre-NAFTA levels. These rates should be levied first on the sector subject to the complaint of failing to effectively enforce the law, but if this is not considered practicable or effective, then other sectors may be considered for suspension of benefits.

The ultimate mechanism for enforcement of fines against Canada is set out as follows: Canada is required to adopt a procedure in the federal court whereby the council's determination can be filed with the court and become an Order of the Court. The commission may take proceedings for the enforcement of the council's determination in court against the party against whom the determination is addressed. A determination that has been made an order of court is not subject to review or appeal in domestic courts; therefore, while not subject to trade sanctions, Canada is still subject to fines which will be enforced through the courts.

One of the key issues yet to be determined is the "buy in" of Canadian provinces. Because the majority of environmental matters fall within the purview of the various provincial governments, it is critical that commitments be obtained from the various provinces. This process of negotiations with the provinces is ongoing, but until provinces representing more than 50% of the population sign on to the agreement, the Canadian body of the Commission on Environmental Cooperation has no real ability to execute its mandate.

6.4   GENERAL AGREEMENT ON TARIFF AND TRADE

The GATT was originally drafted in 1947 as a temporary arrangement until the Havana Charter and the International Trade Organization, envisaged under it, came into being. The Charter was not ratified, and the

GATT (now the World Trade Organization) remains a contract and not a definitive treaty.

One hundred and two countries, which together account for more than 90% of all international trade, are **Contracting Parties** to the GATT. Contracting parties agree to abide by regulations contained within the articles of GATT which set limits on the use of trade restrictions. The regulation covers the use of tariffs (taxes, duties, or charges on traded goods) or non-tariff measures (usually quotas or other quantitative restrictions but sometimes unnecessarily restrictive requirements or standards). Other policy tools which distort trade, such as export subsidies, are also controlled by the GATT.

The main text of the GATT does not address environmental matters directly. Article XX provides for general exceptions to basic principles, including two that are generally construed to exempt some environmental measures from GATT discipline. Although the wording of the exemptions is broad, it has been defined more specifically by recent panel decisions. Two of the parallel agreements signed after the Tokyo Round of Negotiations (1979) have direct bearing on national environmental measures. The agreement on Technical Barriers to Trade, commonly known as the Standards Code, specifies that the signatories will avoid creating barriers to trade when implementing measures for such things as safety, consumer health, and environmental protection. The other agreement deals with subsidies and countervailing measures. It allows industrial subsidies designed to abate pollution under certain specific conditions.

There is general agreement among the trade community that GATT allows nondiscriminatory, product-related environmental standards; however, there still remain broad questions about environmental initiatives within countries and how they are treated under GATT. For example:

- Should a country be allowed to discriminate on the basis of process or production methods to establish a comparative advantage for domestic firms or to induce environmentally correct behaviour in another country?
- Is the additional financial burden that environmental requirements place on producers and importers discriminatory under GATT?
- Do the expanding number of multilateral environmental protocols which allow trade sanctions to encourage membership and/or compliance (e.g. Montreal Protocol on CFC elimination) go against GATT principles?

Recent GATT rulings for cases taken forward on environmental grounds offer a better understanding of the way that environmental issues have been dealt with by GATT.

For 20 years, GATT has had a Working Group on Environmental Measures and International Trade. The group's mandate is to examine "upon request" the impact of environmental measures on the application of the General Agreement. It is significant in itself that the group had its first meeting following a request in February 1991 by the member countries of the European Free Trade Association to consider emerging aspects of the trade/environment interface. The group's mandate is to report to the GATT council on trade provisions in international environmental agreements, transparency of national measures, and new packaging and labelling rules.

There is also currently a Working Group on Export of Domestically Prohibited Goods and Other Hazardous Substances whose mandate is to determine whether or not countries should be allowed to export goods whose sale is domestically banned or severely restricted for health, safety or environmental reasons. It is speculated that the Working Group will recommend the establishment of a notification procedure through which exporters will have to inform authorities in the importing country of the goods' status in the exporter's domestic market.

In the last decade, panels have been formed under the dispute settlement mechanism to examine five disputes in which defendants invoked exceptions to GATT principles on environmental grounds. Four of the five claims that alleged environmental measures were permissible under exceptions to Article XX have been rejected. The countries claiming exemptions were subjected to strict tests of national treatment, and were required to demonstrate that the environmental measures used must be the "least trade restrictive" alternative available. It is worth noting that Canada was involved either directly or indirectly in four of the five disputes.

Perhaps the most important, and most controversial, of the panel's decisions was the one that followed complaints from Mexico about a U.S. embargo on tuna products. The Marine Mammals Protection Act (MMPA) bars entry to the U.S. market of tuna caught in the southeastern Pacific by foreign fleets killing at least 25% more dolphins in the process than competing U.S. fleets. The panel judged the MMPA provisions to be contrary to GATT principles and stated that a country may not use restrictions to its own market to express dissatisfaction with the environmental practices of another country.

The latest round of GATT negotiations, known as the "Uruguay Round" did not, when it was begun in 1986, include a strong emphasis on environmental issues; however, the GATT has come under increasing pressure to accommodate environmental concerns with the result that the latest versions of the negotiation documents include environmental considerations. It has been widely speculated that the next round, to commence at some unspecified point after the completion of the Uruguay Round, will focus on environmental aspects of trade.

6.5 RECENT IMPACTS ON CANADIAN COMPANIES

Because of its international exposure, the Canadian forestry industry has become entangled in several major environment-trade issues. One of these originates in the U.S., where newsprint recycling content initiatives are forcing Canadian newsprint producers to backhaul old newsprint from U.S. municipalities or to establish recycling facilities close to the major U.S. sources of this material.

State regulations prescribing minimum levels of recycled fiber in newsprint were motivated by the desire to find a market for the glut of newsprint being diverted from landfills. Canadian producers generally do not have access to sufficient used newsprint to meet the content initiatives while maintaining present market share. Regulations of this nature have been adopted currently by two dozen states with the net result that Canadian newsprint producers are having to look seriously at the construction of recycling facilities close to major U.S. urban centres.

A second major issue in the forestry industry is the growing resistance in the marketplace to paper products made from chlorine bleached pulp. The primary source of this resistance has been in Europe. Although there is evidence that pulp mill effluent contains chemicals that can adversely affect the environment and human health, the research is inconclusive as to exactly which chemicals pose the greatest risks and the source(s) of those chemicals in the pulp mill. As a result, businesspeople and environmentalists disagree on the desirability of discontinuing chlorine use in pulp bleaching. Both camps are attempting to provide scientific proof to support their case and to refute the other's. Resolution of the problem rests on further research, especially with regard to toxicity properties of organochlorines. In meantime, however, some provinces are moving towards legislation for the elimination of chlorine from pulp operations. It is also expected that European competitors will vie for additional market share, replacing Canadian products with theirs by making claims that their products are produced with "chlorine free" paper. This claim is being disputed because its meaning is unclear; it may in fact mean "low chlorine" or "free of elemental chlorine."

The third area of concern is sustainable forest management. In the medium and longer term, this issue is likely to have the biggest impact on Canadian trade in forest products. Campaigns have painted forest management in Canada as being deficient and non-sustainable. Critics have pointed to the frequency and scale of clearcuts, and at the same time the excessive harvest of old growth forests. At present, there are no universally accepted criteria on which to base a judgement. Several countries and their industries are actively pursuing these criteria through global negotiations. Even though the United Nations Conference on the Environment and Development (UNCED) held in Rio de Janerio in 1992 failed to come to a full-fledged agreement, preliminary steps are now underway.

Forest management and conservation issues represent the clearest challenge to Canadian forest producers because they are likely to affect the market directly, with little or no intervention from government. The recent proclamation of the Forest Practices Code Act in B.C. is being seen by many as a way in which to instill confidence for investors and international markets. The Act addresses riparian management areas, community watersheds, integrated use, clearcutting, biodiversity, and road construction and maintenance.

6.6 FUTURE DEVELOPMENTS

It seems clear that considering everything that has transpired in the past decade, including the GATT negotiations, the environmental side deal for NAFTA, and the UNCED held in 1992, the importance of environmental issues will continue to escalate into the next decade. It is also evident that the influence of environmental concerns on trade issues can give rise to a new set of trade barriers. It is key, therefore, that Canadian businesses get involved and integrate environmental considerations into their daily operations. It also is clear that considerable financial and human resources need to be dedicated to developing national and international positions on environment trade issues.

Environmental groups have already staked strong positions on environmental issues and will continue to press for environmental considerations in trade agreements. In fact, the entire discussion of whether expanding trade agreements are counter to environmental concerns and sustainable development is far from being resolved and may become a key rallying point for environmental groups. It remains for business, led by the multinationals, to demonstrate that trade can indeed be expanded while accommodating environmental concerns and that trade and sustainable development are not incompatible.

The years leading up to the 21st century have been labelled by some industrial observers as the era of strategic alliances. It is incumbent upon business to carry these to unprecedented levels, establishing worldwide networks which can effectively take forward industries' positions to such arenas as ISO TC 207 international standard development as well as WTO and other multinational trade and environmental agreements. Nationally, businesses must work cooperatively with environmental groups on long-term national strategies such as Canada's Green Plan and their blueprints for action.

The UNCED highlighted in its report (Agenda 21) the critical role that small and medium enterprises (SMEs) currently play within the world economy and the escalation of this role in the future. We know from Canadian studies that this is the case, and that the primary growth markets for Canada and most countries will be in exports. Therefore, it is critical that SMEs be supported in the movement towards a global environmentally sustainable culture.

Looking at an action plan for business into the 21st century, the following elements should be considered:

- Establish strategic alliances among business to direct the development of national and international standards and policies on the environment. Bodies such as the Canadian Environmental Council, newly formed to guide the development of Canadian standards and Canada's position in relation to the ISO, must be strengthened and supported.
- Integrate EMSs within business focused on the internationally developing standards to minimize the impact of future requirements to certify under those international standards. Companies in Europe are already certifying their operations to the BS 7750 standard.
- Establish strong national business bodies to focus on the SMEs, eliminating the current environmental fears and developing rudimentary environmental management practices within their organizations which can accommodate future national and international requirements.
- Move forward with environmental reporting both internally and externally as well as involving all stakeholders (employees, management, shareholders, environmentalists, and the general public) in the development of the reports. Experts agree that within a few years, security commissions will require some form of environmental reporting to shareholders.
- Train individuals to deal effectively in international trade and with the interrelated environmental considerations (through programs such as the Canadian Forum for International Trade Training).
- Focus on the sustainable development target by participating in new technology development and exploring possible avenues such as the newly emerging concept of Industrial Ecology (patterning industrial systems both internally and externally, through strategic alliances, to mimic natural ecological systems).

The development of environmental concerns nationally and internationally is not all negative toward business. The escalating environmental agenda continues to create a need for new business enterprises to address the concerns being raised. Whether these be the requirements for consultants, especially in developing countries, or for environmental protection and prevention technology development and production, the environmental sector is one of the fastest growing business segments in

Canada. Needs should continue to expand as businesses and nations attempt to address environmental concerns.

New technology as diverse as new accounting practices for full cost pricing through the full life cycle evaluation of products, to robotic disassembly systems for consumer goods, will be sought in the years ahead. It is important that business not lose sight of these possibilities and be prepared to exploit spin-off technologies which may develop from the natural evolution of business operations.

The way ahead is no doubt difficult and, as in the past, only the fit and innovative will survive. And it will become progressively more difficult to survive alone. Strategic alliances must be established, trade associations and other organizations should be strengthened and molded into useful tools for the future, and SMEs need to be nurtured and supported.

7

Non-Government Organizations

by
J.D. Phyper, Phyper & Associates Limited
Brett Ibbotson, Angus Environmental Limited

7.1 TYPES OF NON-GOVERNMENT ORGANIZATIONS

Given the widespread interest in the design, implementation, and maintenance of EMSs, it is not surprising that many non-government organizations (NGOs) have examined EMSs and created some of the better EMS guidance documents.

In this chapter, NGOs are divided into three groups: standard-setting organizations, industrial associations, and business groups. The standard-setting organizations include national bodies such as the Canadian Standards Association (CSA) and international agencies such as the International Organization for Standardization (ISO). The growing influence of these NGOs is discussed in Section 7.2.

Industrial associations are groups of companies with similar types of products or operations (i.e. all the members are chemical manufacturers or all the members have mining operations). Industrial organizations promote members to learn from one another and to pool resources when investigating issues of mutual interest or concern. There are many industrial associations in Canada and the environmental management principles endorsed by five of these organizations are examined in Section 7.3.

Business groups are similar to industrial associations except that the membership in business groups can cut across many types of operations and products. Section 7.4 examines recent environmental initiatives by a Canadian business group (the National Round Table on the Environment and the Economy) and by the International Chamber of Commerce.

Many of the ideas and recommendations that come from NGOs reflect the collective experience and judgement of their members. And while these recommendations deserve close scrutiny, they should not be adopted by a specific company or organization before their applicability is assessed. Applicability can be tested by asking the following questions:

- Does the EMS component or concept being considered "fit" with the company's current system of overall management?
- Is the component or concept being used by other companies in the same sector?
- Is the component or concept being used by customers or suppliers?
- What will it cost to implement and maintain?
- Will it save the company money? If so, how and when?
- Will the component or concept reduce, mitigate, or eliminate incidents of non-compliance or litigation?
- Will implementing the component or concept contribute to a defense of reasonable care or due diligence?

7.2 STANDARD-SETTING ORGANIZATIONS

7.2.1 Canadian Standards Association

The Canadian Standards Association (CSA) is a not-for-profit, independent, private-sector organization that serves the public, governments, and business as a forum for national consensus in the development of standards. The CSA has facilitated the development of over 1,000 standards, and approximately one-third of these have been incorporated into legislation by provincial and federal authorities.

To assist Canadian businesses and organizations in improving their environmental performance, the CSA uses a multi-stakeholder consensus process to develop an Environmental Management Program series of documents. The documents are intended to offer guidance on such matters as:

- A Voluntary Environmental Management System (Z750-94)
- Environmental Auditing: Principles and General Practices (Z751-94)
- Phase I Environmental Site Assessments (Z768-94)
- Environmental Performance Reporting (Z765)
- Environmental Life Cycle Assessment (Z760-94)
- Emergency Planning for Industry (Z731-M91)
- Emergency Planning for Industry (#2) (MIACC Partnership) (Z731-95)
- Environmentally Responsible Procurement (Z766-95)
- Requirements for the Competency of Environmental Analytical Labs (Z753-95)
- Environmental Labelling (Z761-95)
- Risk Analysis Requirements and Guidelines (Q634-M91)
- Stakeholder Participation and Consensus Processes (draft Z764)
- Pollution Prevention (Z754)

- Competing Leaner, Keener and Greener: A Small Business Guide to ISO 14 000 (Plus 1117)
- Life Cycle Assessment in Practice (Plus 1107)
- Environmental Terminology for Canadian Business (Plus 1109)
- Environmental Principles and Policies (Plus 1113)

The CSA is also working on Environmental Risk Assessment and Phase II ESA documents.

CSA Information Product Z750 was developed to assist companies to set up EMS programs. The document outlines the elements of environmental management and provides a sequence of steps for implementation. However, recent discussions with CSA representatives indicate that the CSA most likely will adopt the ISO 14 000 series when it is completed.

The EMS model described in CSA Z750-94 assumes that the people of an organization subscribe to the following four principles, each of which can be translated in components of an EMS:

- The organization must focus on what needs to be done - it must have **purpose**. Purpose comprises environmental policy, risk assessment, environmental objectives and targets, and EMS design.
- People in the organization should have the **commitment** to take the appropriate action to support the EMS. Commitment includes shared values, alignment and integration, and responsibility and accountability.
- The organization must have the **capability** of performing in support of its objectives. Capabilities can include knowledge skills, training, systems, information technology, operation processes and procedures.
- An organization should be continuously **learning** how to perform better in the pursuit of its objectives, to improve its own management, and to improve the way(s) that it learns. Learning comprises measuring/monitoring, communications and reporting, system audits and management reviews, and continuous improvement.

CSA Z750 has been used as a major seed document in the development of the ISO 14 000, an Environmental Management Guidance Document which is still in draft form. ISO 14 000 will likely be adopted in Canada when it is released in final form in 1996.

The discussion of each principle in CSA Z750-94 includes self-assessment questions and practical advice. Additional information on the CSA environmental management program can be obtained by calling the CSA at (416) 747-4155/2277.

7.2.2 British Standards Institute

The British Standards Institute (BSI) is an independent, standard-setting body. The BS 7750:1994 standard is entitled *Specifications for Environmental Management Systems*. The document was designed to assist organizations establish effective EMSs. It echoes several management system principles found in the BS 5750 documents (see Section 7.2.3) and other internationally recognized quality system standards. The BS 7750 specification divides an EMS into subcomponents and requires organizations to:

- establish procedures to set environmental policy and objectives
- achieve compliance with environmental policy and objectives
- report to the public on the degree of compliance

BSI defines an EMS as the organizational structure, responsibilities, practices, procedures, processes, and resources for implementing environmental management. The standard also specifies that an EMS is comprised of the following elements:

1 Commitment from Senior Management
2 Environmental Policy
3 Organization and Personnel
4 Environmental Effects
5 Objectives and Targets
6 Management Program
7 Management Manual
8 Operational Control
9 Records
10 Audits
11 Reviews

The "Environmental Policy" is defined in the standard as a public statement of the intentions and principles of the organization regarding its environmental effects. The standard requires that the policy include a commitment to continual improvement of environmental performance and provide for the setting and publication of environmental objectives.

"Organizational and Personnel" includes defining and documenting the responsibility, authority, and interrelations of key personnel whose work affects the environment, verification that resources and personnel are adequate to fulfil objectives, appointment of senior personnel to ensure that desired level of environmental performance is achieved, and the establishment and maintenance of environmental awareness training.

The term "Environmental Effects" includes compiling a register for legislative, regulatory, and other policy requirements, and establishing and maintaining procedures for receiving, documenting, and communicating the results with relevant interested parties. Prior to establishing the register, methods must be established for examining and assessing the environmental effects (both direct and indirect) of its activities, products, and services.

The organization must set "Objectives and Targets" for all relevant levels. The objectives and targets should include both those stipulated by regulatory requirements and those developed in response to the environmental effects register and the financial, operational and business requirements of the organization, and pertinent stakeholders.

A "Management Program" should be developed which allows the organization to achieve its environmental objectives and targets. It should include the designation of responsibility for targets at each function and level of the organization, and the means by which they are achieved.

The "Management Manual" should be prepared which contains the environmental policy, objectives, and targets, and program; documents key roles and responsibilities; describes interaction of the EMS; and provides direction to related documents. This section of the standard also describes appropriate procedures for the control of documents.

The "Operational Control" element of the EMS requires management to define responsibilities for control, verification, measurement, testing and corrective action response within the organization and ensure that they are adequately coordinated and effectively performed.

A system of "Environmental Records" should be established and maintained to demonstrate compliance with the requirements of the EMS. The records should also contain the status of environmental performance in comparison to the proposed company's objectives and targets.

"Environmental Audits" should be employed to determine whether the EMS conforms to the environmental management program, is implemented effectively, and fulfils the organization's environmental policy.

The "Review" should allow for a check of the continuing relevance of the environmental policy, an update of the evaluation of environmental effect, and a check of the efficacy of the audits and follow-up actions.

Additional information on the BSI specification document can be obtained by contacting Milton Keynes at 011-44-908-221166.

7.2.3 International Organization for Standardization

The International Organization for Standardization (ISO) was established in 1947. Its membership is comprised of over 90 countries, representing more than 95% of the world's industrial production. ISO Technical Committee 207 (ISO/TC 207) is currently developing standards for environmental issues. These standards are designated the "14 000 series" and will share some similarities with the two other ISO series of standards:

- the ISO 9 000 series of documents related to quality management and quality-assurance standards
- the ISO 10 011 series of documents related to auditing quality systems

For the 14 000 series, ISO is considering developing standards for the following environmental issues:

- ISO 14 000 — Guide to Environmental Management Principles, Systems and Supporting Techniques
- ISO 14 001 — Environmental Management Systems Specification with Guidance for Use

- ISO 14 010 — Guidelines for Environmental Auditing: General Principles of Environmental Auditing
- ISO 14 011 — Guidelines for Environmental Auditing: Audit Procedures - Part 1: Auditing of Environmental Management Systems
- ISO 14 012 — Guidelines for Environmental Auditing: Qualification Criteria for Environmental Auditors
- ISO 14 024 — Environmental Labelling: Practitioner Programs - Guiding Principles, Practices and Certification Procedures of Multiple Criteria (Type 1) Programs
- ISO 14 040 — Life Cycle Assessment General Principles and Practices
- ISO 14 060 — Guide for the Inclusion of Environmental Aspects in Product Standards

It is anticipated that several of the ISO 14 000 series standards (e.g. 14 000, 14 001, 14 010, 14 012) will be available in early 1996. Additional information on the status of the ISO 14 000 series can be obtained by contacting the Secretariate for ISO/TC 207 on Environmental Management Systems at the CSA.

Refer to Section 6.2 for additional discussion on ISO 14 000 series documents.

7.3 INDUSTRIAL ASSOCIATIONS

7.3.1 Background

In response to increasingly stringent and complex legislation, and public perception that most industry is "bad for the environment," several industrial associations have developed industrial standards, guidelines, initiatives, and codes of conduct that promote voluntary environmental stewardship. These activities encourage association members to develop a more positive image and keep current with changing trends in environmental management and compliance.

These voluntary programs have also assisted industrial sectors to lobby for voluntary measures as opposed to "command and control" legislation. The voluntary approach usually allows industry to implement more cost-effective solutions.

Examples of Canadian industrial associations which have prepared environmental policies, guidelines, or codes of practice include:

- Canadian Chemical Producers' Association
- Canadian Manufacturers' Association
- Canadian Petroleum Products Institute
- Canadian Pulp and Paper Association
- The Mining Association of Canada

EMS contributions made by each of these associations are described in this section. Table 7.1 summarizes common concepts found in the policies and principles of these associations.

7.3.2 Canadian Chemical Producers' Association

The Canadian Chemical Producers' Association (CCPA), founded in 1962, currently has a membership of more than 60 companies which produce a broad range of chemicals, inorganic chemicals, and other organic and specialty chemicals (CCPA, 1992).

> The mission of the CCPA is to provide leadership to its members in achieving their vision of a Canadian chemical industry which is respected, operating in a safe and environmentally responsible manner, which competes effectively in domestic and international markets in chosen fields of operation, and which provides an equitable return to its shareholders, opportunities for growth, career opportunities for its employees, and benefits to Canadian society.

To meet this mandate, the CCPA has identified three **"strategic focus areas"**.

- Significant and visible changes in Canada's business climate in comparison with our trading partners which results in a clear competitive advantage in the immediate future.
- Commitment to significant improvement in health, safety, and environmental performance, as a demonstration of Responsible Care®, with particular near-term emphasis on emission reductions, which result in acceptance of voluntary approaches, by the public, governments, media, and our stakeholders.
- The spirit of Responsible Care® embraced throughout the chemical and related industries, and an active reaching out to communities, which results in public confidence in our responsible management of products and services.

Responsible Care®: A Total Commitment

Formal commitment to the principles and codes of practice of Responsible Care® is a condition of membership. Responsible Care® is the means by which member companies fulfil their commitment to the responsible management of their products throughout their life cycle. This commitment means meeting and exceeding both the letter and the spirit of the law. It includes such areas as community outreach and emergency response programs, product development protocols, manufacturing safeguards, distribution and transportation practices, and safe management of wastes.

Implementation support is provided through formalized networking, procedures manuals, seminars, and assistance from association staff and member companies.

CCPA member companies subscribe to the following **guiding principles** of the Responsible Care® Program:

- ensure that its operations do not present an unacceptable level of risk to employees, customers, the public, or the environment
- provide relevant information on the hazards of chemicals to its customers, urging them to use and dispose of products in a safe manner, and make such information available to the public on request
- make Responsible Care® an early and integral part of the planning process leading to new products, processes, or plants
- increase the emphasis on the understanding of existing products and their uses, and ensure that a high level of understanding of new products and their potential hazards is achieved prior to and throughout commercial development
- comply with all legal requirements which affect its operations and products
- be responsive and sensitive to legitimate community concerns
- work actively with and assist governments and selected organizations to foster and encourage equitable and attainable standards

To assist members, the CCPA has developed **codes of practice** that address community awareness and emergency response (includes a policy on community right-to-know), research and development, manufacturing, transportation, distribution, and hazardous waste management.

All of the codes of practice have an underlying theme of protecting people and the environment through the responsible management of chemicals, chemical products, and processes of operations.

It would be prudent for any company handling significant amounts of hazardous chemicals to become a member of CCPA or, as a minimum, to be aware of the components of Responsible Care.® CCPA distributes a booklet on Responsible Care® free of charge. The CCPA can be contacted at (613) 237-6215.

7.3.3 Canadian Manufacturers' Association

The Canadian Manufacturers' Association (CMA) has prepared the following environmental policy:

> The Canadian Manufacturers' Association is committed to assisting member companies to maintain and enhance their profitability and competitiveness in an environmentally responsible manner in Canada and abroad. CMA will advocate and work with its members to support their continuing improvements toward enhanced environmental performance to secure a safe and healthy environment and a sound and prosperous

economy for employees and shareholders and for the future generations of all Canadians.

The CMA encourages its members to include environmental issues in long-term strategic planning and advocates compliance with standards which exceed the current legal requirements to avoid making costly changes in response to legislative changes. CMA urges members to:

- implement environmental polices
- perform environmental audits
- perform research programs involving environmental issues
- exercise the three Rs (reduce, re-use, recycle)
- exchange used material with other manufacturers who could use them productively
- accept responsibility for cradle-to-grave environmental impact of products
- co-operate with government agencies
- participate in public debates on regulatory processes
- educate the government on how to protect the environment without endangering Canadian competitiveness in the global market

The CMA has published the following documents related to environmental management:

- *Guide for Chief Executive Officers*
- *Handbook for Environmental Co-ordinators*
- *A Simplified Guide to Emergency Planning*

The first two documents were developed to assist member companies in their ongoing efforts to ensure a safe and healthy environment and a sound and prosperous economy. The *Guide for Chief Executive Officers* includes a self-assessment questionnaire, an overview of the basic components of an EMS, and a discussion of continuous improvement of environmental performance.

The *Handbook for Environmental Co-ordinators* (CMA, 1994) describes the following areas of EMS:

- roles and responsibility of the environmental coordinator
- preliminary assessment of company's environmental performance
- legislative/regulatory framework
- spills and emergency preparedness
- use of company site plan for environmental purposes
- methods to check the company's compliance with environmental standards
- energy efficiency
- water conservation — protecting supply and quality
- employee work practices and procedures
- preparation of the executive report on the preliminary assessment of the company's environmental performance

- company's proactive environmental performance strategy

The CMA can be contacted at (613) 233-8423 for additional information on programs and publications.

7.3.4 Canadian Petroleum Products Institute

The Canadian Petroleum Products Institute (CPPI) was created in 1989 as a non-profit association of Canadian refiners and marketers of petroleum products. Institute members are involved in one or more elements of the petroleum business — refining, distribution, or marketing — which supplies domestic and industrial consumers with petroleum-based products.

CPPI's mission is to serve and represent these elements of the petroleum industry with respect to environmental, health, safety, and business issues. The CPPI seeks to work with all levels of government and public-interest groups to establish and maintain relationships based on mutual respect, cooperation, and open dialogue.

To guide its members, CPPI has developed a *General Policy and Guiding Principles* for the environment, health, and safety.

General Policy: CPPI members are committed to continuous efforts to safeguard the health and safety of employees, customers, and the general public, and to improve environmental protection. The general policy emphasizes anticipation and prevention:

1) Ensure that reasonable steps are taken so that environmental, health, and safety hazards associated with operations and products are identified, assessed, and responsibly managed through internal reviews of management systems, facilities, and operating practices and procedures.
2) Adhere to the spirit and intent of the law as the minimum acceptable standard of performance
3) Work in cooperation with governments and other stakeholders on setting priorities and on the development of effective legislation and regulations
4) Share information with appropriate stakeholders on the environmental, health, and safety aspects of operations and products
5) Integrate environmental, health and safety considerations into business planning, facilities and product design, operating practices, and training programs.

Endorsement of this policy and commitment to the implementation of the principles are requirements of CPPI membership. Members review and reconfirm this commitment annually to the CPPI board of directors.

Guiding Principles: The following is a summary of the CPPI *Guiding Principles* which address refining, distributing, marketing, research and communications.

Refining, Distributing, and Marketing

CPPI members will endeavour to manufacture, transport, store and handle raw materials, products, and wastes in a manner that seeks to protect the environment and the health and safety of employees, contractors, customers, and the general public. Members will:

a) Operations

    1 Monitor and assess impact and take corrective action

    2 Use reasonable efforts to reduce persistent toxins

    3 Strive continuously to improve energy efficiency

    4 Train employees in hazards

    5 Use only contractors trained in proper operating practices

    6 Perform regular monitoring and inventory control

b) Facilities and Sites

    7 Use safe and environmentally responsive technology

    8 Consult stakeholders during clean-up of sites

    9 Disclose information on sites to purchasers, tenant, or owner

    10 Remediate contaminated sites and off-site damage

c) Waste Management

    11 Continue to reduce waste at source

    12 Endorse the four Rs (reduce, re-use, recycle, recover)

    13 Ensure proper storage and licensed carriers/disposal sites

    14 Support waste management by associates/customers

d) Emergency Response

    15 Develop and improve emergency response capability

    16 Work in cooperation with other stakeholders

    17 Ensure that personnel have proper training

e) Products and Services

    18 Offer information to customers, associates, and employees

Research

CPPI members companies will encourage, support, and promote excellence in research on the environmental, health, and safety aspects of their raw materials, products, processes, and waste materials. Members will:

1) Make scientific knowledge on environmental, health, and safety an integral part of planning, development and management of new products, facilities, and processes.

2) Support work with governments, scientific, and academic communities to identify research needs, coordinate activities, and disseminate non-proprietary results.

3) Support joint funding and research on priority environmental, health, and safety issues.

Communications

CPPI member companies will promote dialogue with their employees, customers, and the general public with respect to relevant information on their raw materials, processes, products, wastes, and emergency preparedness for the protection of health, safety, and the environment. Members will:

1) Support multi-stakeholder consultation on environment, health, and safety polices and programs.

2) Encourage the input of stakeholders on environment, health, and safety issues in business decision-making process.

3) Broaden general understanding through the sponsoring and participating in public and industry technical seminars and workshops.

4) Provide relevant information on the nature of hazards associated with raw materials, processes, products, wastes, and releases.

5) Promote two-way communication with appropriate stakeholders on emergency response plans.

6) Conduct training and awareness programs to promote employee environmental, health, and safety responsibility.

Copies of the *Environmental Performance Measures* can be obtained by contacting the CPPI at (613) 237-6215.

7.3.5 Canadian Pulp and Paper Association

The Canadian Pulp and Paper Association (CPPA) has published an environmental statement which pledges dedication to a policy of "responsible stewardship" of the environment, aquatic creatures, and wildlife. CPPA advocates the following principles:

- Commitment to excellence in sustained yield forestry and environmental management and will conduct their business in a responsible manner designed to protect the environment and the health and safety of employees, customers, and the public.
- Will assess, plan, construct, and operate facilities in compliance with all applicable regulations.
- Forest resources will be managed and protected for multiple use and sustained yield.
- Will promote environmental awareness amongst employees and the public, and train employees in their environmental responsibilities.
- Beyond or in the absence of regulatory requirements, the companies will apply sound management practices to advance environmental protection and minimize environmental impact.
- The industry will work with governments in the development of regulations and standards based on sound, economically achievable technologies, and the analysis of environmental impact.

- The industry will continue to advance the frontiers of knowledge in environmental protection through the support to of scientific research and, as appropriate, apply such knowledge at its facilities.

Additional information on CPPA principles and programs can be obtained by calling (613) 233-2221.

7.3.6 Mining Association of Canada

The Mining Association of Canada (MAC) has established an environmental policy that addresses many of the same issues noted in the preceding discussions of other Canadian Associations. Member companies are committed to the concept of sustainable development which requires balancing good stewardship in the protection of human health and the natural environment with the need for economic growth. Diligent application of technically proven and economically feasible environmental protection measures will be exercised throughout exploration, mining, processing, and decommissioning activities to meet the requirements of legislation and to ensure the adoption of best management practices. To implement this policy, whether in Canada or abroad, the member companies of MAC will:

- assess, plan, construct, and operate their facilities in compliance with all applicable legislation providing for the protection of the environment, employees, and the public
- in the absence of legislation, apply cost-effective, best management practices to advance environmental protection and to minimize environmental risks
- maintain an active, continuing, self-monitoring program to ensure compliance with government and company requirements
- foster research directed at expanding scientific knowledge of the impact of industry's activities on the environment, of environment /economy linkages, and of improved treatment technologies
- work proactively with government and the public in the development of equitable, cost-effective, and realistic laws for the protection of the environment; and
- enhance communications and understanding with governments, employees, and the public.

Additional information on MAC initiatives can be obtained by calling (613) 233-9391.

7.4 BUSINESS GROUPS

7.4.1 National Round Table on the Environmental and the Economy

In 1986, Canada's federal and provincial governments established the National Task Force on Environment and Economy. The Task Force recommended that round tables be established as a means for discussing how to achieve sustainable development practices. In 1988, the National Round Table on the Environment and the Economy (NRTEE) was created. Provincial round tables have also been established. They share common objectives enunciated by the NRTEE in its report entitled *Sustainable Development: A Manager's Handbook* (Conklin *et al.*, 1991):

1) Stewardship

We must preserve the capacity of the biosphere to evolve by managing our social and economic activities for the benefit of present and future generations.

2) Shared Responsibility

Everyone shares in the responsibility for a sustainable society. All sectors must work towards this common purpose, with each being accountable for its decisions and actions, in a spirit of partnership and open cooperation.

3) Prevention and Resilience

We must try to anticipate and prevent future problems by avoiding the negative environmental, economic, social, and cultural impacts of policy, programs, decisions, and development activities. Recognizing that there will always be environmental and other events which we cannot anticipate, we should also strive to increase social, economic, and environmental resilience in the face of change.

4) Conservation

We must maintain and enhance essential ecological processes, biological diversity, and life support systems of our environment and natural resources.

5) Energy and Resource Management

Overall, we must reduce the energy and resource content of growth, harvest renewable resources on a sustainable basis, and make wise and efficient use of our non-renewable resources.

6) Waste Management

We must first endeavour to reduce the production of waste then reuse, recycle, and recover waste by-products of our industrial and domestic activities.

7) Rehabilitation and Reclamation

Our future policies, programs, and development must endeavour to rehabilitate and reclaim damaged environments.

8) Scientific and Technological Innovation

We must support education and research and development of technologies, goods, and services essential to maintaining environmental quality, social and cultural values, and economic growth.

9) International Responsibility

We must think globally when we act locally. Global responsibility requires ecological interdependence among provinces and nations, and an obligation to accelerate the integration of environmental, social, cultural, and economic goals. By working cooperatively within Canada and internationally, we can develop comprehensive and equitable solutions to problems.

10) Global Development

Canada should support methods that are consistent with the preceding objectives when assisting developing nations.

Further information about NTREE activities and publications can be obtained from the NTREE office at 1 Nicholas Street, Suite 520, Ottawa, Ontario, K1N 7B7.

7.4.2 International Chamber of Commerce

In 1974, the International Chamber of Commerce (ICC) published "Environmental Guidelines for World Industry." The guidelines have been revised on several occasions (i.e. ICC, 1991). The following set of guidelines are published in the ICC's *Business Charter for Sustainable Development Principles for Environmental Management.*

1) Corporate Priority

To recognize environmental management as among the highest corporate priorities and as a key determinant to sustainable development; to establish policies, programs, and practices for conducting operations in an environmentally sound manner.

2) Integrated Management

To integrate these policies, programs, and practices fully into each business as an essential element of management in all its functions.

3) Process of Improvement

To continue to improve policies, programs, and environmental performance, taking into account technical developments, scientific understanding, consumer needs, and community expectations, with legal regulations as starting point; and to apply the same environment criteria internationally.

4) Employee Education

To educate, train, and motivate employees to conduct their activities in an environmentally responsible manner.

5) Prior Assessment

To assess environmental impacts before starting a new activity or project, and before decommissioning a facility or leaving a site.

6) Products and Services

To develop and provide products or services that have no undue environmental impact and are safe in their intended use, that are efficient in their consumption of energy and natural resources, and that can be recycled, reused, or disposed of safely.

7) Customer Advice

To advise, and where relevant educate, customers, distributors, and the public in the safe use, transportation, storage, and disposal of products provided; and to apply similar considerations to the provisions of services.

8) Facilities and Operations

To develop, design and operate facilities and conduct activities taking into consideration the efficient use of energy and materials, the sustainable use of renewable resources, the minimization of adverse environmental impact and waste generation, and the safe and responsible disposal of residual wastes.

9) Research

To conduct or support research on the environmental impacts of raw materials, products, processes, emissions, and wastes associated with the enterprise and on the means of minimizing such adverse impacts.

10) Precautionary Approach

To modify the manufacture, marketing, or use of products or services or the conduct of activities, consistent with scientific and technical understanding, to prevent serious or irreversible environmental degradation.

11) Contractors and Suppliers

To promote the adoption of these principles by contractors acting on behalf of the enterprise, encouraging and, where appropriate, requiring improvements in their practices to make them consistent with those of the enterprise; and to encourage the wider adoption of these principles by suppliers.

12) Emergency Preparedness

To develop and maintain, where significant hazards exist, emergency preparedness plans in conjunction with the emergency services, relevant authorities and the local community, recognizing potential transboundary impacts.

13) Transfer of Technology

To contribute to the transfer of environmentally sound technology and management methods throughout the industrial and public sectors.

14) Contributing to the Common Effect

To contribute to the development of public policy and to business, government and intergovernmental programs and educational initiatives that will enhance environmental awareness and protection.

15) Openness to Concerns
To foster openness and dialogue with employees and the public, anticipating and responding to their concerns about potential hazards and impacts of operations, products, wastes or services, including those of transboundary or global significance.

16) Compliance and Reporting
To measure environmental performance; to conduct regular environmental audits and assessments of compliance with company requirements, legal requirements, and these principles; and periodically to provide appropriate information to the board of directors, shareholders, employees, the authorities, and the public.

7.5 FUTURE ROLES OF NGOs

NGOs already have had a strong influence on the evolution of EMSs. The five industrial associations described in Section 7.3 represent several of the industrial sectors that have been key contributors to the growth and prosperity that has occurred in Canada. Their influence on environmental management policy extends well beyond their members.

As shown in Table 7.1, several common themes are present in the environmental policies and principles endorsed by these associations and their members. Two of these common themes likely offer some insight into the future role of industrial associations and business groups:

• Work cooperatively with government agencies to help develop equitable, attainable environmental legislation and standards. Promote environmental protection without endangering the competitiveness of Canadian businesses.

• Communicate with the public and other external stakeholders. Share environmental information, promote awareness and understanding, participate in open discussions of environmental management and regulation.

Both of these themes urge companies to be pro-active – to help shape the legislative regime in which they will operate, and to participate in open discussions of environmental issues with the public. They urge members to share information on the premise that better decisions can be made when information is available. Environmental management decisions will not get easier to make. By sharing information and perspectives, companies, government agencies, and the public will be better informed and environmental management will evolve in ways that have a better chance of achieving the goals of being equitable and attainable.

And what does the future hold for standard-setting organizations? In the last few years, standard-setting organizations have taken on a prominent role in EMS development. This key role seems certain to continue for the next few years at least. As economies and trading patterns become increasingly globalized, this role of organizations such as the ISO may be inevitable. If your clients or suppliers are just as likely to be located across an ocean as they are to be down the street, there is a certain comfort in knowing that an international standard of care has been met. If the environmental standards from the ISO are generally perceived as being appropriate and reasonable, buyers of goods and services will use them as a prerequisite, while providers of goods and services may use them to illustrate their qualifications, even when not required to do so.

Table 7.1
COMMON ENVIRONMENTAL CONCEPTS ENDORSED BY CANADIAN INDUSTRIAL ASSOCIATIONS

On Meeting Legal or Legislative Requirements:
CCPA - comply with all legal requirements
CPPI - adhere to the spirit and intent of the law as a minimum
CPPA - comply with all applicable regulations
MCA - comply with all applicable legislation

When Legislative Requirements Have Not Been Developed:
CPPA - apply sound practices to minimize impacts
MCA - apply cost-effective, best management practices

On the Need to Communicate with the Public and Other External Stakeholders:
CCPA - be responsive and sensitive to community concerns
CMA - participate in public debates on regulatory process
CPPI - share information on environment, health, and safety
CPPA - promote awareness among employees and the public
MCA - enhance communications and understanding

On the Goals of Working Cooperatively with Government Agencies:
CCPA - help foster equitable, attainable standards
CMA - promote environmental protection without endangering Canadian competitiveness
CPPI - help develop effective legislation
CPPA - help develop regulations based on sound, economically achievable technologies

MCA -   help develop equitable, cost-effective, realistic laws for environmental protection

On Managing Risks and Hazards:
CCPA - ensure that operations and products do not pose unacceptable risks; inform customers of hazards

CPPI - take all reasonable steps to responsibly manage hazards

CPPA - protect the health and safety of employees, customers, and
the public

On the Need for Further Environmental Research:
CMA -   to better understand environmental issues

CPPA - to advance knowledge in environmental protection

MCA -   to understand potential impacts, treatment technologies, and
environment-economy linkages

Note: see Sections 7.3.2 through 7.3.6 for details.

REFERENCES

British Standards Institute (BSI), 1992. *Specifications for Environmental Management Systems*, BSI 7750.

Canadian Chemical Producers' Association (CPPA), 1992. *The Canadian Chemical Producer's Association: What It Is/What It Does*. August.

Canadian Manufacturers Association (CMA), 1994. *Handbook for Environmental Co-ordinators*.

Canadian Petroleum Producers Institute (CPPI). *General Policy and Guiding Principles*.

Canadian Standards Association (CSA), 1994. *A Voluntary Environmental Management System*. Publication CSA Z750-94.

Conklin, D.W., Hodgson, R.C., and Watson, E.D., 1991. *Sustainable Development: A Manager's Handbook*. National Round Table series on Sustainable Development.

International Chamber of Commerce (ICC), 1991. *Environmental Guidelines for World Industry*.

8

The Organizational Component

---

by
J.D. Phyper
Phyper & Associates Limited

8.1 ENVIRONMENTAL POLICY AND SUPPORT DOCUMENTATION

8.1.1 Setting Principles and Objectives

One common theme of the EMS publications discussed in Chapter 7 is the need for the persons at the highest levels of an organization to "set the pace" by providing a corporate environmental policy and support documentation which can include guiding principles, objectives, and a rational document.

The **corporate environmental policy** should be aligned to the constraints placed on the company by internal and external stakeholders and be approved by the board of directors. It should state in clear, concise terms the overall direction of the company with regard to environmental management.

The corporate policy should be translated into **guiding principles**. Guiding principles assist in the development of a common vision and culture within an organization. They are broad statements or codes of conduct adopted by an organization that will shape specific corporate policies.

Objectives should then be developed to transfer the guiding principles into measurable tasks that are to be completed within specific time periods. In a recent survey of Canadian companies, 76% of respondents indicated that environmental objectives are already part of their company's business plans (Ernst & Young, 1994).

Both guiding principles and objectives need to be compatible with the government's regulatory direction, the requirements of financial institutions, and public concerns. It is also important that the guiding principles and objectives be employed in all major production, marketing, investment, and human resource decisions.

A **rationale document** should be prepared explaining the environmental policy statement and guiding principles to senior management and others responsible for ensuring the implementation of the objectives. This document should assist in obtaining support from management and employees. It should also present definable expectations which management can use to develop plans for implementation of the guiding principles and objectives within a specific department, operational unit, or facility.

Objectives for specific departments and/or facilities should also be prepared and be based on the corporate rationale document as well as specific corrective action reports and risks. Figure 8.1 presents the "paper" components of an effective EMS. The four plant-specific components are discussed in Chapter 9.

The development of the corporate environmental policy and support documentation can be organized into six steps:

1) Review guidance offered by standard-setting organizations or industrial associations.
2) Consult with internal and external stakeholders.
3) Review policies, guidelines, and objectives of other companies in the same industrial sector.
4) Identify strategic placement of company (e.g. compliance versus risk reduction).
5) Develop corporate environmental policy, guiding principles, and objectives specific to your operations and goals.
6) Communicate policy and associated documentation to all stakeholders.

In the following sections, each step is discussed in detail.

8.1.2 Guidance from Standard-Setting Organizations

The Canadian Standards Association (CSA) defines corporate environmental policy as follows (CSA Z750, 1994):

- to establish an overall sense of direction that sets the parameters of actions for the organization
- to define the boundaries of what an organization will attempt to do, what it will not do, the kinds of actions by its people that are acceptable, and those that are not

The policy should be relevant to the company's activities, products, and services; be consistent with the organization's values, beliefs, and relevant guiding principles; and provide for the setting of environmental objectives and targets.

Figure 8.1
"PAPER" COMPONENTS OF AN EFFECTIVE EMS

CORPORATE ENVIRONMENTAL POLICY
One to two paragraphs stating corporate policy. Very general in nature.

GUIDING PRINCIPLES
The Guiding Principles support the Corporate Policy and relate to major activities.

CORPORATE OBJECTIVES
Definable expectations which management can use to develop plans for implementation of the policy within a specific department. Should include measurable targets and anticipated schedule for each objective.

RATIONALE DOCUMENT
Document that explains the Corporate Policy and Guiding Principles to senior management and others responsible for ensuring the implementation of the policy and objectives.

PLANT ——————————— CORPORATE DEPARTMENT

PLANT OBJECTIVES
Plant- or department-specific objectives should be based on corporate objectives and plant-specific issues.

PLANT-LEVEL POLICIES
Plant-level environmental policies should be prepared covering all areas of environmental compliance.

PROCEDURES FOR POLLUTION CONTROL EQUIPMENT
Detailed procedures for the operation and maintenance of critical pollution control equipment should be developed. The procedures should make reference to allowable permit levels and internal limits (standards).

STANDARDS
Engineering standards, control of pollution control equipment, and scientific standards to prevent adverse effects should be developed.

CORPORATE ENVIRONMENTAL POLICIES
Companies with centralized purchasing and engineering departments may require corporate environmental policies for new chemicals/projects and waste disposal.

The British Standards Institute (BSI) outlines five key issues that management should address when developing and implementing an environmental policy (BSI 7750, 1994):

- be relevant to a company's activities, products, and services and their environmental effects
- be understood, implemented, and maintained at all levels in the organization
- be publicly available
- include commitment to the continual improvement of environmental performance
- provide for the setting and publication of environmental objectives

BSI also stipulates that the policy should be consistent with other corporate policies, such as those for health and safety or quality.

8.1.3 Consulting with Stakeholders

Both the CSA and BSI indicate that the environmental concerns and requirements of external and internal stakeholders need to be identified prior to the development of the policy. External stakeholders may include shareholders, financial institutions, suppliers, customers, government agencies, general public, environmental groups, and the local community. Internal stakeholders include management staff, employees, and union.

An example of the impact that external stakeholders may have on a company's performance is illustrated by recent events related to the Canadian forestry industry:

Government	- Placed restrictions on the types of areas to be harvested (i.e. old growth forest and the method of harvesting).
	- Required state-of-the-art pollution control technology to be installed at pulp and paper mills.
	- Municipalities enacted policies and by-laws requiring recycling of newsprint, cardboard, and office paper.
Customers	- Printing industry is requiring recyclable paper as part of the marketing of services to their customers.
	- Some customers have asked printers not to use paper from old-growth forest on Vancouver Island if non-recyclable newsprint is required.
Environmental Groups	- Pressure on European companies may have potentially caused the loss of contracts for the Canadian forestry sector.
	- Pressure on government agencies has resulted in a reduction in the available acreage for cutting and more stringent legislation for effluents.

| Public | - Employees are receiving negative feedback from some members of the community on corporate performance related to logging practices and water and air (odour) emissions from the mills. |
| Employees | - Growing awareness of environmental issues has resulted in a reduction in the number of spills through human error and generation of cost-effective ideas on pollution prevention. |

8.1.4 Review Documentation from Other Companies

Prior to developing a policy, guiding principles, and objectives for your operation, documentation developed by companies in similar industrial sectors should be reviewed. Policies and guiding principles are available in annual financial reports, annual environmental reports, or through contacting a member of the environmental affairs department. The environmental objectives of the company may not be published as widely as the policy, but should be available by contacting the company.

The following three examples of corporate environmental policies and guiding principles clearly state each company's direction while recognizing its core business.

Noranda Forest Inc. — Noranda Forest operations are committed to the principles of sustainable economic development. They will strive to be exemplary leaders in forest, land, and environmental management by minimizing the environmental impact on the public, employees, customers, and property, and by supporting the application of scientific research, limited only by technological and economic viability. Specifically:

1) The potential risks of new projects or processes to employees and the environment must be addressed so that effective control measures can be foreseen and taken and all parties made aware of these facts.

2) Noranda Forest Group operations will implement site-specific forest land management, environmental, health, hygiene, safety, and emergency response policies in the spirit of environmental leadership as well as in conformity with applicable laws and regulations.

3) Noranda Forest Group operations will constantly evaluate and manage risks to human health, the environment, and physical property, and will be subjected to periodic forest land management, environmental, health, safety, and emergency preparedness audits. A report on forest land management, environmental performance, health, safety, and emergency preparedness will be presented annually to the board.

Avenor Inc. — Avenor Inc. is committed to protecting the environment. The Company has been entrusted with the stewardship of extensive renewable natural resources and accepts the responsibility of managing these resources on a sustainable basis to ensure their productive use and enjoyment for future generations. The Company will undertake:

Forest Management — Plan and conduct our forest management activities in a manner which respects the value of the forest and recognizes the principles of biodiversity, sustainability, and multiple use of forest lands.

Operations — Design and manage our manufacturing and forestry operations in a manner which incorporates good environmental practices and ensures compliance with government regulations. Take prompt corrective action in the event of any accidental discharge. Support research and development to ensure that our processes and products are environmentally acceptable and of a quality which meets customer requirements.

Communications — Continually inform and encourage meaningful input from employees, customers, governments, and the public about our operations and their impact on the natural environment.

Audits — Conduct operational audits on a regular basis and initiate action plans, where required, to ensure compliance with Company policies and standards and government regulations. Ensure the audit programs and methods are periodically reviewed by independent experts.

We recognize that the long-term viability of our operations and the well-being of our employees and their communities are dependent upon a healthy, natural environment.

Northern Telecom — Recognizing the critical link between a healthy environment and sustained economic growth, we are committed to leading the telecommunications industry in protecting and enhancing the environment. Such stewardship is indispensable to our continued business success. Therefore, wherever we do business, we will take the initiative in developing innovative solutions to those environmental issues that affect our business. We will:

- Integrate environmental considerations into our business planning and decision-making processes, including product research and development, new manufacturing methods, and acquisitions/divestitures.
- Identify, assess, and manage environmental risks associated with our operations and products throughout their life cycle, to reduce or eliminate the likelihood of adverse consequences.
- Comply with all applicable legal and regulatory requirements and, to the extent we determine it appropriate, adopt more stringent standards for the protection of our employees and the communities in which we operate.

- Establish a formal Environmental Protection Program and set specific, measurable goals.
- Establish assurance programs, including regular audits, to assess the success of the Environmental Protection Program in meeting regulatory requirements, program goals, and good practices.
- To the extent that proven technology will allow, eliminate or reduce harmful discharges, hazardous materials, and waste.
- Make reduction, reuse, and recycling the guiding principles and means by which we achieve our goals.
- Prepare and make public an annual report summarizing our environmental activities.
- Work as advocates with our suppliers, customers, and business partners to jointly achieve the highest possible environmental standards.
- Build relationships with other environmental stakeholders — including governments, the scientific community, educational institutions, public interest groups, and the general public — to promote the development and communication of innovative solutions to industry environmental problems.
- Provide regular communications to and training for employees to heighten awareness of, and pride in, environmental issues.

For information on environmental policies and guiding principles developed by industrial associations refer to Section 7.3, "Industrial Associations."

Environmental objectives should be consistent with the corporate policy and guiding principles and provide specific information as to "what," "when," and "how much." The inclusion of numerical values and dates allows for subsequent assessments to be made on the status of achieving the objectives. In general, there are four types of environmental objectives:

- voluntary programs promoted by government agencies (e.g. CCME National Packaging Program and Ontario Waste Reduction Program)
- voluntary programs promoted by industrial sectors and government agencies (e.g. ARET program and U.S. EPA Industrial Toxics Project)
- voluntary programs proposed by individual companies (e.g. Chrysler Windsor Van Plant's elimination of chlorinated solvents or the Dow Chemical river separation project at its Sarnia, Ontario facility to virtually eliminate spills and discharges from the plant to the St. Clair River)
- stipulated by legislation for future compliance (e.g. prohibition of the use of ozone-depleting substances)

An assessment of voluntary initiatives by government agencies (federal and provincial) and industrial associations indicates that approximately 100 of these programs have been proposed in recent years in Canada.

The following are four examples of voluntary programs which require Canadian industry to commit to reduction objectives.

The Accelerated/Reduction Elimination of Toxics (ARET) chemicals program, proposed by the New Direction Group, a committee of industry representatives and non-government organizations, and subsequently adopted by Environment Canada. Industry and government agencies are to pledge to reduce emissions of toxic chemicals selected from a list developed jointly by government and industry.

The Pollution Prevention Pledge Program (P4) invites facilities in Ontario to develop pollution reduction goals which exceed existing provincial, federal, or municipal regulatory requirements and to share them with the Ministry of the Environment and Energy. Program objectives include reducing releases of chemicals into the environment, lowering the use of toxic chemicals, and diminishing the generation or disposal of hazardous or liquid industrial wastes. P4 is one of the programs being employed by the Ontario government to reduce 50% of non-hazardous waste by the year 2000.

The National Packaging Protocol (NAPP) of the Canadian Council of Ministers of the Environment (CCME) includes six packaging policies which constitute a plan of action and includes waste reduction targets and schedules. The three reduction targets include 20% by 1992, 35% by 1996, and 50% by 2000.

The Industrial Toxics Project proposed by the U.S. Environmental Protection Agency (EPA) calls for the reduction of 18 chemicals by 33% in 1992 and 50% by the end of 1995. The pollutants were selected by the U.S. EPA because they are emitted in large amounts, have an impact on the environment, and that technology is available to reduce them.

For additional information on voluntary initiatives, it may be appropriate to contact the provincial environment ministries, Environment Canada, and/or a representative of an industrial association for which your company is a member. Telephone numbers for several Canadian industrial organizations are provided in Chapter 7.

8.1.5 Identify Strategic Placement of Company

Increasingly, organizations are seeking to go beyond compliance to ensure that the environmental integrity of their activities, products, and services meets the expectations of stakeholders.

The following questions can be used to determine if going beyond compliance should be part of a company's EMS strategy:

1) Do we strive to be average or above average in environmental performance for the industrial sector in which the company operates?

2) Do we strive to be as environmentally friendly as companies in other industrial sectors?

3) Do we strive to achieve compliance with regulatory standards representative of the country in which the head office is located if those standards are more stringent than those of the country in which the plant is located?

4) If we strive to go beyond regulatory compliance, what is the primary goal:
   • reduced probability of accidental releases to the environment,
   • savings through waste reduction,
   • "green" marketing of products and/or services,
   • compliance with future legislation,
   • a response to a perceived moral obligation?

If the answer to question number 4 is yes, it may be appropriate to perform a preliminary cost/benefit analysis of complying with the proposed policy for significant environmental issues. It is better for a company to adopt a "less aggressive" policy and adhere to it than propose "100% environmentally friendly operations" which cannot be met due to technical and/or financial constraints. The same approach holds true for objectives as they should be easier to quantify.

In a recent survey of Canadian companies, 72% of respondents indicated that compliance was the main goal of their environmental planning effort. After planning for compliance, the desire to improve performance was the most important factor driving the planning effort. Pressure from head office was second, followed by community concerns (Ernst & Young, 1994).

8.1.6 Developing Environmental and Support Documentation

The corporate environmental policy statement should be relatively brief — one or two paragraphs — with specific information being provided in the guiding principles. Guiding principles typically cover the following issues as they relate to the environment: planning; consultation with stakeholders; compliance; waste reduction; product stewardship; corrective action; emergency response; and research. Draft copies of the policy can be submitted to interested stakeholders to ensure that it addresses their concerns and requirements.

8.1.7 Communicate the Policy to Stakeholders

Once the policy has been developed and accepted by the directors, the following activities should be performed:
   • The policy should be communicated to all levels of the organization.
   • The board of directors and senior management should clearly illustrate commitment to the policy in their communications with all stakeholders.

- Overall and specialized environmental objectives, consistent with the corporate policy, that provide details as to "what," "when," and "how much" should be prepared.
- The resources necessary for implementing the policy and objectives should be identified and made available.
- Periodic checks should be performed to ensure that the policy is understood, complied with, and being implemented effectively by all levels of the organization.

8.2 ORGANIZATIONAL STRUCTURE AND ALLOCATION OF RESOURCES

8.2.1 Initial Review

Following the development of a corporate environmental policy, individuals must be assigned responsibilities for components of the EMS and be held accountable for ensuring ongoing compliance and the achievement of objectives. Prior to assigning responsibilities, it may be appropriate to perform the following activities:

1) Identify key areas of environmental risk to the organization (refer to Chapter 10 for a detailed discussion of risk identification and assessment).

2) Identify the organizational relationships between environmental, health and safety, and risk (loss prevention) issues.

3) Review the resources used to implement the EMS (and potentially the health, safety, and risk management systems) at similar organizations.

4) Select the overall organizational structure for the EMS (i.e. centralized vs. decentralized).

5) Estimate the amount of resources (in particular the number of personnel) needed to address environmental risks.

6) Assess the need to assign environmental responsibilities to personnel on either a full-time basis, part-time (i.e. part of other job functions) basis, or as part of a task force to deal with issues on a case-by-case basis.

The findings of these activities can be used to prepare a "resource allocation" table. Two distinct types of structures (centralized vs. decentralized) for managing environmental issues are shown in Table 8.1.

Figure 8.2 presents an environmental organization structure for a company with several facilities. Note that the smaller the company, the less the number of reporting levels and the more "job" sharing between environmental functions and other duties.

Table 8.1
STRUCTURES FOR MANAGING ENVIRONMENTAL ISSUES

	Steel Company	Printing Operation
General Information		
- Structure	Central	Decentralized
- Facilities	2	50
- Employees/site	3000 - 4500	50-125
Senior Person		
- Position	Vice-President	Director of Environment
- Other Roles	Health & Safety	None
- Report to	Board of Directors	Vice-President
Corporate Env. Dept.		
- Staff (total)	10 (includes H&S)	3
- Responsibilities	Proposed legislation, new permits; expert advice on air, water, and waste issues; training, audits, and incident inspections	Proposed legislation; advise on air, water, and waste issues; periodic inspections
Plant Environmental Personnel		
- Number	4	1
- Assignment	Full-time	4 full-time and 46 part-time
- Responsibilities	Daily water monitoring,waste classification and inventories,and the preparation of government reports	Waste classification and shipments, preparation of permits, and annual water sampling

FIGURE 8.2
POTENTIAL ORGANIZATIONAL STRUCTURE OF AN EMS

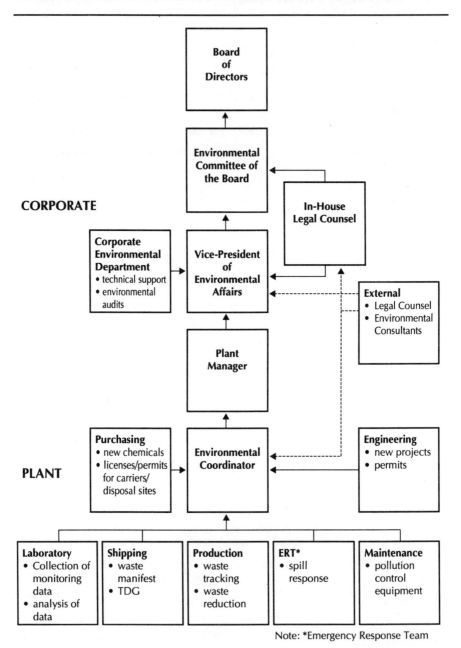

Note: *Emergency Response Team

8.2.2 Assigning Responsibilities

It is critical that the structure of a company's environmental organization fit into the company's current general management system as opposed to creating a new and separate system. The following descriptions of environmental responsibilities are generic and therefore not suitable for every organization.

Board of Directors — In most provinces, legislation holds the directors ultimately responsible for environmental compliance. As such, the directors should:

- be aware of the standards in their own industry, as well as other industries that may deal with similar environmental concerns
- delegate responsibilities for environmental matters to a person in senior management
- ensure that the delegate is properly educated
- be informed of and react to "significant" issues which affect the company as quickly as possible
- review EMS system on an ongoing basis, usually annually
- ensure that minutes of the board of directors' meeting reflect adequate consideration of environmental matters

A detailed discussion of what are "significant" issues is presented in Section 8.3.2.

Committee of the Board — If environmental issues potentially pose a significant risk to the corporation and/or its officers and directors, it may be appropriate to establish a special committee comprised of members of the board of directors. The committee's objective would be to ensure that environmental issues are being addressed and report the status to the board. Typically, it is this committee that performs the review of the company's EMS.

Senior Environmental Management Representative — The board may choose to delegate its responsibilities to officers of the corporation who in turn may pass on some of the responsibility to a senior management representative. In large organizations, the senior environmental person may be an officer of the corporation. As indicated in Chapter 3, the board and corporate officers must ensure that a system of adequate and effective supervision is in place and that they are kept regularly informed of environmental matters affecting the corporation. In order to avoid potential conflicts of interest, the senior environmental management representative's position is typically independent of the manufacturing operations.

The requirement to be independent of manufacturing is proposed to ensure that significant environmental issues are passed to the board of directors in their entirety and not downplayed because of production concerns, and that the allocation of resources (e.g. budget, equipment, manpower, etc.) reflect those concerns. During poor economic conditions, some companies reduce expenditures on environmental control systems with expected results (i.e. increased spills, violation, fines, and staff turnover). As indicated by the court in the *R. v. BATA Industries Limited* judgment, "the environment must not be a sacrificial lamb on the alter of corporate survival."

The position of this individual and hence reporting structure will be a function of the size of the company and liability associated with environmental issues. In a larger organization with potentially significant environmental risks, this individual may be assigned a title such as Vice-President of Environment or Environment, Health, and Safety (EHS) and be an officer of the company who reports directly to the board of directors. At the other end of the scale, the senior environmental representative at a company with few environmental risks will combine more than one job duty. Typically, the term "environmental manager" or "environmental coordinator" would be added to their existing title (e.g. manager of engineering and environment, or manager of environment, health, and safety).

The following are potential tasks that the senior environmental management representative would perform:

- prepare corporate action plan including budget estimates and objectives
- assign components of the EMS to other members of the organization
- regularly monitor the effectiveness of the EMS
- oversee performance of periodic environmental audits
- report regularly to the corporate officer and/or board of directors regarding environmental performance

The individual should have a knowledge of both environmental and manufacturing issues and good communication skills. The latter will be a significant benefit when responding to various stakeholders (e.g. government agencies, employees, community groups, and officers and directors). The individual should also be given appropriate authority to make decisions. A title with little real authority is merely window dressing and may cause more harm than benefit. A potential test of the appropriateness of the senior environmental management representative's authority is to compare their "signing limit" with individuals who have similar titles and responsibilities.

Corporate Environmental Department — Typically, the corporate environmental department oversees the following activities:

- interact with government agencies on proposed legislation
- compile summary data on environmental performance for senior management, government agencies, and public inquiries
- implement special studies on environmental impacts of operations
- interact with other departments on environmental issues

- manage the resource centre for technical or regulatory inquiries by plant personnel
- perform or commission environmental audits
- participate in the purchase or divestment of properties and facilities

Individuals in this group typically include expert(s) in the fields of air, water, waste management, or auditing, as well as junior staff to assist in data compilation.

Plant Manager — More and more companies are including the responsibility for environmental performance — and in particular, compliance — in the plant manager's job description. The management of environmental issues is considered no different than those associated with health and safety, production, sales, etc. As such, the plant manager must ensure that:

- environmental issues are being identified
- information on outstanding environmental issues is being compiled and presented to the manager
- corrective action is being taken to mitigate outstanding environmental issues

Typically, the plant manager assigns operational responsibilities for environmental issues to either facility environmental staff or other plant personnel. Key decisions to make prior to the delegation of responsibility include:

- Will the person be assigned to environmental matters on a full-time or part-time basis? One commonly used approach for the latter is the inclusion of health and safety or risk with the person's responsibilities. Another is the use of utilities or engineering personnel to address environmental issues (e.g. periodic sampling or preparation of permits, on an as-needed basis).
- Will individuals be assigned responsibilities according to environmental compartments (e.g. air, water, or waste) or production units (e.g. coke ovens, steel making, finishing, etc.)?

Environmental Coordinator — The environmental coordinator "links" environmental issues together. The role of the environmental coordinator can take on many forms, as illustrated by the following three examples:

1) Perform all activities related to environmental issues, for example:
   - monitor the releases of emissions and effluents into the environment
   - prepare environmental policies and procedures
   - complete forms, surveys, or reports required by government agencies
   - prepare waste shipments (including Transportation of Dangerous Goods requirements)
   - respond to complaints from neighbours and/or government agencies
   - establish and implement spill response plan

- coordinate activities of other individuals assigned environmental responsibilities
- perform periodic inspections to assess compliance with legislation and conformance to plant policies/procedures and industry codes of practice
- prepare report to plant manager.

2) Perform some activities related to environmental issues and oversee others performed by individuals assigned to specific day-to-day activities (e.g. waste shipments).

3) Coordinate environmental activities performed by others in various departments, resolve outstanding issues, and prepare reports for the plant manager.

Role of Other Departments — Depending upon the type of operations, the following departments may undertake EMS tasks and be considered part of the EMS:

Engineering Department	- prepare permit applications
	- select, design, and install pollution control systems
	- select equipment processes that produce less waste and require fewer hazardous chemicals as feedstock
Purchasing Department	- screen new chemicals
	- ensure that waste carriers and disposal companies have proper licenses and permits
	- ensure that all on-site contractors perform activities in compliance with environmental legislation and company requirements
Maintenance Department	- perform maintenance on pollution control and spill response equipment
Production Department	- ensure that operations are within permit requirements, waste minimization activities, and detection and initial response to spills
Shipping Department	- ship waste off-site and receive/ship dangerous goods
Security	- initiate spill response plan, especially during off hours

By including these departments in the EMS, or by recognizing their role in EMS activities, their activities can provide the greatest benefits.

Individuals should be made aware of their duties formally (e.g. inclusion in job description or environmental manual), lines of communication, and receive additional training where appropriate. Accountability is critical if the organization is to achieve its goals and objectives and prevent incidents of non-compliance.

8.2.3 Ensuring Acceptance of Responsibilities

Once individuals have been assigned environmental responsibilities, it may be appropriate to perform the following activities:

- Prepare a figure similar to Figure 8.2 which clearly illustrates the reporting structure (both normal and during incidents) for environmental issues. It may also be appropriate to include in the figure the frequency and types of reports to be generated (see Section 8.4 and Figure 8.3).

- Include environmental responsibilities in job descriptions of all personnel considered part of EMS. Refer to Chapter 10, "The Cultural Component" for additional discussion on job responsibility and qualifications.

- Organize training for all persons involved in environmental issues. Management training should focus on overall responsibilities of legislation and corporate policy. Additional discussion of training needs and types of programs is presented in Chapter 10.

- Prepare environmental policies, procedures and/or standards which document regulatory requirements in easy-to-understand language and technical specifications of pollution control equipment. Chapter 9 presents a detailed discussion on the preparation of an environmental manual for each facility which contains environmental policies, procedures, and/or standards.

- Select an appropriate type of performance protocol (i.e. penalties versus incentives, for individuals with environmental responsibilities). Refer to Chapter 10 for additional information on potential performance protocols.

- Prepare an in-house policy on the role of corporate or external legal counsel in the event of charges being laid against an employee while conducting his or her duties.

Resources, including personnel, required by the organization should constantly be reviewed as stakeholders' expectations and requirements change.

8.3 REPORTS/REVIEWS AND CORRECTIVE ACTION

8.3.1 Assess Reporting Requirements

To define the content of a report it is critical to understand the "needs" of the users at all levels of the organization. In the case of the board of directors there exists a need, as stipulated by legislation, to obtain information on significant environmental issues and mitigate those issues in a timely manner. Shareholders may need information to assess the company's overall environmental performance before investing or quantify the costs associated with historical environmental impairment or future pollution abatement activities.

This chapter presents examples of some of the types of environmental reports which may be generated by a company. Other special reports commonly prepared by companies include quarterly or annual newsletters to employees, environmental audit reports, property transfer and/or decommissioning environmental site assessment reports, and special studies (typically task forces) of the impact of proposed environmental legislation. The types of reports will vary from company to company depending on the type of structure (central versus decentralized), size of company and individual facilities, and environmental risks.

8.3.2 Report to the Shareholders and Public

Figure 8.3 presents an overview of reports which may be generated by a company. At the top is a report submitted to the shareholders and the public that can either be part of the annual financial report or a separate document dealing only with environmental issues. If it is part of the annual financial report, its content is regulated by Generally Accepted Accounting Practices (see Chapter 4).

Currently, there is no generally accepted format for environmental reports. The following format was recently proposed by the Canadian Institute of Chartered Accountants (CICA, 1994):

Organization's Profile	- activities and products and their impact and effect on the environment
Documentation	- environmental policy, objectives, and targets
Management Analysis-	- discussion of how organization is achieving environmental objectives and targets
Performance Analysis	- presentation of key performance indicators and measurements, analysis of environmental impacts and effects, and activities being taken by the organization

The CICA also indicates that a Glossary and Third-Party Opinion may be appropriate, but consider these components to be optional.

It is critical that the objectives and targets in the Organization's Profile address the aspects of "What," "When," and "How Much" (including units of measure). Failure to include all three components makes it difficult, if not impossible, to objectively assess performance.

FIGURE 8.3
POTENTIAL REPORTING COMPONENTS OF AN EFFECTIVE EMS

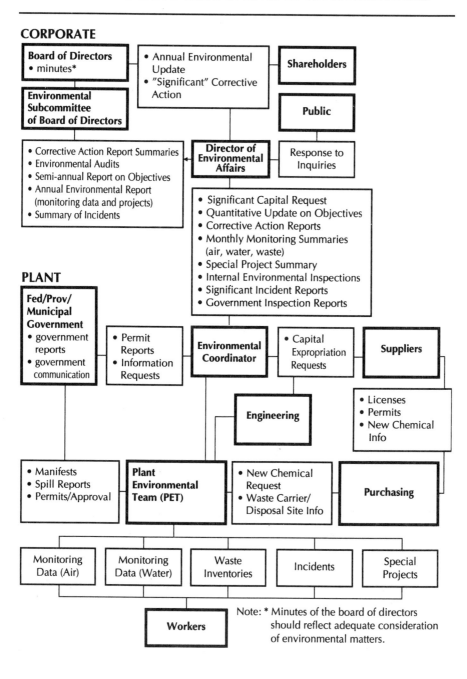

CORPORATE

Board of Directors
• minutes*

Environmental
Subcommittee
of Board of Directors

• Annual Environmental
Update
• "Significant" Corrective
Action

Shareholders

Public

• Corrective Action Report Summaries
• Environmental Audits
• Semi-annual Report on Objectives
• Annual Environmental Report
  (monitoring data and projects)
• Summary of Incidents

Director of
Environmental
Affairs

Response to
Inquiries

• Significant Capital Request
• Quantitative Update on Objectives
• Corrective Action Reports
• Monthly Monitoring Summaries
  (air, water, waste)
• Special Project Summary
• Internal Environmental Inspections
• Significant Incident Reports
• Government Inspection Reports

PLANT

Fed/Prov/
Municipal
Government
• government
  reports
• government
  communication

• Permit
  Reports
• Information
  Requests

Environmental
Coordinator

• Capital
  Expropriation
  Requests

Suppliers

Engineering

• Licenses
• Permits
• New Chemical
  Info

• Manifests
• Spill Reports
• Permits/Approval

Plant
Environmental
Team (PET)

• New Chemical
  Request
• Waste Carrier/
  Disposal Site Info

Purchasing

Monitoring
Data (Air)

Monitoring
Data (Water)

Waste
Inventories

Incidents

Special
Projects

Workers

Note: * Minutes of the board of directors
should reflect adequate consideration
of environmental matters.

Typically, the Performance Analysis comprises the majority of this type of report. Some components of this analysis are relatively straightforward (e.g. the discussion of compliance with environmental legislation or number of environmental incidents). Others may be difficult to present in a meaningful and objective manner. An example of the latter is the reduction in emissions. If a facility reduces total suspended solids loading by 40% yet maintains previous levels of metal loadings in the water discharge, is it fair to report that emissions have been reduced by 40%? Another example of potential misrepresentation of data would be to report that solid waste was reduced by 50% when in actuality the volume of waste was reduced, not mass, due to the use of a compactor. As a result, the following two key components of reporting emissions should be clearly identified:

- "binning" of chemical (e.g. metals, chlorinated and non-chlorinated organics, solid non-hazardous waste, etc.)
- unit of measure (volume, mass, etc.)

8.3.3 Report to the Board of Directors

Directors must ensure that they are regularly informed of significant environmental issues so that they may react in a timely manner. As indicated in Chapter 3, issues reported to the board of directors should cover three distinct areas:

1) Matters which indicate non-compliance with environmental laws and regulations.

2) Environmental "incidents," including spills and discharges, which could give rise to substantial fines, personal liability, or publicity.

3) Anticipated initiatives by the company, governments, or other organizations which could significantly affect the company and/or its business activities.

To avoid the risk of over- or under-reporting environmental issues, an arbitrary threshold should be established by the board defining which matter should be brought before it and which matters should be dealt with by management. The threshold may include one or more of the following components:

- matters, including spills and discharges, resulting in potential liability exposure over a specified dollar amount in fines or clean-up costs must be reported to the board
- matters which involve potential personal liability must be reported to the board, and
- environmental matter which may raise potential public concern must be reported to the board.

The specified dollar amount should reflect the nature of the company's business and the level to which the board has delegated responsibility for environmental matters.

Usually, reports are prepared by the senior environmental management representative for each board meeting or meeting of the environmental committee of the board, and a summary environmental report is prepared on an annual basis.

8.3.4 Plant Manager's Report

In some companies, the environmental coordinator interacts directly with the corporate environmental department, providing periodic updates to the plant manager. The current trend, however, is to report all plant environmental issues directly to the plant manager on a regular basis (e.g. monthly). Typically, this is accomplished by one of the following methods:

- The environmental coordinator prepares a brief report on environmental issues, usually in checklist format with a brief description provided for all areas of concern.
- A monthly meeting is held (in some cases weekly) whereby all department heads report on the status of environmental issues affecting their operations.

The plant manager either uses the environmental coordinator's report or creates a separate report on environmental issues which is sent to the senior environmental management representative. In organizations with several facilities, the corporate environmental manager summarizes the plant manager's reports and submits this document to the officer of the company responsible for environmental issues.

8.3.5 Reports to Regulatory Agencies

Depending on the type of emissions being discharged and waste generated, and the jurisdiction in which the facility operates, numerous reports may be required by environmental legislation or site-specific permits. As indicated in Chapter 2, it is critical that these reports be identified, that their preparation be assigned to an individual, and that they are critically reviewed prior to submission. Examples of regulatory reports commonly prepared by Canadian companies include:

- reports on water quality for provincial, federal, or municipal levels of government depending upon the location of discharge and industrial sector
- reports on waste generated and stored in inventory (in some provinces)
- waste manifests for shipment of specific types of waste (to the provincial government for domestic shipment and the federal government for the importing or exporting of waste)
- reports detailing the storage of special chemicals (PCBs) or storage containers (e.g. underground storage tanks)

- reports on air emissions if a significant emitter as per permit requirements (provincial or federal if transboundary requirement)
- National Pollutant Release Inventory (NPRI) report to the federal government if the facility uses or manufactures specified chemicals in prescribed amounts

A list of reports required on a regular basis by government agencies should be prepared for the facility along with the following information:

- short description of report
- pertinent legislation and section number
- name of government agency(ies) to receive the report
- frequency of report submission
- persons (and job title) preparing the report
- reviewer (and job title) of report
- time required for the report to be kept on file

The storage time for most types of records is two years; however, it is usually prudent to store records for ten years. It may also be appropriate to store records related to potential historical risk (e.g. underground storage tanks, use of special chemicals such as PCBs and some forms of herbicides) for the life of the facility.

8.3.6 Corrective Action

Management must respond to violations or non-compliance by performing prompt remedial or mitigative actions. A written procedure, clearly communicated to employees, should be developed to ensure that corrective action is carried out in a timely manner and communicated to senior management. It is critical that the corrective actions be documented (e.g. "Corrective Action Reports"). Typically, these types of reports will be generated and tracked following inspections and or audits. The company must show that is moving forward to reduce potential impairment.

Corrective action, where possible, should be subdivided into short- and long-term activities. The latter are usually more resource intensive. This allows the facility to initiate corrective action in a timely manner as opposed to waiting for the funding of larger projects. The following example illustrates a sequence of short- and long-term responses to elevated levels of Total Suspended Solids (TSS) in a discharge to a municipal sewer system:

- enter into a Compliance Agreement with the municipality (i.e. an agreement by which activities will be performed by the company or its delegate within a specified time period to resolve non-complying concentrations, during which time the municipality will not charge the company for said non-compliance)
- assess upstream sources of TSS and their relative contributions (both mass and concentration)
- perform additional sampling to identify average and maximum con-

centrations and flows; if possible, assess fluctuation in levels as a function of the hour of the day and day of the week if the process is not consistent

- assess relative costs of reducing upstream sources, entering into an overstrength agreement with the municipality, or installing on-site pollution control equipment (including sludge disposal cost). Overstrength agreement allows a company to pay the municipality for discharge loadings in excess of those allowed by the by-law limits for selected parameters.
- select preferred alternative: if on-site treatment may be appropriate, select a consultant or assign the task to appropriate personnel in maintenance/engineering and/or utilities departments
- either enter into an overstrength agreement or install selected system

8.4 MANAGEMENT REVIEWS

Management should, at appropriate intervals, review the EMS to ensure its continuing suitability and effectiveness. On an quarterly or semi-annual basis, the review may include the following:

- assessment of the results from internal inspections and audits if performed
- status of achieving targets and/or objectives
- status on the implementation of action plans derived from inspections, audits, or management reports

On an annual basis, the suitability of the following should be performed:

- environmental policy
- environmental targets and objectives
- environmental management program
- environmental manual and other related documentation
- training programs

Many factors will influence how "suitability" is defined during the annual reviews. These factors include emerging/growing environmental concerns in specific areas, developing a better understanding of environmental issues, being aware of proposed and potential regulatory developments as well as concerns from internal and external stakeholders, keeping abreast of changes in the activities of the organization, and profitability. The information can be summarized in an annual report by the senior environmental management representative to the board of directors.

Environmental audits are discussed in detail in Chapter 11. During a recent survey of Canadian companies, 83% indicated that they do some form of environmental auditing (Ernst & Young, 1994).

REFERENCES

Ernst & Young Environmental Services Inc. October 1994. "Survey of Environmental Management in Canada highlights strengths, weaknesses and dangers of current approaches." *Canadian Environmental Regulations and Compliance News* 5 (10): 730.

9

The Operational Component

by
J.D. Phyper
Phyper & Associates Limited

9.1 KEY OPERATIONAL FEATURES

In Chapter 1, "components" are defined as the functional resources that a company can use to deal with challenges. The resources that comprise the "operational component" include the procedures a company uses to accomplish its tasks and the standards by which it judges its efforts and level of success. Subsequent sections of this chapter examine six key features of the operational component that are addressed in successful environmental management sysytems:

- **Pollution Prevention** — Traditionally, the selection of pollution control equipment and its proper operation have been the cornerstones of complying with environmental requirements. In recent years, many companies have started to shift emphasis to reducing contaminants at the source and recycling or re-using materials previously disposed as waste. Pollution prevention initiatives over the last few years include the federal Accelerated Reduction/Elimination of Toxics (ARET) Program and the Pollution Prevention Pledge Program (P4) in Ontario.

- **Spill Prevention and Response** — Despite the training, procedures, and many other precautions that may be taken, unscheduled releases or discharges of materials to the environment still occur as a result of equipment failure, mishandling, transportation accidents, and human error. More than 5,000 spills a years are reported in Ontario alone.

- **Documentation** — The documentation associated with an EMS can take many forms. Examples include policies and procedures, training manuals, documents that contain copies of environmental permits, and associated correspondence with the regulatory agencies. Efforts spent developing policies, training staff, or installing pollution control equipment can fail to realize their potential if up-to-date documentation is not readily available to those who need to consult it.

- **Ongoing Monitoring and Estimating Emissions** — Environmental monitoring can serve several functions. It can demonstrate if environmental control systems are operating effectively. Increasingly, monitoring is a regulatory requirement. Monitoring is also used to determine the amounts of materials being emitted or released to the environment or reaching off-site locations. In some instances, actual measurements can be replaced or augmented with estimation methods. Since monitoring is largely an exercise in gathering statistics, care needs to be taken to ensure that the appropriate protocols are used when taking the measurements.

- **Data Storage, Assessment, and Reporting** — As environmental management becomes increasingly complex, it requires ever-increasing amounts of data to measure performance, assess compliance, and make decisions. The need to organize, assess, store, and retrieve environmental data has prompted some companies to create customized data management systems and has resulted in computerized systems becoming widely available.

- **Interaction with External Stakeholders** — External stakeholders include regulatory agencies, members of the local community, and non-government organizations (NGOs). Interaction with those stakeholders can range from government inspections and interviews to public meetings or articles in the media. Since interaction with regulatory agencies are often centred around compliance issues, the people involved need to understand the purpose of the interaction and have the proper information at hand. Interaction with the local community and NGOs are discussed in detail in Chapter 5.

9.2 POLLUTION PREVENTION

9.2.1 Existing Processes

The collective experience of several Canadian companies points to four steps that can be used to prevent pollution where existing processes are to continue.

Step 1 — Eliminate/Phase Out Persistent Toxics at the Gate

A conceptually simple and aggressive action towards reducing hazardous materials in the workplace is to stop purchasing those materials. This approach has been used by Chrysler Canada at its van production plant in Windsor, Ontario. The first task undertaken by Chrysler Canada was to identify the chemicals that were to be "prohibited" based upon a review of occupational and environmental impacts. The department responsible for purchasing was instructed that these products are no longer to be purchased without the approval of the environmental department. Approval by the environmental department is only given if the user of the chemical can show that no alternative is available due to quality, performance, or substantial cost differences. As a result of this program, the use of all chlorinated solvents has been eliminated at the plant.

An additional activity which is being employed by some companies is to develop databases of "environmentally friendly" products for various applications and "prohibited" chemicals. The information can be used by purchasing departments to select preferred chemicals and users of chemicals can consult the database to become better informed about potential substitutes.

Step 2 — Prepare Emissions/Waste Inventory

An inventory of emissions (air and water) and waste streams should contain the amount of each chemical being emitted and the estimated operating cost of treatment or disposal at each emission point. The inventory can have several applications:

- to demonstrate compliance with regulatory requirements
- to provide baseline levels which can be used to assess future activities
- to assign rankings to the relative importance of emission sources
- to identify those pollution control activities and/or disposal methods that are relatively costly

There are both federal and provincial requirements to prepare emission/waste inventories:

- National Pollutant Release Inventory (NPRI) is a federal initiative to gather information for more than 170 chemicals when used or generated at facilities above specified amounts.
- Legislation in some provinces requires annual inventories of hazardous waste to be submitted by those who produce or store such wastes.
- Legislation in some provinces requires non-hazardous waste inventories to be prepared at establishments in excess of specified size and/or number of workers.

Step 3 — Develop Rules

Once emissions have been quantified, rules need to be developed that prioritize how available resources are to be used. As discussed in Section 8.1.5, possible reasons for going beyond compliance in efforts to prevent pollution include the following:

1) Reduce the probability of accidental discharges and environmental impairment (i.e. risk reduction).
2) Obtain savings through waste reduction.
3) Assist in marketing (i.e. green marketing).
4) Comply with requirements of future legislation.
5) Respond to a perceived ethical obligation.

If risk reduction is the objective, additional work may be required to identify areas of high risk, their probability of failure and the potential impact (e.g. a HAZard and OPerability — HAZOP assessment). A more detailed discussion of risk assessment is presented in Section 9.3.

Companies that have savings as an objective typically proceed with a project if the return on investment (ROI) is less than one year. Some companies assign this role to a specific group/team, while others encourage all staff to contribute to waste reduction efforts. A detailed discussion of getting employees to "buy in" is presented in Chapter 10, while the 3M Pollution Prevention Pays program is discussed in Chapter 12.

Step 4 — Implement Pollution Prevention Programs

In 1993, the Business Roundtable, an association of business executives in the United States, commissioned a study to determine the common elements of successful facility-level pollution prevention programs. Key findings of the study included the following (The Business Roundtable, 1993):

- Facilities were successful when they were not told how to approach pollution prevention. The freedom to choose the best method to reach pollution prevention goals was key to their success.
- A majority of the facilities stated that the corporate role should be to establish corporate goals with facility input, develop and deploy pollution prevention technology transfer across the company, and forecast future compliance issues.
- Facilities had the ability to report progress against selected goals or initiatives on a monthly to quarterly basis.
- In order for a facility to be able to sustain a pollution prevention program, the projects had to be, on the whole, cost effective. Pollution prevention projects, unlike compliance projects, had to compete in the normal capital process.

- No facility relied exclusively on source reduction techniques to achieve pollution prevention.
- All facilities included recycling and reuse in their pollution prevention efforts and some used the entire waste management hierarchy (i.e. source reduction, recycling, reuse, energy recovery, treatment and disposal).

9.2.2 New Processes and Chemicals

In many instances, there are more opportunities for preventing or minimizing pollution and wastes before a new process is implemented or a new chemical is phased in or purchased. For both new processes and new chemicals, the first step is to develop appropriate screening criteria.

Step 1 — Develop Environmental Screening Criteria

Criteria that can be used to assess new chemicals include:

- potency of material to humans (e.g. allowable occupational exposures) and biota (e.g. toxicity to rainbow trout)
- the potential to bioaccumulate in the environment or organisms (e.g. Biocumulation Factor — BCF)
- persistence in the environment (often expressed as the half-life of a chemical)
- treatability (e.g. ability of the chemical to be removed by commonly used pollution control devices)

It is anticipated that several persistent and toxic chemicals will be banned or phased out within the next few years through regulatory instruments (e.g. Canadian Environmental Protection Act) or voluntary programs proposed by federal or provincial government agencies, and/or industrial associations.

The criteria that can be used assess new processes include:

- energy and water consumption
- availability of raw materials due to restrictions imposed by environmental legislation
- quantity of waste generated (including releases to air, water, ground water and soil)
- costs of pollution control equipment to treat air emissions and water discharges under current and proposed legislation which may come into force during the lifetime of the equipment
- costs of waste treatment, disposal, and/or recycling
- impacts of air emissions (e.g. odours) and water discharges on the environment and humans

- government acceptance of proposed treatment options for air, water, and waste
- public acceptance of proposed treatment options for air, water, and waste
- potential risk to environment in the event of equipment failure and subsequent clean-up cost

It is critical that the costs noted above be included in assessments of the ROI.

Step 2 — Incorporate the Screening Criteria into Decison-Making

Preparing environmental screening criteria and actually using them are two very different activities. The following activities can be used to ensure that the screening criteria are given a meaningful role in decision-making.

Many medium-size and large Canadian companies do not allow new chemicals to be brought on-site unless potential impacts on worker health have been screened by the Occupational Health and Safety (OH&S) department. Environmental screening criteria can be incorporated into decisions concerning new chemicals in several ways:

- Include screening criteria in forms used internally to assess OH&S issues. If a form is not currently being used for OH&S issues, develop a form that can be used for both environmental and OH&S issues.
- Develop a purchasing policy that requires suppliers to provide specified information to OH&S and environmental department(s) for approval of new chemicals. Only proceed with the purchase of new chemicals with the approval of the OH&S or environmental department.
- Develop databases of environmentally acceptable chemicals and "prohibited" chemicals (refer to Step 1 for existing processes and chemicals).

The ways in which screening criteria can be used to assess new processes are different from those applied to new chemicals.

- Questions based on screening criteria can be incorporated into evaluations of capital expropriation requests (e.g. estimated cost of pollution control equipment and waste disposal/treatment, measures being taken to reduce energy and water consumption, and list of persistence toxic chemicals being used as raw material or potentially created as by-products)
- Require that a senior person in the environment group or department sign capital expropriation requests to verify that environmental issues have been identified and addressed.

9.2.3 New Products

There is growing pressure on companies to minimize packaging materials and recycle non-hazardous waste (metal, glass, plastic, paper, and cardboard). Within the next few years, additional pressure in the form of new environmental or trade legislation and/or industrial association initiatives likely will result in the recycling of most parts associated with automobiles, durable goods, and business equipment. The proposed legislation requires manufacturers and distributors to have cradle-to-grave responsibility for products, including the "take back" and disposal of used equipment at the seller's or manufacturer's expense.

Life Cycle Assessment (LCA), also known as cradle-to-grave assessment, is a tool that may be used to quantify environmental burdens associated with the life cycle of a particular product. The LCA processes consists of four essential phases (CSA, 1994):

- Initiation — This is a screening or scoping process intended to define the problem and establish assessment objectives.
- Inventory — This phase is used to quantify inputs and releases (energy, water, material requirements, air emissions, waterborne effluents, solid wastes, and other environmental burdens) during the life of the product, process, or service.
- Impact Analysis — Technical, quantitative, and qualitative processes are used to characterize and assess the effects of the environmental release identified in the Inventory phase.
- Improvements analysis — This is a systematic evaluation of the needs and opportunities to reduce the environmental burden.

The Canadian Standards Association (CSA) has prepared guidelines entitled "Environmental Life Cycle Assessment" (Z760-94) and "User's Guide to Environmental Life Cycle Assessment: LCA in Practice" (Plus 1107-94).

Design for the Environment (DFE) is another approach proposed by the American Electronics Association Design for the Environment (DFE) Task Force to minimize environmental impacts associated with producing electronic components. The DFE Task Force identifies several key factors as "process enablers":

- give environmental considerations a status similar to that of other factors such as quality, low cost, and fast time-to-market
- implement a system that recognizes and rewards high-quality DFE
- use a system for marking materials and develop specifications for recycled material consistent with national/international standards

- integrate DFE considerations into the product delivery process; consider total life cycle costs in the product concept stage
- communicate design guidelines, rules, standards, or practices within the company
- educate and train engineers in DFE requirements and applications
- share the DFE ethic and considerations with vendors and suppliers early in product design
- review/assess designs at appropriate stages of product delivery process

The following examples illustrate accomplishments using DFE.

BMW designed a car that can be disassembled in 20 minutes and recycled. More than 80% of the car is made of recyclable materials including the doors and bumpers, and front, rear, and side panels. The pilot disassembly plant has already been developed.

Canon and Hewlett Packard have instituted return programs for printer cartridges whereby usable parts are reclaimed and reused, plastics are recycled and remoulded, and remanufactured cartridges are produced.

IBM is using DFE concepts in personal computer designs. Future designs will employ snap-fit technology and one recyclable thermoplastic.

Xerox is developing a strategy for recylcing equipment and parts. Key components of the strategy include designing for disassembly, recycling, and refurbishment.

9.3 SPILL PREVENTION AND RESPONSE

Most spill prevention and response programs can be divided into a few basic components, the first of which is **identifying areas of significant risk**. This component is necessary if resources are to be allocated in a cost-efficient manner. In general, risk assessments answer fundamental questions such as: What can go wrong? How likely is it that a spill will occur? What are the consequences?

The CSA describes the following steps for identifying these types of risk (CSA, 1991a):

- scope definition — describe the system to be assessed, operating conditions, and boundaries (both physical and functional)
- hazard identification - describe the potential sources and impacts
- risk estimation - estimate the risks based upon the nature (quantity, composition, and release/use characteristics) of the originating hazard (may use frequency analysis and consequence analysis)
- documentation — document the risk analysis process

- verification — review the process to confirm the integrity and correctness of the analysis
- analysis update — have the ability to update risk analysis throughout the life of the facility

The CSA document also provides a frequency-severity matrix which assists a user in determining whether a detailed quantitative, semi-quantitative, qualitative, or no-risk assessment is required.

Preventative maintenance and backup equipment should be in zplace to ensure ongoing compliance. Equipment failure often contributes to spills, either directly or indirectly. Because many spills result from the failure of equipment, backup equipment is often critical to prevent the release of material into the environment. Preventative maintenance and backup equipment are seen by regulatory agencies as necessary parts of a spill prevention program.

Proper chemical (waste) storage is critical to spill prevention. Important factors include proper primary and secondary containment, good housekeeping techniques, material compatibility, and security. In recent years, several pieces of legislation have been passed in Canada regulating the storage of chemicals — in particular, petroleum products. The legislation typically requires that only licensed contractors install the storage vessel and associated piping, and that corrosion protection and secondary containment be in place.

Material compatibility of toxic or hazardous substances with container materials and proximity of storage to other chemicals and hazards (such as ignition sources) should also be assessed. The design and operation of all chemical (waste) storage facilities and transfer stations should be reviewed for possible noncompatible chemicals.

Good housekeeping techniques can include the neat and orderly storage of bags and drums of chemicals, prompt spill clean-up to prevent significant runoff, and clearing of dry chemical accumulations by sweeping and vacuuming.

Accidental or intentional entry to a facility resulting in sabotage, theft, etc. should be prevented by incorporation a security system. The main emphasis is the prevention of toxic chemical discharge from unauthorized entry.

Emergency/spill response systems include clean-up equipment and material, trained staff, and communications systems. The latter allows for the prompt contact of government agencies, the local fire and police departments, and spill clean-up contractors. The type of equipment and materials should be a function of the chemicals present at the facility, the types of conditions that can result in spills, and the probability of release. Examples of guidance documents on setting up an emergency planning system are the CSA "Emergency Planning Industry" (CSA, 1991b) and the Canadian Manufacturing Association "A Simplified Guide to Emergency Planning" (CMA, 1990). Some of the key steps described in the CSA publication are listed in Table 9.1.

It is critical that an emergency plan has the ability to address releases from all vital points (i.e. areas in which hazardous chemicals are stored, transferred, or processed) at the facility. Unfortunately most facilities in Canada employ generic emergency/response plans which may not adequately address site-specific issues.

An eight-step process can be used to assess the appropriateness of a company's spill prevention program:

Step 1   Identify all vital points.

Step 2   For each vital point, identify pollution control equipment, primary and secondary containment, and back-up equipment.

Step 3   Identify actual and manufacturers' proposed schedule and activities for maintenance. Also record the maintenance requirement, if any, imposed by permits. Note that some manufacturers "over specify" maintenance to reduce claims of equipment failure. Unless a manufacturer agrees in writing to reduced maintenance, any deviation may be seen by the courts as being less than the appropriate standard of care.

Step 4   Identify the potential impact of failure for each piece of equipment: environmental impact (fish kill, discoloured water, visible or odorous emissions, etc.); requirement to perform clean-up; stoppage or reduction in operations; and regulatory response.

Step 5   Identify the potential probability of failure (e.g. once a year, every ten years, etc.) employing available records and published information on failures, and discussions with plant personnel.

Step 6   Translate the potential impacts for each vital point into costs (e.g. clean-up costs, civil litigation costs, regulatory fines, lost production, etc.).

Step 7   Estimate the overall risk by multiplying the aforementioned costs by the probability of the event.

Step 8   Develop and implement mitigation options for those risk considered to be of unacceptable costs.

Table 9.1
KEY STEPS OF EMERGENCY PLANNING SYSTEMS

Development of Emergency Plan:

- identification of planning coordinator and committee
- perform risk analysis
- identification of requirements of legislation and codes of practice
- identification of organization, roles, and responsibilities
- identification of available resources
- preparation of mutual aid agreements
- preparation of telephone list
- establishment of communication system
- development of public relations plan

Emergency Response:

- activation of emergency plan
- mobilization of resources
- defining appropriate response
- notification and reporting obligations
- establishing an emergency operations centre
- obtaining site security
- damage/claims assessments
- role of legal counsel and stress counselling

Administration:8

- training of personnel
- testing the plan
- implementation and distribution of plan
- periodic update and audit of plan
- obtaining management and potentially government approval of plan

Reference: CSA, 1991b
Note: CSA has recently released a National Standard of Canada document entitled "Emergency Planning for Industry (#2) (MIACC Partnership)" — CAN/CSA Z731-95

9.4 DOCUMENTATION

The documentation for an EMS can take many forms. An **environmental manual** should be prepared for each facility that should clearly define responsibilities for environmental issues and provide guidance to employees in performing their jobs.

The manual should include the following information:

- corporate environmental policy (discussed in Chapter 8)
- a brief summary of regulatory requirements (may include a diagram similar to Figure 2.1)
- an organization chart for environmental issues
- a brief description of responsibilities and internal reports
- plant specific policies (as discussed in Chapter 8)
- operating procedures and standards
- copies of pertinent permits
- a listing of reference material and companies that can provide environmental services

Policies and/or procedures should be developed that address air and noise emissions, water discharges, waste handling and disposal, spills/emergency response, training, special materials, external contact (government inspections and media), new products, capital expropriation, and assessment of waste carriers and disposal sites. It also may be appropriate to develop a policy on the company's commitment to providing legal services in the event of charges being laid against individual employees.

Procedures should also be developed for the operation of equipment and include permit requirements (limits and conditions) and internal performance limits. These internal performance limits, sometimes referred to as standards, should include both engineering and scientific requirements. Engineering standards would be those imposed on pollution control systems to ensure adequate operation whereas scientific standards relate to the prevention of an adverse effect in the natural environment.

Numeric standards include regulatory criteria or guidelines and objectives and/or internal company values. The latter can be more stringent than government values and used as "red flags" to alert operators to situations before exceeding regulatory values.

Some key points to remember when preparing an environmental manual are as follows:

- it must be easy to understand — avoid technical or legal language where possible
- it must be short and sweet — if it is difficult to lift, chances are it won't be
- it must be updated periodically — manuals that are not updated may lead to non-compliance with changing legislation

Familiarizing employees with the contents of the manual and linking the manual to the EMS are critical. The training component should be considered the "last" chapter of the manual when planning it. Without training, individuals typically believe the manual is just more paperwork and that it will make their job more difficult.

Chapter 10 presents additional information on the assessment, preparation, and presentation of training materials.

It is critical that operations personnel be involved in the process of obtaining **permits** from government agencies to ensure that in the application is correct and that they can achieve compliance with conditions set out in permit. If the proposed activity is significant and will have numerous operating conditions, it may be useful to request a draft copy of the permit for review and subsequent discussion with the regulatory agency prior to receiving the final copy.

It is also critical that the government agency be contacted at an early stage if the proposed process is unusual. Insufficient resources at some government agencies and requirements for public consultation on draft permits in some provinces may significantly increase the time required to obtain a permit.

Copies of finalized permits should be readily accessible to environmental management personnel and operators. It may be appropriate to post copies of the permit at the appropriate emission/discharge points to provide a better linkage between the operation of pollution control equipment and the conditions in the permit.

9.5 ONGOING MONITORING AND ESTIMATION

Ongoing monitoring may be used to assess the quality of emissions from stacks, water discharges and off-site groundwater migration, the quality of ambient air or receiving water body, and classification of waste streams. Monitoring programs should be developed, as needed, to comply with regulatory requirements and to assist in environmental control system evaluations. Critical factors to consider when developing a monitoring program include:

- regulatory requirements
- type of monitoring (calibration, confirmation versus ongoing assessment)
- statistical frequency of monitoring
- use of surrogate parameters
- quality assurance/quality control
- capital and operating cost

The term "calibration" refers to the use of sampling to assist in development of an estimation method for a particular source, whereas confirmation sampling is to confirm the relative accuracy of the estimated value.

Plant inspections should be performed on a periodic basis to ensure compliance. The inspection can be carried out by personnel working in the area or from adjacent areas. Checklists should be developed prior to the inspection to identify deficiencies.

Estimating emissions is commonly employed by industry when the process is relatively constant, accuracy is not required, and/or sampling cost are significant. Three methods are commonly used:

- engineering calculations — for emissions from tanks, lagoons, and/or landfills
- mass balance — for emissions when the majority of the chemical is purchased as opposed to being a by-product and releases to other media are limited
- emission factors — for emissions of particulate matter, acid gases, and by-products of processes

The United States Environmental Protection Agency has prepared data bases of emission factors on CD-ROM disks for frequently sampled parameters emitted from standard industrial processes and activities.

9.6 DATA STORAGE, ASSESSMENT, AND REPORTING

Data gathering is merely the first stage of data management. Once compiled, data can be assessed by being compared to conditions set out in permits, regulations, guidelines, or policies. Statistical analysis can be performed to determine trends and identify potential sources of elevated levels of contaminants.

Systems must be in place to "flag" potential non-compliance to identify trends which may lead to non-compliance, or identify potential impairment when regulatory limits have not been developed. These systems usually take the form of internal performance measures discussed in Section 9.4.

More and more companies are turning to electronic computer-based systems. Such a system can assist in more ways than merely being a repository for environmental data:

- The system can be used to track monitoring requirements and to remind sampling staff when, where, and what sampling is necessary.
- It can include automatic checking capabilities that flag or draw attention to results that are inconsistent with previous results, fail data integrity checks, or appear to be entered incorrectly or incompletely.
- It can include the numerical standards, criteria, and objectives being used to access compliance and directly compare the measured results to those points of comparison.

- The system should be able to generate reports suitable for internal and external uses that summarize results (using various formats including tables and graphs), highlight non-complying results, and identify trends in data over time.
- The system should have the capability to receive data from a Laboratory Information Management System (LIMS) and to transmit data to data-management systems operated by regulatory agencies.

An example of software being used by industrial and government facilities in Canada is the Environmental Data Manager (EDM) developed by Environmental Software Associates Ltd. EDM allows for the electronic input of data from a LIMS, automatic assessment of the data against permits, guidelines, and standards, and the export of data electronically to government programs (e.g. Ontario MIDES and Environment Canada's automated National Pollutant Release Inventory — NPRI — system).

The following factors should be considered when reviewing the potential of using a commercially available data management system.

- Does it have the flexibility to respond to the rapid changing nature of environmental regulations? Can the user make updates? How often does the vendor issue updates? Can the program be expanded or have new modules added?
- Is the system software compatible with your existing databases? Is the system software compatible with other pieces of software such as spreadsheets, word processors, and graphics packages? Does the software have the ability to generate forms or reports in formats suitable for being submitted directly to regulatory agencies?
- What level of technical support does the vendor offer? Does the vendor have the resources to address your questions or problems in a prompt manner?

9.7 INTERACTION WITH EXTERNAL STAKEHOLDERS

9.7.1 Reporting to Government Agencies

Environmental legislation in some jurisdictions requires companies to obtain permits, submit monitoring data, emission estimates and waste inventories, and provide notification of exceedances and spills to government agencies. It is therefore critical to perform the following tasks:

- identify reporting requirements (refer to Chapter 2)
- assign responsibilities to individuals for reporting (refer to Chapter 8)
- develop internal review process for all reports (whether generated internally or by a consultant) being submitted to a government agency to ensure that material is factual and does not include speculation

Communications given to one department/branch within a government agency may be provided to another during the course of an investigation. Therefore, it is important that matters dealing with potential non-compliance be reviewed, in some cases by legal counsel, prior to being submitted to government agency.

9.7.2 Government Inspections

All provinces have passed acts which provide designated representatives with the right to inspect sites or premises as part of investigations. Analogous powers of inspection are provided in federal legislation including the Canadian Environmental Protection Act (CEPA) and the Transportation of Dangerous Goods Act (TDGA). In this discussion, the term "Officer" is used to refer to representatives from provincial and federal agencies who have these powers of inspection.

The Officer is also responsible for obtaining evidence for prosecution. An Officer must have **reasonable cause** before exercising these powers. It may be difficult to determine if the Officer is restricting activities to those reasonably related to the administration of an act and its regulations, or whether, in fact, an investigation is taking place to obtain evidence for a prosecution.

In addition to the authority granted by legislation, Officers may in certain circumstances be required to obtain an Order of the Justice of the Peace or a search warrant. The latter is obtained by making a sworn declaration to the Justice of the Peace concerning the offense and the items being sought. Recent case law on the Canadian Charter of Rights and Freedoms strongly suggests that provincial Officers should not search premises to seize or obtain evidence of an offense without a search warrant or an order of a court.

In most provinces, an Officer may enter a business premise at any **reasonable time** to check for compliance with an act or regulation. What constitutes a reasonable time may vary with the circumstances. It is generally accepted that routine inspections should be conducted during normal business hours. In contrast, a search based on the suspicion of an offence may be reasonable even if carried out at other times of the day.

In most cases, government agencies will give a company notice of any incident or situation they are investigating. The company and government representatives should attempt to establish procedures for conducting any investigation such as when and where interviews are to be conducted.

If the time suggested by an Officer is not convenient, an alternative time may be requested by the company. It is not unreasonable to request that an inspection be delayed to allow the company to consult a lawyer.

If arrangements have not been made and an Officer arrives to investigate a situation, the Officer should be treated courteously and without delay. Some companies, fearing that incriminating evidence or practices may be uncovered, may refuse entry or assume an uncooperative attitude. This type of conduct may give rise to an charge of obstructing an Officer.

The Officer should be asked to show credentials and then asked questions concerning:

- the purpose of the investigation and/or the nature of the problem
- whether there is a specific date or series of dates that are of concern
- whether a specific location or source is under investigation
- the section of which Act or regulation may have been violated

If the responses indicate that the inspection is with regard to an investigation into a possible violation, copies of the responses should be sent to the company's legal counsel.

In Ontario, a separate branch of the Ministry of the Environment was formed in 1985 — the Investigations and Enforcement Branch (IEB) — to separate abatement and enforcement activities. The purpose of this branch is to investigate potential violations of environmental legislation and, where appropriate, prosecute.

An Officer may take photographs, conduct tests, or inspect equipment as long as the requests are reasonable. Nonrelated pictures should not be taken. To protect confidential business information and prevent the inclusion of extraneous information, the company should have the right to approve pictures used in reports.

All testing and sampling procedures should be reviewed to ensure that they were done properly and allow for a fair conclusion. It may be appropriate to take a duplicate sample and have the sample analyzed by an independent laboratory.

A list should be kept of all documents or photocopies provided to the government representatives.

It is preferable to designate one company representative to show the Officer the facility and coordinate responses to questions. The individual should be familiar with the legal implications of the inspection and should have a working knowledge of the facility. In addition, the employee should take careful notes of what is seen and photographed, who is interviewed and what is said, and sampling procedures and locations.

A company should try to prearrange the procedures used for interviews. Individuals should be briefed by the company in advance of an interview on their individual rights and what is required of them. In cases where this is not possible, or prearrangements have not been made for some other reason, individuals should be made aware of their individual rights at the beginning of the interview.

Individuals should approach interviews with the attitude that statements made may be used in a court of law whether or not the individual being interviewed is charged or not. Some guidelines to remember during an interview include:

1) Stick to the facts, do not speculate.
2) Make sure you understand the question or ask for clarification or a repeat of the question.
3) Take your time answering the questions.
4) Do not wander off topic.
5) Do not volunteer information.
6) If you do not know an answer, say so.
7) Take notes during the interview.

If the sole purpose of the questioning is to obtain evidence of an offense for the purpose of prosecution, a person may refuse to answer. An Officer cannot force a person into self-incrimination. If the Officer has reasonable or probable grounds to believe that the individual being interviewed has committed an offense, the Officer must recognize the rights against self-incrimination and give a warning. During the interview, an individual is required to give only the information that is pertinent to the investigation.

A company can be incriminated and convicted through statements made by an employee during the course of an inspection. Damaging statements given by employees must be made voluntarily without threat, promise, or inducement. Any threat to prosecute the individual employee if he or she doesn't give a statement would remove the voluntary nature of the statement.

An Officer may write a narrative of the answers while interviewing a person and ask the person to sign it as his or her own statement. The statement will be paraphrased in words selected by the Officer to highlight issues which the Officer feels are important. The statement may omit salient facts. None of the laws or regulations require individuals to sign or initial anything. The choice of whether to sign the document or not is up to the individual being interviewed.

9.7.3 Local Community and Non-Government Organizations

Facilities should be aware of concerns raised by the local community groups or non-government organizations (NGOs). Facilities located in areas with an active NGO may be required to implement more stringent control measures by government agencies, especially with regards to odour and dust control. A discussion of potential methods by which to receive input and provide feedback to concerns of the community and NGO is provided in Chapter 5.

REFERENCES

The Business Roundtable. November 1993. "Facility Level Pollution Prevention Benchmarking Study." Prepared with the AT&T Bell Laboratories QUality, Engineering, Software, and Technologies (QUEST) Benchmarking Group.

Canadian Manufacturing Association (CMA). 1990. "A Simplified Guide to Emergency Planning."

Canadian Standards Association (CSA). April 1994. "User's Guide to Environmental Life Cycle Assessment: LCA in Practice." CSA PLUS 1107-94.

_____ March 1994. "Environmental Life Cycle Assessment." CSA Z760-94.

_____ November 1991a. "Risk Analysis Requirements and Guidelines." CSA Q634-91.

_____ May 1991b. "Emergency Planning for Industry." CSA Z731-M91.

10

The Cultural Component

---

by
J.D. Phyper
Phyper & Associates Limited

10.1 THE ENVIRONMENTAL FACET OF CORPORATE CULTURE

All three of the principles endorsed in Chapter 1 recognize that the cultural dynamics of a company or organization are important to the design, operation, and success of an EMS. However, unlike the organization and operational components discussed in Chapters 8 and 9, the **cultural component** largely consists of intangibles that reveal themselves in characteristics such as morale, ethics, and respect.

Purchasing a new piece of pollution control equipment or redesigning an internal reporting system have often been easier tasks than improving the ways that people interact with one another or trying to ensure that people feel that they are making a meaningful contribution.

Numerous methods can be used to raise environmental awareness in individuals as well as within the company or organization. Three methods, discussed in subsequent sections of this chapter, include various forms of training, improving information systems, and linking incentives to performance objectives. The process of selecting which method(s) to use for a specific situation can be based on two general principles.

The first principle is to identify the inter-relationships between the environmental goals of the organization and the job requirements (or performance specifications) of individuals. For example, what do managers, technicians, shop floor workers, etc. need to be able to do their jobs in ways which will support the environmental goals of the department, facility, or company?

In most instances, there will be gaps between actual and optimal employee performance. The second principle is that all the factors affecting performance must be identified and any improvements or interventions planned accordingly. Four factors have been identified as causes of performance problems (Rossett, 1987, 1992):

- lack of knowledge and skills
- lack of motivation
- flawed work environment
- flawed incentives

Often, more than one of these factors is pertinent, and therefore combinations of solutions or methods of intervention are required. Three widely used forms of intervention foster changes in the environment facet of corporate culture:

- holding environmental training sessions or programs to address the lack of knowledge and skills
- communicating environmental training achievements to increase information sharing and to provide motivation
- linking compensation to environmental performance to align incentives to desired goals

This chapter examines the challenge of developing or raising the environmental awareness in an organization and doing so in a way that reaches both the CEO's office and the staff on the shop floor.

10.2 ENVIRONMENTAL TRAINING PROGRAMS

10.2.1 Content

The training of employees is critical to the successful implementation of environmental management activities, especially in departments or facilities with high staff turnover or where regulatory requirements are changing frequently. The contents of training courses can include one or more of the following general topics:

- regulatory requirements
- due diligence or reasonable care
- internal policies and procedures
- environmental auditing and site inspections
- proper handling, storage, and disposal of chemicals
- operation and maintenance of pollution control equipment
- spill prevention and response
- environmental awareness

The terms "due diligence" and "reasonable care" refer to the activities taken to prevent non-compliance. In the event of an incident, the organization may cite these activities as proof that it did everything "reasonable" to prevent the occurrence.

"Environmental awareness" training typically refers to non-technical discussions of the company's environmental policy, objectives, basic regulatory compliance requirements, and pollution prevention programs.

It is critical that the content of a training program be matched to the responsibilities and needs of the individuals being trained. For instance, it is of little benefit to have senior managers receive detailed training on the handling of chemicals or for shipping department staff to be trained extensively on due diligence.

10.2.2 Presentation

A wide spectrum of methods can be used to present training materials. Traditional methods include workshops, seminars, and exercises conducted in the field or at a training centre. Lessons on videocassettes and computer-based instruction have become almost as commonplace as written manuals.

Selecting a particular presentation method should be a function of the content of the training being performed and the resources that are available. Table 10.1 identifies preferred presentation methods for various environmental topics.

The duration of a course can last from an hour (e.g. due diligence presentation to senior executives) to a week (e.g. detailed course on environmental legislation for a complex facility).

A general rule of thumb is that the closer the individual is to operations, the more practical the course should be (e.g. more than 50% of the training provided to individuals responding to spills should be performed with actual equipment and in-field drills).

10.3 COMMUNICATING ENVIRONMENTAL ACHIEVEMENTS

10.3.1 Purpose

Both internal and external stakeholders need to be shown that a company is committed to the sound management of its environmental affairs. Stakeholders can include shareholders, financial institutions, workers, management, and the general public.

Ideally, a corporate environmental policy (see Section 8.1.1) should assist management and employees in deciding the right course of action when environmental issues need to be communicated. Copies of the environmental policy should be included with the annual report and be widely distributed within the company and prominently posted at the company facilities.

Sections 10.3.3 through 10.3.5 discuss three methods of communicating environmental information. Chapter 5, "Public Participation and Involvement," provides additional information on communicating with the public.

Table 10.1
PREFERRED TRAINING METHODS FOR VARIOUS ENVIRONMENTAL TOPICS

Method	Seminar	Workshop	Video cassettes	In-class cases	In-field cases/ drills	Computer-based instruction
Topic						
Regulatory requirements	X	X	X	X		X
Due diligence/ Reasonable care	X		X			
Organization policies/procedures	X	X	X			X
Auditing and site inspections	X	X	X	X	X	X
Chemical handling/ disposal	X	X	X		X	X
Spill prevention/ response	X	X	X	X	X	X
Environmental awareness	X	X	X			X

10.3.2 Identifying Useful Information

One of the major challenges to successful communication is determining the types of information that readers want and/or need. The Canadian Institute of Chartered Accountants recently suggested that this can be determined by assessing information in terms of four key characteristics (CICA, 1994):

Relevance - This is a function of stakeholders' needs. Critical issues include balancing positive and negative aspects; providing a way for readers to respond; achieving the right level of detail; balancing common interests against those of special-interest groups.

Reliability - Information needs to be accurate, capable of being independently verified, and reasonably free of errors and bias.

Understandability - The target audience needs to be able to understand the information that is being presented. The difficulty is that most environmental information is based upon scientific data and most users do not know how to relate it to the effects on the environment.

Comparability - Some readers will want to compare environmental performance data between different organizations and/or examine the performance of an organization over two or more time periods.

10.3.3. Internal/External Publications

In response to requests for information from stakeholders on environmental performance, growing numbers of corporations have taken to preparing **annual environmental reports** or environmental "progress" reports that address specific issues, goals, or actions. Examples of Canadian companies that have published annual reports summarizing environmental activities include Ontario Hydro, Dow Chemical Canada, Trans Alta Utilities Corporation, Avenor, Dupont Canada, Shell Canada Limited, Noranda Forest Inc., and Noranda Minerals Inc.

Several recent publications offer suggestions for the contents of this type of report:

- Canadian Chamber of Commerce — "A Guideline on Corporate Environmental Reporting" (1992)
- Canadian Institute of Chartered Accountants - "Reporting on Environmental Performance" (1994)
- Canadian Standards Association - "Environmental Performance Reporting" (1994)
- Deloitte Touche Tohmatsu International et al., "Coming Clean — Corporate Environmental Reporting" (1993)
- National Round Table on the Environment and the Economy - "Corporate Sustainable Development Reporting" (1993)

In general, industries substantially affected by regulation or environmental issues, or that choose to emphasize environmental issues as part of "green" marketing, tend to provide more comprehensive and detailed information on environmental issues.

The following four-step approach can be used to prepare an annual environmental report:

Step 1   Identify the information needs of stakeholders and readers (refer to Chapter 8).

Step 2   Decide on the communication method (e.g. part of the annual report or a separate document). If the information is to be incorporated within the annual report to stakeholders, it is important to note that comments will be limited to a few key indicators and be presented in a manner that complies with Generally Accepted Accounting Practices (GAAP).

Step 3   Decide if verification by a third party is required. Some stakeholders believe that independent opinions are necessary to add credibility to management's environmental performance claims. Conversely, there is a lack of environmental reporting standards, and changing scientific standards may reduce or even negate the contributions of such an opinion (CICA, 1994).

Step 4   Identify the types of information or performance indicators to be reported and determine when this information will be available. Table 10.2 lists key indicators based on a recent review of annual environmental reports.

10.3.4 Briefings, Seminars, and Site Tours for External Stakeholders

To better communicate environmental activities to external stakeholders, several facilities have "opened" their doors by providing briefings, seminars, and site tours. The Canadian Chemical Producers Association (CCPA) is seen as a leader in this field with its Responsible Care Program® which requires members to hold information sessions with the local community and, where possible, conduct site tours.

Three examples of special programs include:

- educational programs with local high schools, involving plant tours and seminars
- annual "open houses" to communicate environmental activities and, in particular, emergency response capability
- special seminars to industry associations on environmental projects undertaken by the company

10.3.5 Providing Information to the Media

Most managers would probably prefer that the media and the public leave them to do their jobs. Since it is highly likely that the media will persist, it is imperative that managers understand how to communicate effectively and to anticipate the sorts of information that are likely to be of greatest interest. While communication often becomes a source of confusion, the risks of avoiding the media may be far greater than those of working with them (Sandman, 1986).

It is important to remember that a reporter's job is news, not education; events, not issues or principles. The news is the "risky" thing that has happened and not the difficult determination of environmental impacts or risks. A reporter may seek answers to simple direct questions such as What happened? How did it happen? Who's to blame? and What are the authorities/company doing? The media focuses on the politics of risk rather than the science of risk (Sandman, 1986).

Table 10.2
KEY INDICATORS APPEARING IN ENVIRONMENTAL ANNUAL REPORTS

Aspect of Performance	Indicators
Compliance	- number of violations - number of charges - percentage of time or events where compliance is achieved - number of spills
Environmental Expenditures and Liabilities	- total dollars spent - site clean-up costs - pollution equipment cost
Environmental Management	- number of individuals trained - number of audits performed
Pollution Control Equipment	- number of installations - removal efficiencies
Air Emissions	- mass of pollutants released (possibly divided among specific types of pollutants such as greenhouse gases, ozone-depleting substances, or metals - number of odour/dust complaints
Water Discharges	- mass of pollutants released (possibly divided among specific types of pollutants such as suspended solids, metals, organic material - lethal concentration (LC50) of effluents - fresh water consumption rate
Waste Reduction	- total mass of solid waste and percent of pre-set targets or change relative to previous amounts - total mass of hazardous waste and percent of pre-set targets or change relative to previous amounts - total volume of liquid industrial waste - total amount of packaging material generated
Energy	- reduction of energy relative to past usage or expressed as a percentage of a pre-set target
Stakeholder Interaction	- number of meetings with local citizens - publication of newsletters
Special	- number of hectares or acres reforested - number of noise complaints

Reference: CICA, 1994

Environmental stories often turn into political stories in part because political content is more readily available and understood than technical content.

In responding to questions from the media or members of the public, keep the following points in mind:

- provide facts
- if you do not know the answer to a question, say so, but get back to the reporter
- remember that journalists' deadlines are measured in minutes, not months
- decide the main points in advance
- stress main points consistently and repetitively
- leave out technical qualifiers wherever possible or explain their importance to the discussion
- minimize the use of technical jargon and explain technical terms that are essential

The journalists will want the response to be on one side or another of a situation (i.e. safe versus unsafe, legal versus illegal). They do not want to dwell on the complex nuances of intermediate positions as the length of their news story seldom allows for a lengthy response. Managers, scientists, and technical staff often resent the pressure from journalists to dichotomize and simplify an issue.

10.3.6 Providing Information to the Public

Whether through regulatory requirement or as a result of voluntary programs, environmental information about a facility may have to be presented to the public. The CCPA has taken the bold step of establishing a "Community Right to Know Policy" in its Responsible Care® document. The policy recognizes the need and the right of the public to know the risks associated with the operations and products present in, or transported through, communities.

Successful communication begins with the realization that risk perception is predictable, that the public overreacts to certain sorts of risks and ignores others, and that you cannot know in advance whether the communication problem will be generated by panic or apathy (Sandman, 1986). There is no way to present risk data which is neutral, but only ways that are alarming or reassuring in varying degrees.

It is important to remember when communicating to the public that society has reached a near consensus that pollution is morally wrong. Some agencies are quick to realize this and deal with environmental risk in terms of "good-and-evil" instead of "costs-and-benefits."

The use of quantitative risk assessments, risk-benefit calculations, and risk comparisons are difficult for individuals to accept when they are being asked to bear the risks but someone else is making the decision. Consider the example of a town being selected as the future site of a hazardous waste treatment facility. The community, offended at this infringement of local autonomy, prepares to stop the facility by collecting information on the unacceptability of the site and initiates litigation. Both their anger and the legal process itself encourage community members to overestimate the risk of the proposed facility and to resist any argument that a package of mitigation, compensation, and incentives might actually yield a net gain in the community's health and safety, as well as its prosperity (Sandman, 1986).

People will participate more if they exercise some real control over an ultimate decision. In response to this need, regulatory agencies are trying to achieve public participation on various issues. Many previous public participation exercises have been perceived as being too little too late and often involving only draft decision. As a result, many members of the public believe that they will not be taken seriously.

Table 10.3 presents rules and guidelines published by the U.S. Environmental Protection Agency for effective risk communication. Rules and guidelines like these can be used as a foundation for a company's environmental communication program and lead to a constructive interaction with the community.

Chapter 5 provides additional information on communicating with the public.

10.4 LINKING COMPENSATION TO ENVIRONMENTAL PERFORMANCE

Compensation for environmental performance can be divided into monetary and non-monetary remuneration. Non-monetary compensation may include everything from verbal praise from senior management, the presentation of plaques and certificates, notices in internal newsletters, and awards banquets. An example of a highly successful non-monetary program is 3M's "3P" program (Pollution Prevention Pays) which is discussed in Chapter 12.

Monetary remuneration typically falls into the following categories: a) bonus payment based upon environmental performance, or b) a cash award based upon savings to the company.

The first type of remuneration is normally paid to members of environmental departments and/or plant managers and can be a function of the number of non-compliance items in the environmental audits/inspections, violations of environmental legislation, and/or environmental spills/incidents. For senior environmental personnel, the evaluation criteria may be related to corporate environmental objectives/targets, implementation of new programs, and company-wide compliance with environmental legislation and corporate policies and procedures.

The second type of compensation is usually an extension of existing programs to compensate workers for ideas leading to increased profitability of the company. The amount of remuneration may take the form of a percentage of the savings or a fixed value. If a system is selected which employs monetary compensation, especially for bonus payments, it is critical that the evaluation criteria be measurable, equitable (especially between plants), and clearly documented.

Table 10.3
EPA RULES AND GUIDELINES FOR EFFECTIVE RISK COMMUNICATION

Rule 1   ACCEPT AND INVOLVE THE PUBLIC AS A LEGITIMATE PARTNER
Guideline: Demonstrate your respect for the public and your sincerity by involving the community early, before important decisions are made. Make it clear that you understand the appropriateness of basing decisions about risks on factors other than the magnitude of the risk. Involve all parties that have an interest or a stake in the particular risk in question.

Rule 2   PLAN CAREFULLY AND EVALUATE PERFORMANCE
Guideline: Begin with clear, explicit objectives such as providing information to the public, motivating individuals to act, stimulating emergency response, or contributing to conflict resolution. Classify the different subgroups in your audience. Direct your communication at specific subgroups. Recruit spokespersons who are good at presentation and interaction. Train your staff including technical staff in communication skills; rewarding outstanding performance. Whenever possible, pre-test your messages. Carefully evaluate your efforts and learn from your mistakes.

Rule 3   LISTEN TO YOUR AUDIENCE
Guideline: Do not make assumptions about what people know, think, or want done about risks. Take the time to find out what people are thinking. Use techniques such as interviews, focus groups, and surveys. Let all parties that have an interest or a stake in the issue be heard. Recognize people's emotions. Let them know that you understand their point of view, addressing their concerns as well as yours. Recognize the "hidden agendas," symbolic meanings, and broader economic or political considerations that often underlie and complicate the task of risk communication.

Rule 4 BE HONEST, FRANK, AND OPEN

Guideline: State your credentials, but do not ask or expect to be trusted by the public. If you do not know an answer or are uncertain, say so. Get back to people with answers. Admit mistakes. Disclose risk information as soon as possible (emphasizing any appropriate reservations about reliability). If in doubt, lean toward sharing more information, not less — or people may think you are hiding something. Discuss data uncertainties, strengths, and weaknesses, including the ones identified by other credible sources. Identify worst-case estimates as such, and cite ranges of risk estimate when appropriate.

Rule 5 COORDINATE AND COLLABORATE WITH OTHER CREDIBLE SOURCES

Guidelines: Closely coordinate all inter- and intra-organizational communications. Devote effort and resources to the slow, hard work of building bridges with other organizations. Use credible intermediaries. Try to issue communications jointly with other trustworthy sources such as university scientists, physicians, trusted local officials, and opinion leaders.

Rule 6 MEET THE NEEDS OF THE MEDIA

Guideline: Be open with and accessible to reporters. Respect their deadlines. Provide information tailored to the needs of each type of media, such as graphics and other visual aids for television. Provide background material for the media on complex risk issues. Follow up on stories with praise or criticism, as warranted. Try to establish long-term relationships with editors and reporters.

REFERENCES

Canadian Chamber of Commerce (CCC). 1992. "A Guideline to Corporate Environmental Reporting."

Canadian Chemical Producers' Association (CCPA). Not dated. "Responsible Care; A Total Commitment".

Canadian Institute of Chartered Accountants (CICA). 1994. "Reporting on Environmental Performance." Prepared in association with the Canadian Standards Association, Financial Executives Institute Canada and International Institute for Sustainable Development.

Canadian Standards Association (CSA). 1994. Environmental Performance Reporting. CSA Z765.

Deloitte Touche Tohmatsu International, International Institute for Sustainable Development and Sustainability. 1993. "Coming Clean – Corporate Environmental Reporting."

National Round Table on the Environment and the Economy. March 1994. "Corporate Sustainable Development Reporting in Canada."

Rossett, A. 1992. "Analysis of Human Performance Problems." In H.D. Stolovitch and A.G. Keeps, eds., *Handbook of Human Performance Technology*. San Francisco, CA: Jossey-Bass. Pp. 32-49.

———— 1987. *Training Needs Assessment*. Englewood Cliffs, NJ: Educational Technology Publications.

Sandman, P.M. November 1986. "Explaining Environmental Risk". U.S. Environmental Protection Agency, Office of Toxic Substances, Washington, D.C.

11

Environmental Audits

by
J.D. Phyper, Phyper & Associates Limited
Brett Ibbotson, Angus Environmental Limited

11.1 THE CANADIAN CONTEXT

11.1.1 Defining the Environmental Audit

During the past several years, the term "environmental audit" (EA) has been used to describe various types of environmental studies.

The numbers of EAs being performed has grown rapidly, and confusion has set in over terminology, tasks, and the qualifications needed to be an environmental auditor. To help clarify this situation, the Canadian Standards Association (CSA), in association with the Canadian Environmental Auditing Association (CEAA), prepared a document entitled *Guidelines for Environmental Auditing: Statement of Principles and General Practices* (CAN/CSA Z751-94). This document provides an overview of the principles and practices that are applicable to all types of environmental audits and defines an EA as *a systematic process of objectively obtaining and evaluating evidence regarding a verifiable assertion about an environmental matter, to ascertain the degree of correspondence between the assertion and established standards and criteria, and then communicating the results to the client.*

A verifiable assertion is a declaration or statement about a specific subject which is supported by documented factual data.

The definition is distinctly different than that of an environmental site assessment (see CSA Z768-94), and does not encompass internal plant inspections performed by facility personnel or on-site monitoring programs.

According to the proposed principles, only verification sampling should be performed during the audit. It is recommended that these principles and practices be followed to ensure auditor objectivity and professional competence and due care, and that well-defined and systematic procedures and relevant standards and measures are being used.

The CSA is currently working on developing detailed practices and procedures for EAs. It is anticipated that these practices and procedures for conducting an EA will become generally accepted. The voluntary guidelines on EAs are part of a series of documents under development by the CSA dealing with various aspects of EMS.

11.1.2 Relationship to Regulatory Requirements

Changes to provincial environmental legislation and the Canadian Environmental Protection Act in the late 1980s delineated the responsibilities of corporate officers and directors for communicating information and instructions through the management structure of an organization, and for arranging training, supervision, and monitoring so that adverse effects to the environment are prevented. To reduce potential liability and ensure ongoing compliance, senior management of numerous companies have initiated environmental auditing programs. Recent court decisions (see Chapter 3) and the publication of environmental management standards by various organizations (see Chapter 7) have reinforced the need to perform environmental audits.

Most large industries in Canada perform periodic audits of their operations. The frequency of auditing and procedures employed in the audit may differ, but there is a growing consensus that it is an integral part of an EMS.

11.1.3 Accreditation

The CEAA is an independent association of individuals dedicated to the development of environmental auditing as a profession. The association encourages the development of the profession of environmental auditing and the improvement of environmental management of Canadian private and public organizations through the creation and application of generally accepted environmental auditing principles and standards. The CEAA is currently assessing the accreditation of environmental auditors. It is anticipated that an accreditation system will be in place in late 1995.

11.2 INTERNATIONAL AUDITING ACTIVITIES

Several international organizations have prepared, or are in the process of preparing, guidelines/specifications for EAs. These include:
- International Organization for Standardization (ISO), proposed 14 000 series
- European Community Eco-Management and Audit Scheme
- National Environmental Auditors Registration Board (United Kingdom)

- Environmental Auditing Roundtable (United States)
- Environmental Auditing Institute (United States)
- Environmental Auditing Foundation (United States)

The International Organization for Standardization (ISO)/Strategic Advisory Group on Environment (SAGE) is preparing a draft standard on environmental auditing which includes the following draft definition of an EA: *A systematic, documented verification process of objectively obtaining and evaluating evidence to determine whether specified environmental activities, events, conditions, management systems, or information about these matters, conform with audit criteria, and communicating the results of this process to the client.*

The following standards are currently in draft form:

ISO 14 010   Guidelines for Environmental Auditing — general principles of environmental auditing

ISO 14 011-1 Guidelines for Environmental Auditing: Audit Procedures, Part I — auditing of environmental management systems

ISO 14 012   Guidelines for Environmental Auditing — qualifications criteria for environmental auditors

ISO 14 050   Environmental Management — vocabulary

More standards in this series are to be prepared. The *ISO Guidelines for Auditing Quality Systems* (ISO 10 011) may be a useful reference until the EA guidelines are available.

The European Union (EU), formerly the European Community, recently adopted a proposal for a Council Regulation allowing voluntary participation by companies in its Eco-Management and Audit Scheme.

The objective of the Council Regulation is to promote continuous improvement in the environmental performance of industrial activities by:

- the establishment and implementation of environmental policies and programs on management systems
- regular environmental auditing, and
- the provision of information on environmental performance to the public (Keyworth, 1994)

The policy of continuous improvement in environmental performance is qualified with the clause that the commitment is made with a view to reducing environmental impacts to levels not exceeding those corresponding to the "economically viable application of best available technology."

The EAs are to be performed every three years and will involve a comprehensive analysis of the environmental issues and impacts, and performance relating to a site. Following the audit, an environmental statement regarding the performance of a company's environmental activities must be made public. The audit methodology and procedures currently must be undertaken in accordance with the guidelines set out in ISO 10 011 and the principles and requirements of the Council Regulation. It is anticipated that ISO 14 011 will be adopted by the EU for this purpose once it has been finalized.

11.3 PRE-AUDIT DECISIONS

11.3.1 Prerequisites

Regardless of the reason(s) for undertaking an EA, there are several prerequisite elements that need to be in place if the full benefits of the audit are to be realized. Whenever a company decides that an EA is to be performed, it is necessary that:

- the audit is supported by the company's senior management
- the audit team is given the authority, resources, and training to conduct a thorough and proper job
- the audit receives good cooperation from staff at the facility to be audited, and
- the company's management is prepared to respond to any deficiencies identified during the audit

ISO 14 010 recommends that the auditor should not undertake an audit if, in the auditor's opinion there is not sufficient or appropriate information about the subject matter of the audit, or there are not adequate resources to support the audit process.

11.3.2 Objectives, Scope, and Boundary Conditions

The objectives, scope, and boundary conditions of an EA will depend upon who is requesting the audit and the reasons why the audit is to be undertaken. These aspects need to be conveyed to the auditor before the audit begins. Uncertainties in the scope of the EA may result in large variances in quotations to perform the work, or the writing of a report which does not respond to the objectives of the client.

Objectives will normally make reference to the types of criteria to be employed (e.g. compliance with environmental legislation or conformity to published EMS standards, industrial codes of practices, and corporate policies and procedures). In the case of an EMS audit, the objectives may also include determining the suitability and effectiveness of the way the EMS has been implemented. The objectives should be clearly documented prior to initiating the EA.

The **scope** should define the activities required to meet the audit's objectives and summarize the boundary conditions discussed below. As a minimum, an EA report will present findings. The extent to which the findings are translated into conclusions, recommendations, and/or the development of an action plan should be discussed in advance with the client and defined in the scope of the work.

Boundary conditions identify what is to be audited and may draw attention to specific items that are to be included or excluded. For example, the boundary conditions for an EMS audit could include the following:

- section of company to be assessed (e.g. facility and/or corporate)
- departments (e.g. inclusion of purchasing)
- time period (i.e. current and/or past operations)
- on-site subcontractors/lessees
- interaction with government agencies
- involvement of third parties, and
- inclusion/exclusion of occupational issues
- development of an action plan

It is important that the role of the relevant boundary conditions be documented clearly in the scope of the EA.

11.3.3 Types of Environmental Audits

Environmental audits can be divided into several broad categories according to the type of material being audited or the objective of undertaking the EA.

A **compliance audit** is directed toward determining whether or not a facility meets all of its current environmental regulatory requirements. The requirements can be subdivided into legislation which is legally binding (e.g. federal and provincial acts, regulations, permits, standards, and municipal by-laws; and potentially non-legally binding objectives, codes of practices, and criteria and guidelines developed by government agencies. Failure to comply may result in fines or other penalties such as the revocation of permits, issuance of control orders, adversarial relations with regulatory agencies, court injunctions, and even criminal prosecution of corporate officials.

An **environmental management system audit** is a systematic and documented verification process of objectively obtaining and evaluating evidence to determine:

- conformity of an organization's EMS to audit criteria (typically includes a corporation's policies and procedures and published EMS standards)
- effectiveness of an organization's EMS in achieving that organization's policies and procedures

An **environmental statement audit** involves a critical review of a company's publicly available environmental statement. Typically, the environmental statement contains "an assessment of all the significant environmental issues of relevance to the activities concerns" as well as a summary of data on emissions, waste generation, raw materials consumption, energy and water use, and noise (Keyworth, 1994).

11.3.4 Audit Confidentially

Two issues related to confidentiality can arise during an EA. The first is related to **confidentiality between an auditor and the client**. Sensitive information collected during an EA may impact upon a company's competitiveness and reputation if passed along to competitors, members of the financial community, potential purchasers, or the press. The auditor should not, without the expressed approval of the client, disclose information or documents obtained during the EA, or contained in the final report, to any third party.

The second confidentiality issue concerns the **accessibility of audit reports** by government agencies or through court-directed disclosure. Both industry and regulators continue to struggle with this issue. Environment Canada recognizes that EAs are an effective management tool for assessing environmental compliance. Under the Canadian Environmental Protection Act (CEPA), audit reports may be required when federal inspectors or investigators have reasonable grounds to believe that:

- an offense has been committed
- the EA findings will be relevant to a particular violation, necessary to its inspector/investigation specialist, and required as evidence, or
- the information being sought cannot be obtained from other sources through the exercise of the inspector's or investigator's powers (Environment Canada, 1988)

Environment Canada has stated that an EA must not be used to shelter monitoring/compliance or other information that would otherwise be accessible to inspection under CEPA. In addition, the demand for access to an EA during an investigation can be made under the authority of a search warrant. An exception can be made when the delay necessary in obtaining a warrant would likely result in danger to the environment or human health, or the loss or destruction of evidence (Environment Canada, 1988).

Several provinces have adopted similar policies (e.g. Ontario Ministry of Environment and Energy) or are in the process of developing these.

Prior to initiating an EA, a client should discuss the issue of confidentiality with legal counsel. Two schools of thought on the confidentiality of EAs revolve around the concepts of attorney-client privilege and due diligence (or reasonable care).

Option 1: Solicitor-Client Privilege

Several companies use "solicitor-client" privilege when conducting an EA and subsequently for restricting access to the audit report. To be in force, the lawyer must take the lead role and ensure that the following conditions are met:

- the information/study must be requested by the corporation and/or officers and directors
- the request must be in anticipation of litigation
- the advice given by the lawyer must be considered legal advice
- the information/study must be delivered by the lawyer to the corporation and/or officers and directors
- the information/study must be kept confidential

The above conditions do allow for an outside consultant and/or corporate staff to assist the lawyer in the preparation of the report.

Counsel responsible for an EA should develop procedures for maintaining confidentiality and ensure that those procedures are followed by everyone who participates in the audit (see also Section 3.6).

One disadvantage of this approach is that it may deny report access to individuals who will implement the corrective action. To correct negative findings, several companies are preparing two reports: an EA report and an action plan. The latter does not reference the area of non-compliance, but does identify activities that will rectify the problems.

Option 2: Due Diligence (Reasonable Care)

Several companies are choosing the due diligence option (as opposed to solicitor-client privilege) on the premise that the benefits flowing from an auditing program outweigh any negative concerns associated with disclosure (Villeneuve, 1989). Advocates of this approach can argue that a defense of due diligence based on an active EA program which critically and impartially identifies and corrects environmental deficiencies may be the best defense.

11.4 PRE-VISIT ACTIVITIES

11.4.1 Selecting the Audit Team

An essential element of all EAs is that the auditors must be independent of the activities being audited, and reasonably free from bias and influence throughout the process. The auditors may be completely external to the company or in-house personnel provided that their objectivity is not compromised. The use of in-house personnel will not jeopardize independence if certain criteria such as auditor proficiency and non-accountability to the facility are met. Auditors must disqualify themselves when there is an actual or apparent conflict of interest (CAN/CSA Z751-94).

If EAs are to be performed on a regular basis, it may be appropriate to select and train several individuals (i.e. create a pool of auditors) from different facilities to audit their counterparts.

The use of external auditors, especially for a first audit, can be beneficial. External auditors also can be used to train internal audit staff. It may also be appropriate to have external consultants perform periodic audits to assess the adequacy of the internal audit program depending upon the degree of potential non-compliance and regulatory changes.

As discussed in Section 11.1.3, the Canadian Environmental Audit Association (CEAA) is currently assessing accreditation of environmental auditors.

Audit team members should be selected based upon the scope and type of audit to undertaken. Audit team members should include professionals with appropriate specialist skills. Depending upon the type of audit, these skills may include:

- expertise in environmental affairs and policy
- regulatory affairs expertise
- management systems expertise
- specific environmental and engineering expertise
- scientific expertise such as that possessed by biologists, chemists, toxicologists, or hydrogeologists
- familiarity with operations

If the audit is to assess compliance, the team must collectively understand the operations of the facility or company from a technical perspective and also be familiar with the applicable environmental laws and regulations.

The responsibilities of each member of the team must be clearly established. One of the members of the team must be appointed as the lead auditor. The leader should have a general level of familiarity with the facility and auditing principles and practices, and leadership qualities to ensure that audit objectives are met.

The availability of team members for the required time period must be unequivocal. The amount of time required to audit a facility will depend on the objective of the audit, the size of the facility and its complexity, as well as the number of people on the audit team. A two-person team may need two to four days to audit a small or medium-size chemical plant, while a four-member team may require two to five days for a larger facility.

11.4.2 Identification of Audit Criteria

Audit criteria are defined as the policies, practices, procedures, and requirements against which the auditor compares collected evidence about the subject. Depending upon the type of audit to be undertaken, the criteria may include — but may not be limited to — federal and provincial environmental acts, regulations, standards, policies, guidelines, codes of practices, objectives, and municipal by-laws; judges' rulings related to EMS; industrial codes of practice; published guidelines and standards on EMS; and the organization's policy requirements and internal codes of practice.

It may be useful to review rulings on what constitutes due diligence in

Canadian courts, especially for facilities located in the province in which the decision applies. Chapter 3 summarizes recent rulings.

Industrial codes of practice should be used to assess operations for which minimal legislation exists (e.g. in some provinces little if any legislation exists for the storage of non-petroleum products). Codes of practice also should be used if the company's membership is a function of compliance with codes of practice (e.g. members of the Canadian Chemical Producers Association (CCPA) prescribe to the Responsible Care Program®). Codes of practice are discussed further in Chapter 7.

It is critical that the most recent versions of legislation and regulations be used. During the past ten years, many regulatory requirements have changed and widespread changes to legislation are expected. An EA performed without an appreciation of the relevant legislation may fail to identify non-compliance situations. Software is available which contains regulations for all Canadian jurisdictions (see Section 9.6).

11.4.3 Develop an Audit Plan

A plan should be developed for collecting evidence that uses procedures relevant to the objectives of the audit. The plan should contain the objectives of the audit, scope, and boundary conditions; the proposed schedule; names of team members; the evaluation criteria to be used; the auditing procedures; report format, structure, and expected date of issue; and confidentiality requirements. The criteria should be referenced and documented. The audit plan should be communicated to the client allowing for constructive review.

Clearly understood protocols should be implemented to ensure consistency in information gathering and interpretation. The protocols much ensure that only "verifiable assertions" are recorded — a declaration or statement about a specific subject matter which is supported by documented factual data. Much of the information gathered during an audit initially may be recorded on checklists or other types of working documents.

It may also be appropriate to assess the **audit risk** (i.e. the probability of reaching an incorrect conclusion before an audit is undertaken). The level of risk is determined by the type of audit, the objectives of the audit, as well as the materiality, extent, and nature of the collected data and evidence. An example of an audit risk is the practice of randomly selecting transportation manifests to assess compliance. Risks during an EMS audit could include the absence of plant personnel due to vacation, interdepartmental rivalries, or conflicts between union and management (in particular when contracts are being negotiated). Once the potential risks are identified, the audit plan and level of investigation can be formulated so that the risk is reduced to an agreed-upon level.

11.4.4 Working Documents

Working documents are used to record EA findings and results. These documents may include:

- checklists for documenting findings and corresponding references
- methodologies used for evaluating particular components of the audit (e.g. elements of an EMS)
- records of meetings and interviews

Questions in a compliance audit checklist should be worded in such a way that they can be answered "yes" or "no." This allows the audit team to assess quickly and summarize non-compliance with legislative criteria or non-conformity with other criteria. In the case of an EMS audit, the questions may be worded in such a manner that the answers indicate the quality of the EMS (e.g. absent, unsatisfactory, satisfactory, and excellent).

The checklist should require all responses to be referenced. The protocols should document how references are to be recorded (e.g. numerically numbered and presented at the back of the checklists) and whether copies of all pertinent parts of documents (letters, reports, and pictures) indicating non-compliance with legislation or non-conformance with EMS standards or codes of practices are to be copied and attached to the audit report.

The audit procedures should also include **tests** to assess specific items on the checklists. For example, the number of transportation manifests to be randomly selected and reviewed should be identified. The use of specific statistically sound test methods can allow the audit to be conducted in a reasonable amount of time while minimizing the audit risk.

11.4.5 Data Request and Review for a Compliance Audit

Ideally, the audit team should have been provided with various types of information before actually visiting a facility. The request for information will be strongly influenced by the type, scope, and boundary conditions of the audit.

Foremost among the data that should be provided in advance is a **comprehensive site plan**. The plan should show the locations of all buildings, storage and on-site transportation facilities, waste storage/treatment/disposal facilities, waste discharge or release points, environmental monitoring equipment, sewer connections, site drainage, neighbouring properties, and environmentally sensitive areas. Environmentally sensitive areas can include drinking water supplies, streams, wetlands, parks, areas frequented by birds or animals, and any areas used by endangered species.

A **process and emissions block diagram** showing the physical or chemical processes conducted on the site, the handling of raw materials brought onto the site, and all points where waste products (solids, liquids, or vapours) leave the facility also should be provided to the team, or the team should produce one. A typical block diagram is presented on

Figure 11.1. A block diagram is critical since it is impossible to assess compliance if all the emissions or waste streams leaving the facility have not been identified.

Figure 11.1
TYPICAL BLOCK DIAGRAM OF EMISSIONS,
DISCHARGES, AND WASTE STREAMS

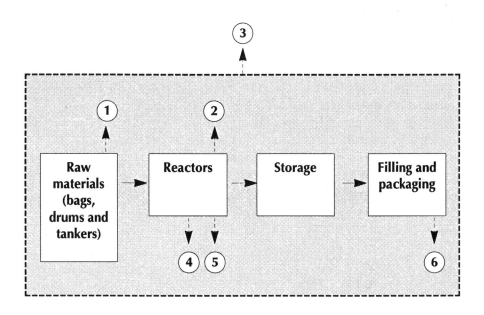

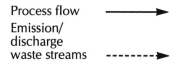

Process flow ⟶

Emission/
discharge
waste streams - - - - - - - ▸

1. Duct from raw material storage
2. Stack for reactor discharge
3. Fugitive emission to atmosphere
4. Water discharge to sanitary sewer
5. Solid waste
6. Spoiled product for off-site disposal

All documentation relating to **previous environmental inspection reports** must be collected. Notices of complaints, violations, and prosecutions should also form port of the pre-audit materials. The audit team should be provided with **hazardous materials reports** that identify the locations of materials such as asbestos insulation, equipment that contains PCBs, radioactive materials, or solvents.

Depending upon the scope and boundary conditions of the EA, it may be appropriate to contact pertinent government agencies to obtain copies of available Certificates of Approval/Permits, waste registration information, complaints and orders, and to discuss any concerns they may have with the facility. A similar request can be made of the municipal representatives to identify potential problems with discharges to sewer system and noise levels.

Travel arrangements may need to be made along with arranging for **permission to inspect** the facility. In most instances, an initial meeting with plant personnel to discuss the audit and a tour of the facility should be set up in advance. The availability of plant personnel must also be established prior to the audit.

At many types of facilities, various forms of safety equipment or special security passes are needed. Safety equipment may range from hard hats and safety glasses to respirators and hazard suits. Passes may be required to ensure security and also safety in the event of an accident. Arrangements must be made prior to the site visit.

11.4.6 Data Request and Review for an EMS Audit

The types of information which auditors may request and review before conducting an EMS audit can include:

- corporate organization chart
- environmental policies and procedures
- environmental operating standards
- environmental reporting chart (normal operations and during incidents)
- copy of internal/external environmental reports
- copy of corporate/plant environmental newsletter, brochures, etc.
- documentation relating to previous audits or reviews
- documentation on previous incidents, non-complying measurements, charges, and convictions

11.5 ON-SITE ACTIVITIES

11.5.1 Opening Meeting and Orientation Tour

A meeting between the audit team and appropriate representatives of the facility being audited should be the first on-site activity. The meeting should introduce the audit team to the auditee's management, allow the groups to review and discuss the scope and objectives of the audit, provide a short summary of the methods and procedures to be used, establish official communication links between team and auditee, identify those personnel who have a responsibility for environment activities and their role in the audit, and confirm the time and date of the closing meeting.

Following this meeting, it may be appropriate to perform an orientation tour to provide an overview of the facility and its operations. The tour is relatively brief and auditors should note areas of concern where further follow-up is required. A site plan should be taken with the audit team as part of the orientation.

The activities described in Sections 11.5.2 through 11.5.4 should all be seen as methods by which to collect **evidence** during the audit. "Evidence" is defined in draft ISO documentation as "qualitative or quantitative verifiable information, records, or statements of fact, based on interviews, examination of documents, observation of activities and condiitons, measurements, tests, or other means within the scope of the audit." Information collected during any audit activities should be tested to an appropriate extent by acquiring corroborating information during another activity.

11.5.2 Record Review

A major component of most EAs is the review of environmental records. All records relevant to questions posed by audit criteria — typically questions on the audit checklist — must be reviewed. In the case of an EMS audit, the review must include the presence or absence of the EMS component and its adequacy.

Depending upon the scope of the audit, records to review may include waste manifests and inventories, data for discharges or releases to the environment, the performance logs of environmental control equipment, calibration reports for measuring devices, written environmental procedures and policies, the results of environmental monitoring efforts, Certificates of Approval or control orders issued by regulatory agencies, and reports of unusual or unscheduled events.

If an EMS audit is being performed, it may be appropriate to examine the basis of the monitoring program and the procedures for ensuring effective quality control of the sampling and measurement procedures.

The review of environmental records can be very time-consuming. The practices and theory from financial accounting can be used to advantage in some instances. For example, the review of manifests for hazardous goods or liquid industrial waste can be time-consuming if every document must be reviewed. Instead, a representative sample of the documentation can be retrieved from the files and reviewed for compliance. As discussed in Section 11.4.5, the number of manifests to be randomly selected should be identified in the audit plan.

Care must be taken to check for any major additions, alternations, or modifications that have occurred since certificates or permits were originally issued. These types of changes may require either an amendment to a current approval or the obtaining of a new permit. Note that in some provinces, sources which have not been modified or altered may be exempt from requiring a permit if constructed before a certain date. They must still be operated, however, in compliance with appropriate legislation covering the quality of discharges/emissions.

11.5.3 Site Investigation

The activities performed during the site investigation are a function of the type of EA. In the case of a compliance audit, all information which indicates potential non-compliance with legislation is relevant (e.g. operation of continuous sampler as per discharge regulation or presence of visible sheen on discharge).

The site investigation may include all operations, equipment, and storage facilities, all pollution control equipment, flow measurement devices, and monitoring equipment (on-line and continuous samplers), and all points where wastes are discharged, removed, or released to the environment. All existing and potential hazards must be noted. The actual information to be collected will be dictated by the questions listed on the audit checklists.

In the case of an EMS audit, the site visit can be seen as a tool to investigate the adequacy of the EMS. The site visit should allow for the "symptoms" of "problems" with the EMS to be identified. The following is an example of a symptom versus an EMS problem (Phyper and McDougall, 1994):

Symptom   *Potential Problem*

Spillage   *Training* of personnel both in terms of regulatory requirements and corporate policy on pollution prevention; *internal reporting* of past spillage to senior management to identify need for additional resources to rectify a problem; *allocation of resources* once a need is identified.

All team members should make sure that they have the appropriate safety equipment to enter all parts of a facility (i.e. hard hat, safety glasses, ear protection, etc.)

11.5.4 Interviews with Plant Personnel

Interviews should be conducted with plant personnel, plant management, and corporate personnel depending upon the scope of the audit or organization of the company (Phyper and McDougall, 1994).

Plant personnel who are aware of current and historical site conditions should be interviewed. Plant personnel may have important knowledge of past chemical and waste storage sites, above/below ground tanks, and spills. It is important to talk to plant personnel who have been at the facility or operation for several years. Former operators may also be interviewed.

The degree of training received by staff to operate pollution control equipment, respond to environmental incidents, and their knowledge of environmental regulations should be assessed during the interviews.

Examples of non-plant personnel who may be interviewed include staff from the corporate environmental management, purchasing, and human resources departments. The purchasing department may be involved to assess the appropriateness of checks and balances on waste disposal companies and haulers or the screening of "environmentally unfriendly" chemicals. Human resources may be contacted during the review of training requirements and records.

Checklists should be used during interviews to ensure that all areas are covered and to confirm or identify discrepancies with information collected during a site tour and record reviews.

11.5.5 Exit Meeting

An exit meeting should be held upon the completion of site-related activities. At this meeting, the key observations and findings should be reported. It also provides the opportunity for site management to point out errors or misconceptions in the audit team's work at a time and place where further verification can be undertaken at a minimal cost.

11.6 POST-SITE VISIT ACTIVITIES

11.6.1 Preparing the Audit Report

The report should be based on the review of the pre-audit materials, the site tour, the review of environmental records, and interviews with plant personnel. As a minimum, the report should describe the objectives and scope of the audit, the procedures and criteria used, the audit team members and audit date, and present the **audit findings**. The audit findings are the correspondence between the collected evidence and the agreed-upon criteria.

Conclusions and/or recommendations may be provided if stipulated in the scope of work. All findings should be fully supported by back-up documentation. Any major obstacles encountered in performing the audit should also be documented.

If the audit was performed under lawyer-client privilege, the draft and final report must be submitted directly to the lawyer. The lawyer can then assess potential non-compliance issues and provide legal advice to the client.

If the report has not been prepared under lawyer-client privilege, it should be marked "preliminary" or "draft" until plant management and legal counsel have had a opportunity to review it and make written comments. The distribution of the report usually will be determined by plant, divisional, or corporate management, and/or corporate environmental staff with some input from legal counsel.

All working papers, procedures used, techniques applied, and the completed audit checklist should be retained along with the final report by the auditor for several years in a secure location. In the case of an audit performed under lawyer-client privilege, all supporting materials should be labelled "confidential and privileged" and kept in a secure location.

11.6.2 Post-Audit Activities

Senior management should be made aware of all audit findings. Ideally, a summary table of the findings should be provided to senior management along with comments from legal counsel if areas of non-compliance have been encountered. If stipulated in the scope of work, cost estimates and a proposed schedule to implement corrective action for areas of non-compliance may be prepared.

The preparation and implementation of an action plan is essential for an effective audit program. In essence, it closes the loop and ensures that all deficiencies are corrected in a timely and cost-effective manner.

Little good is accomplished if the paper trail of positive responses does not result in specific actions. In some cases, inaction on the findings can be damaging. Procedural controls cost little to implement, and large capital projects can be implemented in phases.

11.7 THE FUTURE OF ENVIRONMENTAL AUDITS

Environmental audits have become an essential component of an EMS and may be critical in establishing the defense of due diligence or reasonable care. Recent publications by the Canadian Standards Association (CAN/CSA Z751-94) and similar organizations in Europe and the United States, reinforce the need to perform environmental audits using recognized principles and practices.

Generally, these principals and practices require the use of trained auditors who are independent of the activities being audited, and who follow protocols to provide verifiable assertions about compliance with legislation and/or conformance with company policies and published EMS standards. It is anticipated that in time these principles and practices will be become "generally accepted" — analogous to those employed in financial audits.

Table 11.1
CHECKLIST FOR PERFORMING AN
ENVIRONMENTAL AUDIT

Pre-Visit Activities
- Determine the objective, scope, and boundary conditions of the audit
- Organize audit team and schedule
- Identify audit criteria
- Develop audit plan
- Ensure that client is in agreement with components of audit plan
- Request and review information from the facility
- Request and review information from the government agencies if acceptable to client
- Schedule site visit

On-Site Activities
- Conduct opening meeting and orientation tour
- Review all records dealing with environmental compliance and performance
- Perform site investigation
- Conduct interviews with site personnel
- Conduct exit meeting

Post-Audit Activities
- Prepare audit report
- Prepare action plan if stipulated by client

REFERENCES

Canadian Standards Association 1994. *Guidelines for Environmental Auditing: Statement of Principles and General Practices.* CAN/CSA Z751-94.

Environment Canada. May 1988. *Canadian Environmental Protection Act: Enforcement and Compliance Policy.*

International Organization for Standardization (ISO) and Strategic Advisory Group on Environment (SAGE). October 5, 1994. *Environmental Auditing.* Draft text.

Keyworth, C.J. 1994. "Comparison of the European and U.S. Approach to Environmental Auditing." Air and Waste Management Association 87th Annual Meeting and Exhibition, Cincinnati, Ohio, June 19-24.

Phyper, J.D., and J.D. McDougall, 1994. "Audit Criteria for Environmental Manager Systems: A Canadian Perspective." Air and Waste Management Association 87th Annual Meeting and Exhibition, Cincinnati, Ohio, June 19-24.

Villeneuve, E. 1989. "Overview of an Environmental Auditing Program." Presented at the Environmental Auditing Workshop, 10 and 11 October, University of Toronto.

12

Novacor Chemicals Ltd.
— A Case Study

by
Tek Chin
Ross Burns
Sam Fenimore

12.1 INTRODUCTION

12.1.1 The SHER Management System

This chapter outlines one company's approach to establishing an overall environmental management system (EMS). The approach used at Novacor Chemicals Ltd. is referred to as its integrated SHER (safety, health, environment, and risk) management system. It is designed to meet Novacor's needs, but it draws its inspiration from the Responsible Care® (RC) program developed by the international chemical industry. Therefore, it should contain elements that can be applied to other types of organizations and lessons for those establishing their own EMS.

The core philosophy that underlies the SHER management system has been expressed as follows:

> Some undertake a comprehensive effort in Responsible Care® because they believe it makes good business sense. Others do it so they can stay within governing laws and regulations. Our management team at Novacor does it for different reasons. We fundamentally believe that we owe our hard-working fellow employees the safest work environment possible. We respect the rhythm and beauty of God's creation on this earth and we wish to preserve it. Lastly, we are the fathers and mothers of future generations: we must protect the environment and gently pass it down for our descendants to enjoy.
>
> *John Feick, past-President, Novacor Chemicals Ltd.*

Given this strong expression of support, Novacor Chemicals Ltd. has committed to making safety, health, environment, and risk (SHER) management its foremost priority. Planning and execution of the SHER management system are based on company principles as well as guidance from the industry's RC program. Quality management tenets also play a critical role.

This case history outlines the philosophy underlying Novacor's integrated approach, describes examples of its application, and points to early indicators of tangible and intangible benefits.

12.1.2 Corporate History and Culture

Initially a holding company, Novacor emerged as an operating petrochemical and plastics firm in 1983. The acquisition of Polysar Energy and Chemical Corporation Ltd. in 1988 led to rapid growth. Novacor is now one-half of the Alberta-based company NOVA, which transports and refines the hydrocarbon product stream.

Novacor operates as a decentralized organization with its head office in Calgary, and has manufacturing and research facilities across North America (12 facilities in Canada and five in the U.S.A.) Its main products are petrochemicals such as ethylene, styrene, methanol and fuel products, and plastics such as polyethylene, polystyrene, and polypropylene.

The nature of Novacor's business means the company must place strong emphasis on SHER practices. Problems could arise instantly from a chemical spill, vapour release, or explosion. The company also must be alert to the possible long-term build-up of chemicals in the environment at its facilities. Each situation could potentially affect the environment, the health and safety of workers, or neighbours. The company's decentralized organization also presents a challenge, and an opportunity, to find ways to apply SHER management principles across a diverse corporate culture.

The question becomes, "How does Novacor make fully operational the requirement to protect the environment and human health, and assure regulators and the public it is doing so in a responsible manner?" During the past decade, Novacor's senior management has participated with chemical manufacturers from around the world to develop codes of practice that would make environment, health, and safety an integral part of their business conduct. Today, the industry champions this effort through its RC program and encourages all chemical manufacturers, suppliers, and customers to adopt these codes.

Novacor's first step was to adopt the RC program as the company's ethical foundation. To achieve excellence in safety, health, environment, and risk management, the company decided in 1991 to integrate the RC codes of practice into its overall business strategy. This meant a change from day-to-day SHER management at the facility level to a systematic, long-term approach that provides continual assurance and applies it consistently across the company. To accomplish this goal required a shift from viewing SHER management as a "necessary evil" to recognizing it as a value-added component of Novacor's business plan. More importantly, it is seen as the intrinsically ethical approach to take. As a result, SHER issues have gained a heightened profile within the organization. The integration of associated values is also serving to meld a mosaic of different entities into a more cohesive culture.

Combined with this new corporate attitude are quality management concepts such as cross-functional networking, open communication both within and outside the company, and commitment to continual improvement of SHER performance. Each employee in a SHER role is viewed as a valued professional whose opinion is sought on most decisions. Communication with regulators and the public is expected to be open and direct.

As a company that has grown through acquisitions, one of Novacor's greatest challenges has been to synchronize implementation of this strategy across a decentralized organization. Each business unit and facility brings its own distinct SHER management strengths. The corporation's goal is to draw on the synergies created through the cross-organization network to both expand these strengths and refine the values and visions inherent in the company's culture.

12.2 RESPONSIBLE CARE: THE CATALYST BEHIND SHER

The SHER management system is sustained by the underlying values and standards of the RC program. RC is a powerful environmental, health, and safety initiative undertaken by the international chemical industry and conducted under the auspices of the International Council of Chemical Associations. The concept originated in Canada in 1984 and has since expanded to more than 30 countries worldwide. This comprehensive program is based on the right of all industry shareholders — including the public — to know the facts about risks posed by the industry's operations. It also recognizes the chemical industry's moral obligation to conduct business in as safe a manner as possible and is consistent with the philosophy of sustainable development.

The RC program is built around a set of guiding principles and six codes of practice. Public input is received through advisory panels to the Canadian Chemical Producers' Association (CCPA) and the Chemical Manufacturers Association (CMA) in the United States that critique development and implementation of the program. The panels evaluate how well member companies are applying the codes and assess the performance of industry as a whole. Executive leadership groups provide a forum where senior management can discuss progress, share information, provide implementation assistance, and give feedback. A mutual-assistance strategy identifies and addresses cooperative needs of member companies and develops networks for members to share information. The final aspect of the program provides independently verifiable performance measures that demonstrate ongoing improvement.

Several themes are consistent throughout RC:

Accountability Producers of chemicals are responsible for their products' performance from "cradle to grave," including research, product use, recycling, and disposal.

Dialogue The program recognizes the industry cannot do business in a vacuum. Chemical producers rely on partnerships with suppliers, government, employees, industry counterparts, customers, and shareholders, all of whom have a legitimate stake in the integrity of industry operations. True partnerships based on common goals and open dialogue are essential.

Teamwork RC calls for integrating the best efforts, experience, and thinking inside and among member companies. Applying the program's guiding principles to day-to-day operations is a multi-disciplinary undertaking.

Continuous Improvement Commitment to RC is a commitment to the goal of reducing risk. The goal of zero risk may never be achieved, but ongoing risk reduction is essential to our business and those we serve.

Novacor's first step was to incorporate the Guiding Principles of Responsible Care® into its corporate mission statement: "In accordance with the guiding principles of Responsible Care®, we will, in the execution of our responsibilities, make the protection of human health and the environment our first priority." The following summarizes these guiding principles:
- response to community concerns
- commitment to safety as a priority in manufacture, distribution, use, and disposal
- making SHER issues a priority in all planning
- prompt reporting of hazards
- counselling customers on use and disposal of our products
- operating facilities based on SHER protection
- extending knowledge and working with others to resolve problems
- participating with others to create laws, regulations, and standards to safeguard SHER
- promoting RC by sharing experience and offering assistance to others involved in industry-related activities

Novacor's mission statement is supported by its management structure, including the board of directors, which ensures that Responsible Care® governs all aspects of Novacor's SHER activities. The Novacor Management Committee (NMC) provides leadership and sets direction for the RC program. The NMC, in turn, is supported by the Novacor Responsible Care® council which coordinates the development and application of appropriate corporate-level SHER policies, standards, programs, and systems.

Novacor, as a subsidiary of NOVA, is governed by the NOVA board of directors. Within the board, a Public Policy, Risk, and Environment Committee was established in 1991 to review policies, standards, compliance, programs, and accountabilities.

The RC council prepares periodic summary reports for the NMC and, where requested, for the Public Policy, Risk, and Environment Committee. These reports outline the company's SHER performance, achievements, and continuous improvement efforts.

On the operational side, the corporate SHER network provides support and services for facilities and business units to enable them to meet the company's SHER standards.

In addition, the position of Corporate Environmental Officer for NOVA was created in 1992 to facilitate the flow of environmental health and safety information between divisional line management and the board, to contribute corporate perspective to environmental issues, and to provide primary accountability for ensuring that environmental compliance remains with divisional line management. This officer, a senior vice-president reporting directly to the CEO, also coordinates with divisional line management to ensure appropriate SHER crisis management and due diligence systems are in place.

12.3 FIVE ESSENTIAL CHARACTERISTICS AND KEY ELEMENTS OF THE SHER MANAGEMENT SYSTEM

The Responsible Care® program has galvanized a new company-wide awareness of SHER issues. But without the right type of management support, the initiative could have faded away over time. Instead, Novacor drew on the RC principles and codes of practice combined with quality management precepts to identify the following five "essential characteristics" fundamental to successfully achieving excellent SHER performance.

Top Management Support Company commitment to SHER goals is publicly expressed and senior officers demonstrate personal leadership in this area. This commitment is equal to quality and financial performance, and employees have full knowledge of senior management's goals.

Resource Allocation Sufficient human resources and operating budgets are provided to achieve SHER goals. SHER professionals are well trained and highly motivated. Pollution control and safety equipment is purchased and installed that is the "best available" or innovative. Preventive maintenance programs are undertaken to assure proper operation.

Line Responsibility All business and facility management and operating personnel know that SHER compliance and good performance are their personal responsibilities, and that the role of the SHER professional is to assist them. All SHER professionals feel responsible for providing accurate and timely assistance.

Training and Awareness All new employees receive SHER training and there are ongoing training and awareness programs at all employee levels. The company utilizes a variety of media to heighten employee consciousness about SHER matters and has an employee recognition program. Contractors are treated as if they were company employees with the same access to training.

Continuous Improvement The company constantly searches for improved ways to eliminate or minimize emissions and wastes, and otherwise conducts business in a way which enhances environmental quality and health and safety conditions.

These characteristics have been incorporated in several policy and operation initiatives at Novacor. They appear as 12 elements of the SHER management system (see Figure 12.1).

Policies and Standards Clear and up-to-date, underlining the company's SHER stewardship role.

Organization A strong working network among all functions to support the SHER goals.

Communications Public reporting of SHER performance and improvement objectives.

Planning Process SHER planning is fully integrated with the business planning system.

Integrated Risk Management System A formal system for identifying, assessing and managing all health, safety and environmental risks.

Emergency Preparedness Meeting or exceeding all Novacor's obligations for emergency response planning; maintaining and regularly testing a detailed crisis-management plan to ensure all employees are "emergency ready."

Regulatory Tracking and Influence Monitoring emerging public policy, laws and regulations; trying to exert influence in a manner that responsibly reflects interests of all stakeholders. Systems are in place to communicate SHER laws and regulations to relevant parts of the company.

Management Information Systems MIS team identifies and implements improvements to SHER information systems capabilities. All permits, reports, and training requirements are tracked routinely.

Figure 12.1
NOVACOR CHEMICALS SAFETY, HEALTH, ENVIRONMENT, AND RISK-MANAGEMENT SYSTEM

Elements

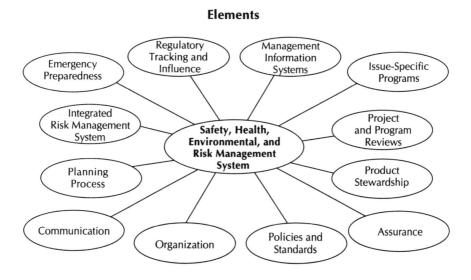

Characteristics

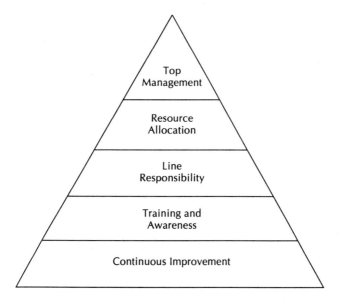

Issue-specific Programs Those addressing future issues that, if properly managed, will reduce Novacor's long-term health, safety and environmental liabilities, such as assessing groundwater quality at all facilities.

Project and Program Reviews Routine reviews of health, safety, and environmental risks at several stages of project or program development; assessment of potential acquisitions and divestitures for their SHER consequences before completion.

Product Stewardship Risk-based life cycle approach to Novacor's products and processes.

Assurance Designing a formal SHER audit program to promote continuous improvement and superior performance; program is certified by an independent body. Periodic benchmarking of Novacor's SHER performance against the best in the industry.

The integrated SHER management system has set lofty goals and, admittedly, implementation has been a challenge. But overall, the approach is achieving initial success. We see the evolution of this strategy as part of our maturing process as individuals, as a company, and as an industry.

12.4 INTEGRATED SHER MANAGEMENT IN ACTION

Novacor is a composite of NOVA, Polysar, Union Carbide, Petrosar, Monsanto, and other companies acquired over the years. It has used the organization's diversity to its advantage by adopting the best proven SHER management practices, and performance-management systems from each location.

A recent review of one element of the company's SHER management system provides an illustration of how best management practices were identified in one area.

In August 1993, a Novacor-wide team of professionals working with Arthur D. Little Canada Ltd. completed a comprehensive review and analysis of our SHER management information systems (MIS). Building upon expertise from site and corporate team members, we identified a number of critical performance elements for MIS and defined specific performance rating criteria. The elements were assessed for consistency with the philosophy, principles, and management practices of RC.

To complete the study, the team appraised the current SHER performance and developed a multi-year continuous improvement action plan for the MIS. This plan began in January 1994 with the ambitious goal of completing more than 20 improvement projects by the first quarter of 1996. The enhanced MIS is being built on many of the existing systems at facilities so that it will be a collection of systems. It is designed to standardize reporting throughout Novacor and eventually will be replaced or linked with new automated Systems Applications and Programs.

Figure 12.2
NOVACOR CHEMICALS RESPONSIBLE CARE® (SHER)
ORGANIZATION PRINCIPLES

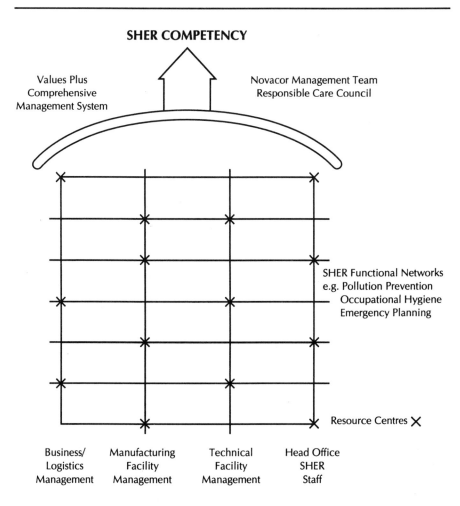

Clearly Defined Roles/Responsibilities

Novacor is now implementing this plan through a company-wide network, or matrix, and through a situational leadership approach. In our SHER functional networks, individuals identified as "resource centres" are recognized as experts with particular knowledge that may be tapped by other parts of the network (see Figure 12.2). As well, leadership for a particular improvement project may come from any part of the organization, not just Novacor's head office. Given Novacor's commitment to decentralization, this approach encourages the type of open and honest communication required for effective team coordination and ensures best use of expertise, no matter where it is located.

Criteria for measuring SHER performance are based on four levels ranging from the first quartile, which describes the highest performance, to the fourth quartile, which outlines the least satisfactory level of performance.

- A **first quartile** evaluation reflects the best SHER practices currently used within the chemical industry, and a proactive performance as defined by Novacor culture.
- A **second quartile** evaluation describes SHER management systems that are adequate, and in some cases that exceed compliance with laws, regulations, and corporate policies. It generally reflects a compliance posture.
- A **third quartile** evaluation reflects SHER management systems that generally need improvement to ensure compliance with laws, regulations, and corporate policies.
- A **fourth quartile** evaluation indicates a general lack of SHER management systems and adequate resources and infrastructure necessary to achieve compliance.

While the quartile definitions are based generally on benchmarking reference criteria from the North American chemical industry, we have also incorporated Novacor's philosophy and values into our definitions.

Two examples of how the quartile measurement characteristics are applied to the MIS element of the SHER management strategy are illustrated in Table 12.1.

Clearly defining performance characteristics within a quartile system has provided several tangible and intangible benefits in the MIS area. First, it has helped Novacor establish the SHER infrastructure vital to first-quartile performance. That structure helps ensure consistent SHER information availability across the company, and has an integrative effect by encouraging information sharing between different facilities and businesses. Other important benefits include facilitation of compliance, local and company performance measures and reporting, staff productivity, and communication with stakeholders. These planned MIS improvements are expected to require minimal incremental cost, currently estimated at approximately $1 million over three years. This expense is primarily for software and hardware used for tracking and measuring and for professional support (internal and external).

Table 12.1
QUARTILE MEASUREMENT CHARACTERISTICS USED IN SHER

Example 1   Category: Regulatory Tracking/Communication
Key Concern: Tracking best available practices/technology

1st Quartile Process and systems are defined for tracking proven best practices and technology. Information is available to all individuals who need it throughout the company. Process and systems are defined for tracking potential technology from R&D facilities, articles, trade magazines, conferences, etc. A system is in place for sharing the results of trials of new practices or technologies.

2nd Quartile Process is defined for sharing best practices and technology between sites. Criteria for information sharing requirements are in place and communicated to all affected individuals. A system is in place to share opportunities and areas of common interest.

3rd Quartile Ad hoc communication occurs within sites. Individuals informally share ideas based on published articles in trade magazines and through attending conferences.

4th Quartile No data kept.

Example 2   Category: Continuous Improvement
Key Concern: Tracking and reporting emissions

1st Quartile Tracking systems are in place to assist in continuous improvement. A pollution prevention plan is in place at each site. Reports are generated at each site comparing actuals to reduction targets. Reports are issued by each site to Nova Head office (NHO) to consolidate release data and to compare with reduction targets. The consolidated information is reported to the Novacor Management Committee (NMC).

2nd Quartile Systems are in place to track all releases of hazardous/toxic chemicals, according to regulatory requirements. Impact analyses for all releases are documented and issued to appropriate personnel. Reports are generated on site for use by site personnel. Reports are issued by the site to regional regulatory agencies as required to meet compliance with legislation, licences, and permits. Hazardous/toxic/other release data are forwarded to NHO for consolidation with all other sites for regulatory and NERM reporting requirements see Section 12.6.2).

3rd Quartile Hazardous/toxic chemical release data are logged for each specific chemical. Data are generally kept in either a manual or automated form.

4th Quartile No data kept.

12.5 NOVACOR'S RESPONSIBLE CARE® AUDIT PROGRAM

This corporate-wide audit program is another critical element in Novacor's SHER management strategy. Established in 1990, the program advises NOVA's board of directors and Novacor's senior management on the environmental regulatory compliance status of our petrochemical facilities. Its objective is to assess and communicate information on the safety, health, and environmental challenges facing the company, includ ing the significance of associated liabilities.

The Audit Program assesses SHER performance against predetermined standards and provides Novacor with the opportunity to document continuous improvement in this area. It is administered by the Audit Committee of the Responsible Care® council. The committee consists of the senior functional SHER managers in the corporate management office, as well as legal counsel.

The program specifically addresses compliance with the Responsible Care® Codes of Practice promoted by the Chemical Manufacturers Association in the United States and the Canadian Chemical Producers' Association. It focuses on all operating facilities of Novacor and its subsidiaries, including manufacturing facilities, feedstock and product pipelines, technical facilities, and terminals. Joint ventures, toll manufacturers, suppliers, carriers, distributors, and customers are considered for inclusion in the Audit Program on a case-by-case basis.

The scope of the Audit Program includes the following functional areas: management systems, environment, safety, emergency planning, health, occupational hygiene, product stewardship, and risk management.

The Audit Program's principal goals are to:
- assist management in identifying and ranking areas and/or practices that need improvement
- reduce liabilities by identifying deficiencies and implementing corrective action
- encourage consistency in environment, health, safety and risk approach and performance
- assist in measuring SHER management performance
- increase all employees' awareness of SHER issues and requirements
- provide consistent SHER training of personnel throughout Novacor

Auditors are selected from across Novacor and professionally trained by external audit experts. Usually the external consulting company participates directly in selected audits to enhance the program's effectiveness and credibility.

Novacor's policy is to retain all audit documentation for two years and final reports for ten years. Among the specific quality assurance steps the Audit Committee routinely performs are:

- reviewing and updating audit procedures and protocols to guide audit teams in conducting future audits
- reviewing and updating roles and responsibilities for managing the Audit Program
- reviewing working papers to ensure audits are conducted in a manner consistent with the goals and objectives of the Audit Program
- reviewing draft audit reports to ensure the findings and observations are reported clearly and accurately and are supported by facts developed during the audit
- soliciting feedback from the managers of audited facilities

A periodic critique of the Audit Program is also conducted by an outside consultant to assess implementation and overall quality of the program.

Novacor's Responsible Care® Audit Program continues to evolve and become increasingly ingrained within the company as part of the way we do business. Not only is it achieving its goals, but its existence is also facilitating preferred access to bank financing and commercial insurance markets.

12.6 OTHER SHER PROGRAMS AND ACTIVITIES

12.6.1 Partnerships in Commitment Program

In 1992, Novacor began a Partnerships in Commitment Program in Canada, expanding it to 500 of its U.S. customers in 1993. This program, part of product stewardship, recognizes business partners committed to the safe handling, storage, use, and disposal of Novacor's products. Novacor is in the process of extending this program to suppliers, distributors, transporters, and resellers of company products.

To become part of the program, customers complete five steps:

- sign a letter of commitment to the program
- complete a self-evaluation of their processes
- receive Novacor's evaluation of the potential risks associated with those processes
- work with Novacor to determine appropriate changes needed to reduce or manage those risks
- make the necessary changes

"Change usually comes from customers' expectations and needs ... this initiative is the other way around with the supplier helping the customer improve for the betterment of the customer, Novacor and future generations," observed Robert Matagliati, president of U.S. Plastics, whose company recently joined the program.

12.6.2 Novacor's National Emissions and Wastes Reduction Masterplan (NERM)

NERM fits under the integrated SHER management umbrella as an issue-specific program within environment. It is a voluntary Canadian initiative, supported by the Canadian Chemical Producers Association under the RC program, requiring submission of detailed emission and waste reduction targets. NERM is the forerunner to the more recent government-sponsored National Pollutants Release Invesntory (NPRI). Under NERM, Novacor has developed a five-year plan for plant modifications and in 1993 spent $20.4 million on capital equipment directly related to environmental improvements.

As part of its commitment to open communication, Novacor published its 1992 emissions and waste data and plans for improvement to demonstrate tangible gains. This report was preceded by communication of the NERM initiative to employees, community members, government, and the media.

"The NERM initiative will help Novacor monitor its emissions carefully under guidelines that are realistic and achievable," says Bud Clark, Novacor's senior vice-president. "We also need to communicate openly. I've heard the public's negative view of the chemical industry places us, on a scale of popularity, just below nuclear power and just above the tobacco industry. To overcome this image we have to demonstrate a complete management of chemicals in all of our activities."

Although production expansion will increase overall emissions by 10% over the next five years before levelling off, plant modifications will actually lower emissions per unit of production. Estimated reductions will range from 6% to 15% per unit, depending on the substance being measured.

Novacor is taking its NERM/NPRI reporting requirements to its U.S. locations to ensure a consistent, company-wide emissions and waste reduction plan. (Unlike NERM, the U.S. Toxics Release Inventory does not require CO_2, NO_x or SO_x reporting and asks for reduction targets for on-site emissions and wastes only. NERM/NPRI includes information on these gases and on transfer of wastes off-site for disposal.)

12.6.3 Pollution Prevention Network

This network of professionals forms another important strand in the integrated management system. Following a request from Novacor's RC Council in early 1993, the Pollution Prevention Network (PPN) was formed, made up of 24 experts on environmental matters across the company. Its mandate is to enhance communication between environmental staff throughout Novacor and to act as a catalyst for achieving and maintaining superior environmental performance. The network does not replace routine line management responsibilities and reporting relationships.

PPN's 1993 objectives included: coordinating the development of performance monitoring measures; tracking environmental technology developments; developing environmental financial disclosure procedures; reviewing Responsible Care® environmental standards; and coordinating implementation of the environmental audit program. The group is currently preparing a comprehensive report on Novacor's chemical emissions and wastes, including the five-year reduction plans.

12.6.4 Novacor Assumes a Leadership Role

Novacor intends to demonstrate leadership in the chemical industry through corporate programs like Partnerships in Commitment and through individual plant initiatives. Recently, the Corunna plant in Ontario played host to 11 smaller chemical companies to explain the RC codes of practice. Particular emphasis was placed on helping these firms understand risk assessment and hazard analysis as well as methods for site assessment.

In the U.S., the Indian Orchard polystyrene plant in Massachusetts set the pace within Novacor for waste reduction. Since launching their program, the plant has reduced waste volumes by 85%. One modified procedure for changing filters not only recovered feedstock but also eliminated disposal costs.

As concrete evidence of commitment to RC, Novacor was the recipient of the 1991 U.S. Conrail and 1992 CNR safety awards for responsible transport of chemicals. In 1993, we received *The Financial Post*'s Silver Award for our report on the company's Responsible Care® program.

These are only a few examples of the programs and activities planned to enhance Novacor's ethical business conduct and ensure continuous improvement in meeting SHER performance goals.

12.7 WHERE DO WE GO FROM HERE?

Novacor's integrated SHER management program is still in its infancy. While we have received excellent support from senior management, some initial resistance to this program was to be expected. Concerns centred on cost and the perception that the company was already a good performer in the industry. Fears about the implications of full disclosure was also expressed. Line managers, understandably, were concerned about bottom-line impact and had difficulty with the concept of intangible gains. Nevertheless, although implementation has not always been easy, some early evidence of benefits is beginning to emerge.

One significant advantage in adopting a cross-functional team approach to SHER issues is that it has enabled us to draw on expertise across Novacor's decentralized organization. The process is already showing results in innovative solutions which have improved the bottom line and in strengthening commitment to RC across the organization. More difficult to measure, but equally important, is that this process has helped to build a more cohesive corporate culture. Drawing on the best each business unit and facility has to offer, in itself, creates a synergy for problem solving within the company.

The integrated SHER management approach has received considerable top-down support to date. Now our challenge is to develop a new protocol of how we work to support RC and SHER management principles, with greater focus on bottom-up initiatives and commitment.

A constant challenge will be the need for continuous improvement to stay competitive and conduct our business responsibly. The move to a family of performance measures will help Novacor meet this challenge by tracking the progress it is making in environment, health, and safety processes. The information, supported by the strengthened Management Information System, will place Novacor in a better position to interpret trends, progress, and improvements needed.

As part of its leadership role, the company is at the initial stages of examining the possibility of using RC as a marketing tool. It may draw on the 12 elements of the SHER management system to provide cost-effective assistance to customers in areas such as risk-management processes, emergency planning, information systems, audits, and issue-specific programs.

Novacor is finding the RC program fits well with other standards developed for the chemical industry. For example, our SHER management system also has the potential to be applied to sustainable development characteristics which balance environmental and economic considerations. We have recently reviewed the SHER management system against the International Chamber of Commerce's (ICC) 16 sustainable development principles and are generally satisfied that Novacor's system conforms with ICC principles.

We are confident the integration of RC into our company through the SHER management system will ensure Novacor moves from the role of follower to leader in safety, health, environment, and risk management. However, we are still in the early stages of the process. The next essential step is to assess efficiency improvements resulting from our array of SHER programs and new integrated management strategy.

One initiative currently being examined is the concept of "full" or "total" cost accounting. Historically, industries have tended to absorb costs for waste disposal and treatment company-wide. In full cost accounting, the true and complete costs of waste generation are identified and used to evaluate company operations, including pollution prevention projects. Some of the costs which could be considered include those related to collection, storage, treatment, disposal, regulatory fees, lost product, and administration. More precise information on these costs could lead to further improvement strategies and, in the end, lower operating costs.

The most significant intangible benefit to date has been the sense of a more cohesive culture across our decentralized company brought about through commitment to the RC philosophy. Novacor recognizes we are in an evolutionary process, one which emphasizes continuous improvement. Progressive empowerment of employees and commitment at all levels of the organization will be required to achieve our goal of consistently achieving first-quartile performance in all SHER functions.

For the future, we aim at nothing less than excellent performance through full integration of SHER requirements in Novacor's business, strategic, and operational planning. We believe strongly that an integrated approach to SHER management is both ethically right and commercially intelligent. Our ultimate goal is to make operational the vision expressed by Novacor's executive.

13

Pollution Prevention at 3M

---

by
Daniel Schmid
Tom Zosel

13.1 INTRODUCTION

From its beginnings as a small manufacturer of sandpaper, 3M has grown to an 87,000-employee, $14-billion global corporation with operations in 58 countries. 3M has more than 60,000 products and services in the consumer, commercial, professional, and industrial markets. There are more than 50 product divisions, subsidiaries, and departments, organized into three business sectors: Industrial and Consumer Information, Imaging and Electronic, and Life Sciences.

Many aspects of the 3M organization and corporate culture have been valuable assets in promoting environmental responsibility and fostering the integration of pollution prevention throughout the organization. Perhaps the most important cultural attributes at 3M are its focus on innovation and change. In some corporations, it is important to maintain the status quo. If a product is acceptable or if a process is functioning adequately, these will not be changed. Such companies function under the banner of "if it ain't broke, don't fix it."

This is not the case at 3M. Innovation and change are a way of life and the basic foundation of the corporate culture. If a product is acceptable in its present form, can it be improved to better meet the customers' needs and expectations? If a process is functioning adequately, can it be changed to increase yield, improve quality, and reduce waste? The majority of pollution prevention projects and those which accomplish the greatest reduction in pollution involve major innovations and changes in products or processes.

As an example, all Magic Tape™ production has been converted from using a solvent-based adhesive to using a water-based adhesive. This eliminated the release of smog-producing organic emissions and the generation of solvent-containing hazardous waste. The new Never Rust™

soap pads are produced from recycled PET. From its inception, the product was based on the concept of using a post-consumer waste stream as a basic raw material.

3M's management structure is also an important contributing factor to the development and implementation of a pollution-prevention culture. 3M management is comprised of individuals most of whom have technical degrees and have been with 3M a minimum of 25 years. There is a strong policy of promotion from within, so that by the time a person is in a top management position, the cultural aspects of innovation and change have become essential elements of the decision-making process.

With regard to their technical capabilities, the last three chief executive officers have been chemical engineers. The present CEO received his degree from McGill University in Montreal, Canada, and started his career in 1957 as a process engineer for 3M Canada.

Having a technically trained management has added immensely in having pollution prevention projects approved. Since these individuals started their 3M careers in the factory or laboratory, they understand the problems, their causes, and their effects. Consequently, they have a technical appreciation as to how pollution prevention projects can reduce or eliminate those problems. This training and educational background has allowed 3M's management to address problems and solutions from the technical perspective and not merely as a financial accounting calculation.

3M's focus on growth and particularly on the development of new products is another important factor in pollution-prevention success. 3M has a corporate goal that, in any one year, 30% of the sales volume will be from new products which have been introduced within the last four years. As these new products are developed and introduced, a focus on environmental improvement is a clear and consistent direction. One way of measuring this focus is through the funds that are spent on Research and Development. 3M's R&D budget is more than 7% of sales. This amounts to an annual R&D budget of more than $1 billion, of which over 15% or $150 million is spent on pollution prevention R&D. With this level of funding, significant accomplishments have been made in the past and will continue to be made into the future.

The final attribute of 3M which has been a major contributing factor to its pollution prevention efforts is the basic environmental organization. At 3M, all of the environmental professionals work in a central corporate staff group which then does the environmental work for the facilities and operating divisions. This centralized group allows the development of a high degree of environmental expertise which is difficult if the environmental function is spread throughout the entire organization. This central group has also developed policies and procedures so that there is a high degree of consistency in the way each operating unit addresses the environmental challenges which it faces.

3M is widely known for environmental innovation and has a long history of environmental leadership. The company has received numerous national awards for its environmental efforts, including the Environmental Achievement Award for 3P from the National Wildlife Federation's Corporate Conservation Council, California Governor's Clean Air Award, the President's Environmental and Conservation Challenge Award, and the World Environmental Center Award.

13.2 THE HISTORY OF ENVIRONMENTAL MANAGEMENT AT 3M

13.2.1 Prior to the 3P Program

3M began organizing in the environmental area in the 1960s. It was a time when regulations were beginning to develop at federal and state governments. 3M formed an Environmental Engineering and Pollution Control group which became the focal point of all environmental activities at 3M at both the corporate and plant levels. This group was staffed by environmental professionals, people who understood and were trained in the technologies of pollution control, wastewater treatment systems, scrubbers, and thermal oxidizers — ways of treating pollution after it had been created at a plant site by the various plant operations.

By the mid-1970s, this group realized that the task of environmental improvement was significant, and that the costs associated with add-on pollution control equipment were having a significant, negative impact on the corporation's financial goals. They also realized that add-on pollution control processes would not achieve a really clean environment. There were always residuals from the control equipment that would add to the environmental burden. They saw that the better way to protect the environment was through pollution prevention —to eliminate pollution from occurring in the first place and to recycle and reuse all residual materials in a way that did not create a negative impact on the environment.

The group also recognized that implementing a broad pollution prevention program was beyond its technical and organizational capabilities. It was only a small group, approximately 40 people at that time, and 3M was a multi-billion-dollar corporation with over 80 manufacturing facilities located throughout the world. While this group was amply trained in pollution control, the individuals did not have the necessary knowledge of 3M products, processes, and operations to make all of the changes needed to reduce the amount of pollution that, indeed, was preventable.

When this group sat back and looked at where 3M needed to be in the future, they realized that every 3M employee would need to take environmental considerations into their daily efforts if the corporation was to make meaningful advances. We wanted our product designers to create new products that eliminated the use of hazardous and toxic materials. We wanted to have our equipment designed to provide maximum efficiency, and to reduce the amount of waste materials that were being generated. And we wanted our manufacturing people to not only increase the efficiency of operations, but also to find ways to reuse, recycle, and reclaim any residual materials that were being created by their processes.

13.2.2 3M's Corporate Policy

With these objectives in mind, 3M created a corporate environmental conservation policy and launched the Pollution Prevention Pays Program in 1975. The environmental conservation policy states as follows:

3M will realize and exercise its responsibility to:
  1) solve its own environmental pollution and conservation problems;
  2) prevent pollution at the source whenever and wherever possible;
  3) develop products that will have a minimum effect on the environment;
  4) conserve natural resources through the use of reclamation and other appropriate methods;
  5) assure that its facilities and products meet and sustain the regulations of all federal, state, and local environmental agencies;
  6) assist whenever possible, governmental agencies and other official organizations engaged in environmental activities.

It is important to understand that this policy was adopted by the 3M board of directors and has remained unchanged since 1975. It has become the foundation of the 3M management approach to environmental issues.

13.2.3 The Evolution of the 3P Concept

The second goal of the corporate policy — that being "prevent pollution at the source wherever and whenever possible" — became the foundation for the 3M Pollution Prevention Pays (3P) Program. The 3P Program is defined as a proactive company-wide effort benefiting both the environment and 3M by taking positive action to reduce pollution early in product or process development, in pilot and facility design, and in production operations. Its objective is to achieve total corporate participation: to have each and every 3M employee reduce pollution and waste in their daily activities.

The third point of the policy, that which states that 3M will "develop products that will have a minimum effect on the environment," is also extremely important to pollution prevention. In reality, this was the forerunner of the present design for the environmental concept. It gave strong guidance to laboratory scientists and product development engineers in that the environmental effects of the products which they were designing must be taken into consideration and efforts put forth to minimize those effects.

This was one of the first corporate policy statements that was developed by any corporation with a focus solely on the environmentally related activities of the entire organization. It was not just a work plan for the environmental group, but set forth a direction which every employee of the corporation was to follow. To have the maximum impact on everyone, the policy was taken to the board of directors and was formally adopted in February 1975. This effort occurred prior to the adoption of the major changes in the U.S. environmental laws of the late 1970s that required U.S. corporations to develop comprehensive environmental compliance plans.

But the adoption of the policy was only the first step on the path of integrating pollution prevention into the corporate culture of the entire corporation. Two bodies of thought along this issue are the concepts of cultural change versus cultural integration. The first is that the entire corporation must undergo a paradigm shift and develop an entirely new culture which has environmental responsibility as a core value. The second is that every corporation has, over the years, developed a culture which can be termed the corporation's personality, and that it is impossible for the environmental efforts to change that basic personality. Consequently, the objective should be to find ways of integrating environmental responsibility, and more particularly pollution prevention, into that existing culture.

This second approach, that of integrating pollution prevention into the existing culture, is highlighted in a study conducted by The Business Roundtable (BRT). The BRT is an organization of 250 CEOs of some of the largest corporations in America. The objective of this benchmark study was to determine how six outstanding pollution prevention initiatives were developed and implemented.

This study found that, in all six cases, success was achieved by integrating pollution prevention into the existing culture and not by trying to make a paradigm shift in the entire corporate personality.

In retrospect, this is exactly the way that pollution prevention was implemented at 3M. There was an existing corporate culture that was based on innovation, change, empowerment of employees, and technical management which was promoted from within. That basic culture was not changed, but its positive attributes were used to create a strong supporting structure for both environmental responsibility and pollution prevention. With the goal of integrating pollution prevention into the entire organization a detailed plan was developed, an organization was created, and actions were put into place.

13.3 THE 3P PROGRAM

13.3.1 Implementation

Initially a program supervisor from environmental engineering was responsible for facilitating the 3P program. Later, a 3P Coordinating Committee was formed that consisted of representatives from several 3M departments including engineering, the Manufacturing Council, the laboratory organization, the Engineering Council, and Health Services and Industrial Hygiene. This group was responsible for developing the initial guidance for the program.

It was determined that projects could be suggested by any employee within 3M. The merits of a suggested project were judged using the following guidelines:

- the project had to accomplish pollution prevention and not pollution control — pollution prevention through source reduction, recycling, reuse, or reclamation
- the project had to have a monetary benefit to 3M, so that there had to be some form of cost avoidance or cost savings associated with the project
- the project had to have additional environmental benefits, such as the reduced use of energy or the reduced use of natural resources
- the project had to have an innovative or technical accomplishment associated with the effort

The same criteria are still in use for judging the acceptability of 3P projects on a worldwide basis.

13.3.2 Promoting 3P within the Corporation

To get pollution prevention adopted as a core philosophy within the entire corporation, a five-point program was conceived and implemented:

1) Total management support
2) A program to reward the creative employees who accomplished pollution prevention projects
3) A measurement system to not only find out how much was being accomplished but to report back to management the successes of the program
4) A way of passing on information so that once a pollution prevention project or technology was implemented in one facility, that information could be passed throughout 3M
5) A way of reporting results so that everyone in the corporation could understand the accomplishments that were being achieved

Perhaps the most critical of these five components was the development of top management support. This support needed to come directly from the chairman of the board, from the CEO, and from everyone else in top management. Fortunately, 3M is a technically managed company. Consequently, when this program was first developed, the top management of 3M understood the concepts and could see that it was easier to design new products and new processes that prevented pollution than it was to spend extensive capital for add-on pollution control. When we first presented the 3P Program, there was overwhelming support from top management. It was not "Should we do this?" but "What can we do to help you accomplish this goal?" It is also important to realize that these goals are being met without massive increases in staffing.

It was very interesting that the initial roll-out of the program included a 12-minute videotape. In that presentation, the chairman and CEO explained the program and asked for total corporate support. The vice-president of research and development aimed his remarks at people in the 3M R&D laboratories who develop new products. Then the vice-president of engineering and manufacturing directed his remarks to the people who design our equipment and operate our factories, again focusing on their contributions to the pollution prevention effort. The next person was the president of international operations who offered his remarks to our international companies in that they themselves needed to play an important role in developing pollution prevention alternatives on an international basis. The last person in the video presentation explained more of the details of the program. This was the vice-president of the environmental organization.

What this video clearly showed to all 3M employees was that management at the very top of the corporation was united in supporting a pollution prevention initiative throughout the entire 3M community. That really began the ball rolling and the movement toward an overall pollution prevention ethic within the entire 3M corporation.

13.3.3 Recognizing Employee Contributions

The second major point to achieve was a recognition program that would reward and recognize the creative employees who are accomplishing pollution prevention objectives. People who develop pollution prevention projects are awarded certificates or plaques for their accomplishments. These awards are presented directly from that person's vice-president at an appropriate awards luncheon, dinner, or special meeting to honour environmental accomplishments. By organizing recognition in this manner, the employees are sent a firm message that management of their division views pollution prevention and environmental achievements as an extremely important part of that division's goals.

3M does not believe in affording direct monetary benefits to its employees for this type of accomplishment. There is a specific reason for that. 3M believes that if monetary rewards are given, there is a reluctance to share that information with other employees. People hold it close to their chest. They want to make sure that they are rewarded monetarily for those accomplishments. However, 3M management wants to make sure that these employees share information. At 3M, you are given as much credit for sharing information throughout the various divisions as you are for coming up with that idea in the first place. Consequently, recognition is not developed on a distinct monetary reward basis. However, because of the long-standing history of the 3P Program and the rewards given for technical accomplishments, 3M employees understand that their rewards will come through merit review increases and job advancement and promotion.

13.3.4 Measuring Pollution Prevention

The measurement system which 3M has used has focused on the degree of pollution prevention and the savings that are realized through each project. But the numbers that we have developed are very conservative. Only the first-year savings and pollution prevented in the first year are measured. If a project lasts for three or four years, we do not measure the extra savings or extra pollution prevention that has occurred. The main reason for doing this is that we did not want to get into a detailed accounting procedure in determining exactly how much savings or how much pollution was prevented. As long as we knew a project was preventing pollution and was saving 3M money, that was sufficient to afford recognition and to be included as part of the program.

The 3P Program has been in effect since 1975. Since that time, the total amount of pollution that has been prevented exceeds 630,000 tons. Pollution Prevention Pays has clearly paid off in environmental improvements. And when we look at the financial aspects since 1975, the program has accomplished savings of over $750 million. In this way, pollution prevention has paid financially for 3M.

13.3.5 Communicating Results

The next area that needed to be addressed was finding ways to pass on the information that was developed at different manufacturing facilities and within different laboratories. There are a number of mechanisms that have been utilized to accomplish this. One of the problems that we had to face is that a high portion of the pollution prevention projects are nonproprietary to 3M. That is, they are developed in ways that contain trade secret or patentable information. Consequently, we had to be very careful as to how we conveyed information throughout the corporation and outside of the corporation to other entities.

This information is conveyed in a number of ways. One of the concepts is what we call idea sheets. These idea sheets are a one-page explanation of the problem, the solution (but the explanation of that solution is in rather broad and nonspecific terms), and then the names of the individual people within 3M that have achieved that success. This accomplishes two things: first of all, other people that may have similar problems can see a summary of that solution and contact the people that were responsible for that development. And second, it gives the people who made the accomplishment a degree of recognition within the corporation.

Another method of passing on information is through specific internal seminars and conferences on specific subjects. A conference might be held on the conversion of pressure-sensitive adhesives to solventless systems. A seminar such as that would involve only the people within 3M who are responsible for the R&D or engineering design for pressure-sensitive tapes. It's a very specific subject and those people involved would get into the highly proprietary developments that are occurring within 3M.

On the other hand, if we have people within 3M who are developing projects or procedures that are proprietary, we encourage their involvement with outside organizations. One group within 3M did an extensive study and research on the advantages of a just-in-time manufacturing process for preventing pollution. Those people, since this was not a proprietary project, have been involved in an extensive number of outside presentations explaining how they have gone about developing and implementing this program within 3M.

And lastly, we needed to report the results of our achievements to our employees. This has been an ongoing process through various newsletters, publications, presentation, etc. This continuing reporting of 3P results also reinforces our corporate pollution prevention philosophy to all employees.

13.4 THE SECOND STEP — 3P PLUS

13.4.1 Changing Times and the Need to Improve

Despite those major accomplishments of the 3P Program, 3M found itself wondering what the future might hold. In the late 1980s, we began looking at where we have been and where we needed to go. Because the regulations of the late 1970s and early 1980s focused on plant-related activities, that really was the original focus of the 3P Program. However, as regulations have expanded, 3M needed to expand its response to those regulations. We did not just need to look at our factories; we needed to look at our products — at not only how they are manufactured but how they are used and how they are disposed. We had to look at transportation issues; how were we moving our raw materials and our processes between manufacturing facilities and into general commerce. And we had to look at our entire operations and evaluate if we were developing operations that were going to have the minimal impact on the environment.

13.4.2 New Goals and Methods of Measuring Progress

We expanded these efforts into what we called Pollution Prevention Plus (or 3P Plus). We have defined that program as methodologies necessary to minimize, while striving to eliminate, the impact of all activities on the environment. For the first time, we established specific goals. Under the 3P Program the objective was to do the best we could, but management said, "Let's set some goals and implement programs that will achieve those goals." The goals we established were that by the year 2000 we would achieve a 90% reduction of all releases to the environment from all 3M facilities worldwide. And, that by the year 2000, we would accomplish a 50% reduction in the generation of wastes.

The establishment of these goals and the development of a measurement method was extremely important. The 3P Program measurement system told us that we were preventing pollution, but it was not geared toward relating the pollution which was prevented to production levels, nor was the system set up to incrementally measure continuous improvement. It was also extremely important to make sure that the goals and the measurement methods were broad enough so that they would cover the activities of all employees. As with the 3P Program, it was an absolute necessity that all employees be able to participate.

In establishing these goals, the 50% reduction in the generation of waste was to be a pollution prevention goal, while the 90% reduction of all environmental releases was to be achieved by including reductions that were achieved through pollution control. Although all employees were to play an integral part in achieving these reductions, the measurements were focused on the plant operations.

The waste-measurement method presented a number of unique challenges in determining what was to be measured and how it was to be measured. To simplify the data collection, it was decided to use available data to the greatest extent possible and to produce a single waste ratio calculation for the entire facility. The first decision was that all measurements would be on a mass basis. This meant that all outputs from a manufacturing facility had to be converted into pounds or tons.

It was then decided that all of the materials which left a plant would be placed in one of three categories:

Products This was the intended output from the manufacturing facility and it was to be measured in the form it was shipped. In this way, all packaging materials were included in the calculation.

By-Product This comprised any residuals from the manufacturing process that were productively reused, recycled, or reclaimed, including solvents that are reused, cardboard that is sent to a recycler, or scrap metal that is sent to a reclaimer.

Waste This is the material that leaves the process and is either sent to a waste-treatment facility or operation, or is directly imposed upon the environment. It is important to note that these measurements are taken before the material is subjected to pollution control. By measuring at this point, it emphasizes the fact that pollution control cannot reduce the amount of waste that is being generated; it can only reduce releases to the environment.

The following is a schematic of how this system works.

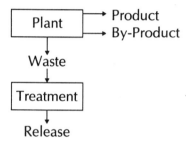

13.4.3 Refining Corporate Infrastructure

To accomplish those goals, we also needed to implement a refined corporate infrastructure. Waste minimization teams were formed within every operating unit and a pollution prevention staff was developed to assist those teams in implementing and developing pollution prevention projects.

The waste minimization teams were interdisciplinary and specific to a manufacturing facility. They included people from manufacturing, the laboratory, engineering, marketing, the environmental organization, logistics, manufacturing, and packaging. We needed to include all disciplines to support the projects and implement the various aspects relative to their area of expertise.

We also implemented another very important structural change. That was the development of detailed environmental management plans by each one of 3M's 50-plus operating divisions. Each one of these plans outlines each of the major environmental issues that is facing that division today and into the foreseeable future, and develops a detailed plan on how that division will address that specific environmental challenge.

3M also looked at how we can find a better way of measuring our success. Now that goals had been established on a percentage basis, we needed to achieve a detailed measurement system. This has been one of the significant accomplishments of the environmental program to achieve our waste reduction goal of a 50% reduction by the year 2000. We established an interim goal of 35% by the year 1995, a goal that we had hoped might be achievable with a concerted effort. That goal then was the driving force behind the development of a waste-measurement system. The purpose of that waste-reduction measurement is to provide a simple method to track major changes in the amount generated by 3M plants and divisions.

When we looked at the subject of waste, we realized that in reality waste is just production inefficiency. It is the inefficient use of our raw materials. As previously put forth, we divided all of the outputs from a 3M manufacturing facility into three groups: products, by-products, and waste.

We then developed a waste ratio for each facility. That waste ratio is the total amount of waste divided by the total of product plus the total amount of by-products plus the total amount of waste — or the total amount of waste divided by the total amount of output from that facility. In reality, it is a material use efficiency measurement.

We have also developed a system in which there are five waste categories. These categories are:

1) Chemical Waste: We define this as all materials that are included in a RCRA manifest. (These are numbers and measurements which a facility is already developing as required by law.)
2) Trash: This is all material that is being sent to a municipal landfill.
3) Organic Wastes: This is accomplished through a mass balance of all organic materials that go to the air and water streams.
4) Particulate Air Waste: This is all material that would be emitted as a particulate material.
5) Discharged Water Waste: In this situation we do not measure the amount of water discharged, but only the pollutants that are in that discharged waste stream.

This measurement system has been in place for the last four years with 1990 as the base year. In 1991, 3M achieved a total amount of waste reduction of 8.3%, and in the three years that the measurement system and the goals have been in place, 3M has achieved more than a 21% reduction in the generation of waste. Consequently, we are on target to achieve a 35% reduction in 1995 and will exceed our goal of a 50% reduction by the year 2000.

13.5 FUTURE GOALS

The Pollution Prevention Pays Program within 3M continues to be alive and well, functioning at a high level of involvement for all 3M employees. And where does 3M want to go in the future? Our long-term goals for the future are zero releases and becoming a sustainable growth company. We understand that zero releases are long-term goals and that we may never actually achieve zero. However, we look at that goal in the same context as the goal of zero defects. You may not achieve it, but it is the goal you strive for.

Our other long-term goal is to achieve sustainable growth. 3M wants to continue to maintain a viable economy for its employees, for its customers, and for the communities in which we live without creating a negative impact on the earth. It's a long-term goal that today we don't know how to measure. But we are moving in that direction, and we hope that in the future we will be able to measure our sustainable growth and eventually achieve an environmentally sustainable economy.